The
TOWER HAMLETS
CONNECTION

A Biographical Guide

by

Harold Finch

Tower Hamlets Library Services
and Stepney Books

ISBN 0 902385 25 9

© 1996 Tower Hamlets Library Service
Bancroft Library
277 Bancroft Road
London E1 4DQ

Produced in association with
Stepney Books
19 Tomlins Grove
Bow, London E3 4NX

Most of the illustrations in this book are from the collection belonging to the Tower Hamlets Local History Library and Archive, the Whiffin Collection is also held there. Enquiries regarding the other pictures should be addressed to the copyright holders whose names appear in italics after the captions.

Typesetting, Design and Printing by
Aldgate Press, Gunthorpe Street Workshops,
Gunthorpe Street, London E1 7RQ

Contents

Preface and acknowledgements	v
Introduction	vi
List of Illustrations and credits	vii
Cumulative Index of Persons	ix
The People	17
Appendices	
General References	162
Bishops of Stepney	164
Mayors of Bethnal Green 1900-1965	164
Mayors of Poplar 1900-1965	164
Mayors of Stepney 1900-1965	165
Mayors of Tower Hamlets 1965-1997	166
The Metropolitan Board of Works 1855-1889;	
Tower Hamlets Representatives	166
The London County Council 1889-1965;	
Tower Hamlets Representatives	167
The Greater London Council 1964-1986;	
Elected Representatives	171
School Board of London 1870-1904;	
Tower Hamlets Representatives	172
Members of Parliament for the Borough 1832-1997	173

Thomas Brooks, Borough of Bethnal Green Councillor, declared his intention to continue to clean chimneys during his mayoral year. *Hulton Picture Co. Ltd*

Preface

Working in Tower Hamlets for twenty seven years as a Youth Officer for the London County Council and Inner London Education Authority enabled me to know some of the people written about. In the course of my work I came to respect and admire the quality of their work and the commitment to it. It was a great learning experience.

Others I have come to know through reading about them and their interests and achievements, they became my companions over many months. In the book there is much poverty, hardship and struggle and the spirit in which this is surmounted is remarkable. While some did much to improve conditions of home and work, others made significant contributions elsewhere. Some must be seen to represent their profession, for there are many other voluntary workers, councillors, teachers, doctors, social and youth workers, local government officers of long and outstanding service.

There should be more women, but those included are exceptional people. The book is meant to be an introduction to show the great diversity of talent and achievement of so many of the Borough's residents. The names of books in the Local History Library are given to follow up any interest. The letters DNB and DLB indicate that there are entries in the *Dictionary of National Biography* or *Dictionary of Labour Biography*.

I have received help from many friends and interested persons, a list is given below, but I am particularly grateful to Anne Cunningham, Denise Jones, Chris Lloyd and Jenny Smith who have painstakingly checked and edited the entries. I must also thank my friend Bill Fishman for kindly writing the Introduction, and not least my wife, Hilda for her great patience and encouragement.

HF

Acknowledgements for contributions and assistance

Rev. G. Daley, Mrs G. Deakin, Mr G. Dellar, Mr D.D. Dunkley,
Professor W.J. Fishman, Mr A.H. French, Mr. P.A.T. Gurnett, Mr J. Harris,
Mr C. Kerrigan, Mr D.S. Levy, Mrs S.W. Manister, Mr S. Park, Mr T. Ridge,
Mr M. Steed, Mrs R. Taylor, Mrs S. Taylor, Miss W.M. Taylor, Mrs C. Thomas,
Mr H. Watton and Mr S. Whiffin.

Introduction

The East End of London has been on the international map, certainly since the nineteenth century. It has produced more than its quota of extraordinary men and women, who have made history, as well as many whom history has unjustly passed by.

Harold Finch, a retired Youth Officer of nearly 30 years service in the old London County Council and Local Education Authority, with special work in this locale, has remedied the last omission. He has produced here a comprehensive biographical dictionary of local notables, mainly those who have made a contribution to the betterment of the human condition, both nationally and internationally. But his choice is more wide ranging. He adds a variety of characters who made an impact, both positive and negative, on the contemporary scene.

Amongst the unsalubrious we discover Rlchard Brandon, a 17th century executioner of Charles I and Archbishops Laud and Stafford, who lived in Royal Mint Street near the Tower, an unworthy contemporary of 'Hanging Judge' Jeffreys, whose victims were hanged in Wapping; Arthur Orton (1834-1898), domiciled in Wapping, the impostor who claimed the family fortune in the famous Tichborne Case (1871-1872), to be subsequently sentenced to 14 years hard labour; and Horatio Bottomley (1860-1933), born in Bethnal Green, the son of a tailor's foreman, who rose to be a successful journalist and founder of the popular *John Bull* magazine, and to elected Liberal MP for South Hackney. He was convicted of fraudulent conversion of funds, expelled from Parliament, and sentenced to seven years penal servitude.

But of the Great and the Good are noted the majority. These range from the famous seaman Captain Cook, whose shore home is listed at 88 Mile End Road, to the leading 'saints' and philanthropists who started their 'missions' to alleviate the sufferings of the poor in the East End. Amongst those are included William Booth (1829-1912), who founded the work of the Salvation Army on the Mile End Waste; Dr Thomas Barnardo (1845-1905) who opened his first lodging place for homeless children at 18 Stepney Causeway; the Rev. Samuel Barnett (1844-1913), the founding father and first Warden of Toynbee Hall, and the more recent Sub-Warden and social insurance reformer, William Beveridge, whose 'Beveridge Report' of 1942 was fully implemented by Prime Minister Clement Attlee (Ex-Mayor of Stepney and MP for Limehouse 1922-1950) in the post second World War Labour Government (1945-1951). All these, and so much more are included in this mine of information about those who left their mark on this, one of the most fascinating areas in our capital.

The author is to be congratulated on this scholarly compendium, the result of laborious study by an insider. It will be invaluable to any student engaged in research into the history of Tower Hamlets.

William J. Fishman

Illustrations

frontispiece
BROOKS, Thomas — Thomas Brooks, Borough of Bethnal Green Councillor, declared his intentio to continue to clean chimneys during his mayoral year. *Hulton Picture Co. Ltd*
ADAMS, David Morgan — Alderman Adams speaking at the opening of Sumner House, Maddams Street, Bromley 28th September 1929
ALEXANDER, David Asher — Wapping Pierhead, built by D. A. Alexander, photographed in 1975
ATTLEE,
    Clement Richard, (Earl) — Attlee, speaking into the microphone at Transport House, Westminster after being elected Chairman of the Labour Party on 8th October 1935 *Whiffin Collection*
BARLOW, Peter William — Barlow's Thames Tunnel shield
BARNARDO, Dr. Thomas John — Wax figure of Dr. Barnardo
BARNETT,
    Henrietta Octavia Weston — Rev. S.A. and Mrs Barnett at the time of their marriage in 1873
BARTLETT, Ernest James — Ernest James Bartlett
BARTLETT,
    Rev. Philip Mandeville — Rev. Philip Mandeville Bartlett
BESANT, Annie — Annie Besant speaking to the strike committee of the Matchmakers' Union
BOOTH, William — A Salvation Army service held by General Booth at the headquarters in Whitechapel Road in 1865
BRADLAUGH, Charles — Charles Bradlaugh
BRUNEL, Isambard Kingdom — I.K. Brunel, third from the left, with J.S. Russell, first from the left, at the launch of the Great Eastern *Brunel University Library*
BURDETT-COUTTS,
    Baroness Angela Georgina — Baroness Burdett-Coutts
CASLON, William — William Caslon
CAVELL, Edith — Edith Cavell at the time she was at the London Hospital, 1899 *Royal London Hospital Trust Archives*
CHARRINGTON,
    Frederick Nicholas — Frederick Nicholas Charrington
COLET, Rev. John — Rev. Dean Colet's House, Stepney in 1797
COOK, Captain James — Noticeboard outside St. Paul's Church, Shadwell with details of the Cook family connection with the parish
CRESSALL, Nellie Frances — Earl Attlee congratulates Councillor Cressall on her receiving the Freedom of the Borough of Poplar on the 8th April 1959
CROMWELL, Thomas — Thomas Cromwell
CROOKS, William — Will Crooks and Sir Alfred Yeo, Poplar's MP, seeing off mothers and children for a country holiday in 1917 *Whiffin Collection*
CULPEPER, Nicholas — Nicholas Culpeper
DEEDES, Sir Wyndham Henry — Sir Wyndham Henry Deedes
DENNIS, Harold Escott — Three Freemen of the Borough of Poplar, Nellie Cressall, Charles Key, and Harold Dennis, on 8th April 1959
ENTICK, Rev. John — Rev. John Entick
FREEDMAN, Barnett CBE — Portrait of Barnett Freedman by Rothenstein
GERBIER, Sir Balthazar — Sir Balthazar Gerbier
GOSLING, Harry — Memorial to Harry Gosling in Transport House, Westminster
GREEN, Rev. John Richard — Rev. John Richard Green
GRESHAM, Sir Thomas — The signature of Sir Thomas Gresham
GROSER, St. John Beverley — Father Groser in 1962
HENRIQUES,
    Sir Basil Lucas Quixano — Portrait of Sir Basil Henriques
HOWELL, George — George Howell
JACKSON, Rev. Thomas — Rev. Thomas Jackson

vii

JACOBS, William Wymark	William Wymark Jacobs *National Portrait Gallery*
JAMES, Mary Eleanor Elizabeth	Mary James
JAMRACH, Johann Christian Carl	The shop front of Jamrach, the wild animal dealer, in St. George Street, about 1896 *and* Inside the shop.
JEFFREYS, Baron George	Judge Jeffreys in the disguise of a sailor seized at Wapping
KEY, Charles William	Charles Key receiving the casket containing the Freedom of the Borough scroll from Councillor Guy, Mayor of Poplar on the 9th November 1953
LANSBURY, George	George Lansbury in 1921
LAWRENCE, Arabella Susan	Susan Lawrence in November 1923 *Newham Library Service*
LAX, Rev. William Henry	Rev. Lax, the Mayor, at the Old English Fair which he opened in Poplar Recreation Ground in August 1919
LEAKE, Sir John	Sir John Leake
LESTER, Muriel	Muriel Lester with Councillor Gillender, Mayor of Poplar at her 80th birthday party on the 9th December 1963
LEWIS, Ted (Kid)	Ted (Kid) Lewis photographed in about 1915 *East London Advertiser*
LÜCKES, Eva Charlotte Ellis	Eva C.E. Lückes *The Royal London Hospital Trust Archives*
MARCH, Samuel	Councillor Sam March, Mayor, speaking in Poplar Recreation Ground to raise funds to carry on the fight for equalization of rates in August 1921
MEAD, Rev. Matthew	Rev. Matthew Mead
MODEL, Alice	Alice Model
MONTAGU, Sir Samuel, Lord Swaythling	Sir Samuel Montagu
MORRISON, Arthur	Arthur Morrison
MOSES, Miriam OBE	Miriam Moses, photographed in 1965 *Jewish Chronicle*
OKEY, Thomas	Thomas Okey
PANKHURST, Estelle Sylvia	Sylvia Pankhurst, circa 1915, in the mother and infant clinic in Old Ford Road
RALEIGH, Sir Walter	Sir Walter Raleigh's house at Blackwall, demolished to make way for the Tunnel
ROBERTS, Dr. Harry	Dr. Harry Roberts
ROSENBERG, Isaac	Isaac Rosenberg
RUSSELL, John Scott	John Scott Russell
SCURR, John	Alderman John Scurr and Councillor Mrs Julia Scurr
SHEPPARD, Jack	Jack Sheppard
STEEVENS, George	George Steevens
STEPHENSON, Rev. Thomas Bowman	Rev. Thomas Stephenson *and* The National Children's Home, in Bonner Road, Bethnal Green *National Children's Home*
TATE, Henry Edward	Mayor Tate presents a bravery award certificate to Mrs Florence Howard on 24th November 1949
TILLETT, Benjamin	Benjamin Tillett
TRUMAN, Sir Benjamin	Sir Benjamin Truman
TRUMAN, Charles Samuel	Charles showing children an early map of Stepney (1965)
VALE, George Frederick	George Vale receives a testimonial from Mayor Clark after 31 years service, 25th January 1951
WATERS, Elsie and WATERS, Doris	'Gert' and 'Daisy' serve tea from mobile canteens they presented to Poplar during the second World War (October 1941) *Whiffin Collection*
WILLIAMS, John	John Williams
WOODIN, William Samuel	William Samuel Woodin
ZANGWILL, Israel	Israel Zangwill

Cumulative Index of Persons

ADAMS, David Morgan	Labour Leader	1875-1942
ADAMS, William	Navigator and Merchant	1564-1620
ADAMS, William	Engineer and Inventor	1825-1904
AINSW0RTH, Robert	Lexicographer	1660-1743
ALEXANDER, David Asher	Architect	1768-1846
ALEXANDER, Dr. Frederick	Medical Officer of Health	1859-1937
ALLEN, William	Chemist	1770-1843
AMES, Joseph	Historian of Printing	1689-1759
ANDERSON, Dr. Elizabeth Garrett	Physician	1836-1917
ANGELL, Moses	Headmaster	1818-1898
APPLETON, Rt. Rev. George	Archbishop in Jerusalem	1902-1993
ARMSBY, Eva	Labour Councillor	1905-1991
ARNOLD, Matthew	Poet	1822-1888
ASHBEE, Charles Robert	Architect	1863-1942
ATKINSON, Dr. Stanley Bean	Doctor and Lawyer	1873-1910
ATTLEE, Clement Richard, (Earl)	Prime Minister	1883-1967
ATTWELL, Mabel Lucy	Illustrator	1879-1964
ATTWOOD, Edward Lewis	Naval Architect	1871-1940
AYLWARD, Ellen	Labour Councillor	1894-1988
BAILEY, Nathan or Nathaniel	Lexicographer	died 1742
BAILLIE, Robert	Engineer and Bridge Builder	1818-1899
BANCROFT, Francis	City Officer	1667-1727
BANNISTER, Charles Acres	Resident	1868-1901
BARLOW, Peter William	Civil Engineer	1809-1885
BARNARDO, Dr. Thomas John	Founder of Homes for Destitute Children	1845-1905
BARNATO, Barney	Financier	1852-1897
BARNETT, Henrietta Octavia Weston OBE	Social Reformer	1851-1936
BARNETT, Rev. Samuel Augustus	Founder of Toynbee Hall	1844-1913
BARON, Bernhard	Philanthropist	1850-1929
BARTLETT, Ernest James	Antiquary	1870-1942
BARTLETT, Rev. Philip Mandeville	Priest	1885-1958
BEAUMONT, John Thomas Barber	Philanthropist	1774-1841
BEDFORD, Peter	Silk Merchant and Reformer	1780-1864
BEKE, Dr. Charles Tilstone	Explorer	1800-1874
BELL, Edward	Labour Leader	1860-1954
BENN, Sir John Williams	Publisher	1850-1922
BENN, Rev. Julius	Dissenting Minister	1824-1883
BENTHAM, Jeremy	Philosopher and Legal Reformer	1748-1832
BERG, Jack (Kid)	Boxer	1909-1991
BESANT, Annie	Social Reformer	1847-1933
BESANT, Sir Walter	Historian and Writer	1836-1901
BEVERIDGE, Lord William	Economist	1879-1963
BHOWNAGGREE, Sir Mancherjee Merwanjee	Barrister and Member of Parliament	1851-1933
BILLIG, Hannah MBE,GM,FRCGP,MBBS	General Practitioner	1901-1987
BIRCH, Canon John Godfrey	Priest	1880-1965
BISHOP, Sidney Macdonald	Footballer	1900-1949
BLIZARD, Sir William	Surgeon	1743-1835
BOLT, Daniel	Deputy Borough Surveyor, Poplar	1873-1946
BOMBERG, David Garshen	Painter	1890-1957
BONN, Issy see LEVIN, Benjamin		
BONNER, Bishop Edmund	Bishop of London	1500(?)-1569
BOOTH, Catherine	Mother of the Salvation Army	1829-1890
BOOTH, Charles	Ship Owner and Social Reformer	1840-1916

BOOTH, William	Founder of the Salvation Army	1829-1912
BOROUGH or BURROUGH, Sir William	Navigator	1536-1599
BOTTOMLEY, Horatio William	Journalist and Financier	1860-1933
BOWKETT, Dr. Thomas Edward	Building Society Pioneer	1805-1874
BOXALL, Elizabeth see BANNISTER, Charles Acres		
BRABAZON, Reginald, Lord Meath	Pioneer of Open Spaces	1841-1929
BRADLAUGH, Charles	Social Reformer	1833-1891
BRANDON, Richard	Executioner	died 1649
BRAY, Rev. Dr. Thomas	Philanthropist	1656-1730
BRESSLAW, Bernard	Actor	1934-1993
BRIDGEMAN, William Walter	Footballer	1883-1947
BRINE, Elizabeth see LANSBURY, Elizabeth		
BRINSON, William	Labour Councillor	1894-1984
BRODETSKY, Professor Selig	Mathematician	1888-1954
BRONOWSKI, Dr. Jacob	Scientist	1908-1974
BROOKS, Thomas, JP	Chimney Sweep	1886-1954
BROWN, Georgia	Singer	1933-1992
BROWNFIELD, Dr. Matthew	Doctor	1825-1908
BRUCE, George see DRUCE, Joseph		
BRUNE, Walter and Rosea	no occupation designated	circa 1190
BRUNEL, Isambard Kingdom	Civil and Marine Engineer	1806-1859
BRUNEL, Sir Marc Isambard	Civil Engineer	1769-1849
BRYANT, William	Match Manufacturer	1804-1874
BURDETT-COUTTS, Baroness Angela Georgina	Philanthropist	1814-1906
BURKE, Thomas	Writer	1886-1945
BURMAN, William VC	Soldier	1897-1974
BUXTON, Sydney Charles, (Earl)	Liberal Statesman	1853-1934
BUXTON, Sir Thomas Fowell	Brewer and Social Reformer	1786-1845
CASLON, William	Typefounder	1692-1766
CASS, Sir John	Merchant	1666-1718
CASTRO, Thomas see ORTON, Arthur		
CATCHPOOL, Egerton St. John (Jack)	Founder of the Youth Hostels Association	1891-1971
CAVELL, Edith	Nurse	1865-1915
CHARRINGTON, Frederick Nicholas	Missioner	1850-1936
CHAUCER, Geoffrey	Poet and Chronicler	1340(?)-1400
CHESWORTH, Donald Piers OBE	Warden of Toynbee Hall	1923-1991
CHEYNEY, Peter	Writer of Crime Novels	1896-1951
CHICKEN, George Bell VC	Mercantile Marine Officer	died 1860
CHUDLEIGH, Rev. Frederick William	Methodist Preacher	1878-1932
CHURCH, Henry Tyrrell (H.Tyrrell)	Secularist	1821-1859
CIBBER, Caius Gabriel	Architect and Sculptor	1630-1700
CLARK-KENNEDY, Archibald Edmund	Physician and Author	1893-1985
CLORE, Sir Charles (Charlie)	Businessman	1904-1979
COBORN, Charles see McCALLUM, Colin		
COBORN, Priscilla or Prisca	Founder of Coborn School	1622-1701
COHEN, General Morris Abraham	Soldier	1887-1970
COLET, Dame Christian	Mother of John Colet	circa 1466
COLET, Sir Henry	Mercer	died 1505
COLET, Rev. John	Scholar and Preacher	1467(?)-1519
COLLINS, Brenda M.	Liberal Democrat Councillor	1946-1990
COLQUHOUN, Patrick	Magistrate	1745-1820
CONRAD, Joseph	Writer	1857-1924
COOK, Captain James	Navigator	1728-1779
CORNER, Dr.Edred Moss	Surgeon	1860-1928
CORNER, Dr. Matthew Cursham	Physician and Surgeon	1873-1950
COTTON, William	Philanthropist	1786-1866

CRAB, Roger	Hermit	1621(?)-1680
CRESSALL, George OBE	Labour Councillor	1880-1951
CRESSALL, Nellie Frances	Labour Councillor	1882-1973
CROMWELL, Thomas	Statesman	circa 1485-1540
CROOK, Lillian	Labour Councillor	1914-1986
CROOKS, William	Labour Leader	1852-1921
CUBITT, Sir William	Builder and Politician	1791-1863
CULPEPER, Nicholas	Herbalist and Writer	1616-1654
CURRIE, Sir Edmund Hay	Philanthropist	1834-1913
CUTNER, Samuel CBE	Concert Pianist	1902-1988
DANCE, George (The Elder)	Architect	1700-1768
DARBISHIRE, Henry Astley	Architect	1838-1908
DASH, Jack	Dockers' Leader	1906-1989
DAVENANT, Rev. Ralph	Rector of Whitechapel	died 1680
DAVIES, Micky	Youth Worker	1910-1954
DAY, Thomas	Writer	1748-1789
de BLANK, Rev. Joost	Bishop of Stepney	1908-1968
DEEDES, Sir Wyndham Henry	Soldier and Community Worker	1883-1956
DENMAN, Alice see BANNISTER, Charles Acres		
DENNIS, Harold Escott OBE	Town Clerk of Poplar	1880-1973
DENT, Joseph Malaby	Publisher	1849-1926
DIAMOND, Alfred	Businessman and Community Worker	1902-1978
DICKENS, Charles	Writer	1812-1870
DICKIN, Maria Elizabeth	Founder of the PDSA	1870-1951
DITCHBURN, Joseph	Engineer	1801-1870
DODD, Robert	Marine Artist and Engraver	1748-1816(?)
DOLLOND, John	Optician and Mathematician	1706-1761
DORÉ, Gustave	Painter and Book Illustrator	1832-1883
DOREE, George	Weaver	1844-1916
DOWNHAM, Rev. Denis	Rector of Spitalfields	1921-1979
DRAKE, Corporal Alfred George VC	Soldier	1893-1915
DRIFFIELD, Rev. George	Priest	1817-1901
DRUCE, Joseph	Maori Chief	1777-1819
DUCKETT, Sir George	Canal Builder	1777-1856
DUNBAR, Duncan	Ship Owner	1790-1862
DUTCH SAM, (ELIAS, Samuel)	Bare Knuckle Fighter	1775-1816
DYCHE, Rev. Thomas	Lexicographer	died 1727
EAST, Mary	Publican	1715-1780
EDWARDS, Walter	Member of Parliament	1900-1964
ELBOZ, Annie	Labour Councillor	1899-1985
ELIAS, Samuel see DUTCH SAM		
ENSOR, Sir Robert Charles Kirkwood	Journalist and Historian	1877-1958
ENTICK, Rev. John	Schoolmaster and Writer	1703(?)-1773
ERASMUS, Desiderius	Dutch Humanist	circa 1469-1536
FAIRBAIRN, Sir William	Engineer and Shipbuilder	1789-1874
FATHER JOE see WILLIAMSON, Father Joe		
FELS, Joseph	Soap Manufacturer	1854-1914
FISHER, Dorothea Kate E.M.W. OBE	Barge Owner	1894-1974
FITZGERALD, Canon Thomas	Priest	1895-1968
FLANAGAN, Bud OBE	Comedian	1896-1968
FOXE, Rev. Richard	Bishop	1448(?)-1528
FRANKEL, Daniel	Member of Parliament	1900-1988
FRANKLIN, Sydney	Merchant Banker	1887-1970
FREEDMAN, Barnett CBE	Artist	1901-1958
FROBISHER, Sir Martin	Navigator	circa 1535-1594
FROST, Samuel	Footballer	1879-1926

FRYE, Thomas	Founder of Bow Pottery	1710-1762
GANDHI, Mohandas Karamchand	Indian Political Leader	1869-1948
GARFORD, James	Magistrate	1772-1850
GARRICK, David	Actor Manager and Dramatist	1717-1779
GARTHWAITE, Anna Maria	Silk Designer	1690-1763
GASCOYNE, Joel	Cartographer	died 1705
GAVIN, Dr. Hector	Surgeon and Pioneer in Public Health	1816-1855
GERBIER, Sir Balthazar	Courtier and Adventurer	1591(?)-1667
GERSON, Phyllis Josephine MBE, JP	Social Work Administrator & Magistrate	1903-1990
GERTLER, Mark	Painter	1891-1939
GIBSON, Nicholas	Merchant	died 1540
GILBERT, Sir Humphrey	Navigator	1539(?)-1583
GILBERT, Tony	Worker for Human Rights	1914-1992
GODLEY, Sidney Frank VC	Soldier	1869-1957
GOMPERS, Samuel	American Trade Union Leader	1850-1924
GOSLING, Harry	Labour Leader	1861- 1930
GRANT, Clara Ellen	Teacher & Founder, Fern St. Settlement	1867-1949
GRANT, Julius	Forensic Scientist	1901-1991
GREEN, George	Shipbuilder and Philanthropist	1767-1849
GREEN, Rev. John Richard	Historian	1837-1883
GREEN, Richard	Shipbuilder	1803-1863
GREENHILL, Rev. William	Dissenting Minister	1591-1671
GRENFELL, Sybil Vera MVO,CBE	Social Worker	1902-1990
GRENFELL, Sir Wilfred Thomason	Missionary Doctor	1865-1940
GRESHAM, Sir Thomas	Merchant and Ambassador	1519(?)-1579
GROSER, St. John Beverley	Priest	1891-1966
GULAMAN, Solomon see BANNISTER, Charles Acres		
GURLE, Leonard	Gardener	circa 1621-1685
HANBURY, Cornelius	Pharmacist	1796-1869
HANBURY, Sampson	Brewer	1769-1835
HARRIS, Betsey	Resident	1809-1831
HARRIS, Sir Percy	Politician	1876-1952
HARRISON, Dr. John	Surgeon	1718-1753
HAWKSMOOR, Nicholas	Architect	1661-1736
HEADLAM, Rev. Stewart Duckworth	Priest	1847-1924
HECKFORD, Nathaniel	Founder, E. London Children's Hospital	1842-1871
HENDERSON, Robert	Headmaster	1884-1958
HENDERSON, Rev. William John	Baptist Preacher	1843-1929
HENRIQUES, Sir Basil Lucas Quixano	Community Worker and Magistrate	1890-1961
HENRIQUES, Lady Rose	Community Worker and Artist	1890-1973
HESSEL, Phoebe	Female Soldier	1713(?)-1821
HILLS, Arnold Frank	Shipbuilder	1857-1927
HILSDON, George Richard	Footballer	1885-1941
HILTON, Marie	Pioneer of the Creche	1821-1896
HIRD, James Wynne	Salesman & Promoter, Football to Russia	1887-1959
HOBBS, Horace Edwin	Dog Lover	1896-1935
HODGSON, Joseph Ray	Lifesaver	1829-1908
HODSON, Bishop Mark Allin	Rector of Poplar	1907-1985
HOLLAND, Sydney George, Lord Knutsford	Chairman of the London Hospital	1855-1931
HOOLE, Rev. Samuel	Priest	1770-1839
HOLMAN, Francis	Marine Painter	1729-1784
HOW, Bishop William Walsham	Hymn Writer	1823-1897
HOWELL, George	Labour Leader	1833-1910
HUDDART, Joseph	Marine Surveyor & Rope Manufacturer	1741-1816
HUFFAM, Christopher	Ship's Chandler	1771-1839
HUGHES, Mary	Social Worker and Philanthropist	1860-1941

ISAACS, Adelaide Mary *see* REEVE, Ada		
JACKSON, Sir Cyril	Educationalist	1863-1924
JACKSON, Rev. Thomas	Methodist Preacher	1850-1932
JACOBS, William Wymark	Writer	1863-1943
JAMES, Mary Eleanor Elizabeth MBE	Social Worker	1859-1943
JAMRACH, Johann Christian Carl	Importer of Wild Beasts	1815-1891
JEFFREYS, Baron George	'The Hanging Judge'	1648-1699
JEROME, Jerome Klapka	Writer	1859-1927
JONES, Rev. Richard Cynfyn	Anglican Clergyman	1873-1964
JOSEPH, Ernest Martin	Architect	1877-1960
KENTON, Benjamin	Vintner and Philanthropist	1719-1800
KEY, Charles William	Schoolmaster and Politician	1883-1964
KNUTSFORD, Lord *see* HOLLAND, Sydney George		
LANE, James Charles (Jimmy)	Wrestler and Weightlifter	1884-1956
LANE, William	Publisher	1745(?)-1814
LANSBURY, Elizabeth Jane	Suffragette	1860-1933
LANSBURY, George	Politician	1859-1940
LAWRENCE, Arabella Susan	Politician	1871-1947
LAX, Rev. William Henry	Methodist Preacher	1868-1937
LEAKE, Sir John	Admiral	1656-1720
LEAN, Sir David	Film Director	1908-1991
LEDINGHAM, Professor John (Jack)	Professor of Medicine	1916-1993
LEIJONHJELM, Baroness Emma	Seamen's Friend	1847-1937
LESTER, Muriel and LESTER, Veronica Doris	Founders of Kingsley Hall	1886-1965 & 1883-1968 respectively
LEVIN, Benjamin	Music Hall and Radio Entertainer	1903-1977
LE WALEYS, Henry *see* WALEYS, Henry Le		
LEWIS, Ted (Kid)	Boxer	1894-1970
LIEBERMAN, Aaron	A Founder of Socialist Zionism	1849-1880
LINTON, William James	Engraver, Poet and Political Reformer	1812-1898
LITTLE, Dr. William John	Physician and Surgeon	1810-1894
LONDON, Jack	Writer	1876-1916
LOSS, Joshua Alexander (Joe) MVO,OBE	Band Leader	1910-1990
LOWDER, Rev. Charles Fuge	Priest	1820-1880
LÜCKES, Eva Charlotte Ellis CBE	Matron, The London Hospital	1855-1919
LUCY, Joseph (Joe)	Boxer	1930-1991
McCALLUM, Colin Whitton	Comedian	1852-1945
MACCOBY, Rabbi Hayim Zunden	Maggid-Preacher	1858-1916
McDOUGALL, Sir John	Miller	1844-1917
McMILLAN, Margaret	Educationalist	1860-1931
MACPHERSON, Annie P.	Founder of the Home of Industry and Bethnal Green Medical Mission	1824-1904
MALLON, James Joseph	Warden of Toynbee Hall	1875-1961
MANN, Sir Edward	Brewer	1854-1943
MANN, Tom	Trade Union Leader	1856-1941
MANNING, Rev. Henry Edward	Cardinal	1808-1892
MANSBRIDGE, Albert	Founder, Workers' Educational Assoc.	1876-1952
MARCH, Samuel	Labour Leader	1861-1935
MARE, Charles John	Shipbuilder	1815-1898
MARTELL, Philip	Conductor and Director of Film Music	1906-1993
MARX-AVELING, Eleanor	Socialist	1855-1898
MAY, Francis	Match Manufacturer	1803-1885
MAYHEW, Henry	Journalist	1812-1887
MEAD, Rev. Matthew	Minister of Stepney Meeting House	1630(?)-1699
MEAD, Dr. Richard	Physician	1673-1754
MEARS, Kid *see* SOLOMONS, Jack		

MEATH, Lord see BRABAZON, Reginald		
MENDELOFF, Gershon see LEWIS, Ted (Kid)		
MENDOZA, Daniel	Prize Fighter	1764-1836
MERCERON, Joseph	Magistrate	1763-1839
MERRICK, Joseph Carey	'The Elephant Man'	1862-1890
MIKARDO, Ian	Politician	1908-1993
MODEL, Alice	Community Worker	1856-1943
MONTAGU, Sir Samuel, Lord Swaythling	Merchant Banker	1832-1911
MONTEFIORE, Robert M. Sebag	Barrister	1882-1915
MORLEY, Lord see PARKER, Edward		
MORRISON, Arthur	Writer	1863-1945
MOSES, Miriam OBE	Community Worker	1886-1965
MUDD, Captain Henry	Sailor	died 1692
MUSSELL, Ebenezer	Antiquary	died 1764
MUSTO, Sir Arnold Albert	Civil Engineer	1883-1977
NEALE, Thomas	Master of the Mint	died 1699(?)
NEWLAND, George Alexander	Borough Librarian	1891-1975
NEWTON, Sir Isaac	Mathematician and Physicist	1642-1727
NEWTON, Rev. John	Priest and Hymn Writer	1725-1807
NEWTON, William	Politician and Newspaper Publisher	1822-1876
OKEY, Thomas	Basket Maker and Professor of Italian	1853-1935
ONSLOW, Joseph William see BANNISTER, Charles Acres		
ORTON, Arthur	Imposter	1834-1898
PACE, Rev. Richard	Priest and Diplomat	1482(?)-1536
PANKHURST, Estelle Sylvia	Suffragette Crusader	1882-1960
PARKER, Edward, Lord Morley	Public Servant	1555-1618
PARMITER, Thomas	Silk Merchant	died 1682
PASSMAN, Florrie	Youth Worker	1888-1986
PATER, Walter Horatio	Writer	1839-1894
PENN, William	Founder of Philadelphia	1644-1718
PENNETHORNE, Sir James	Architect	1801-1871
PEPPERELL, Elizabeth OBE	Champion of Working Women	1914-1971
PEPYS, Samuel	Diarist and Secretary of the Admiralty	1633-1703
PERKIN, Sir Henry William	Chemist	1838-1907
PERRY, John	Shipbuilder	1743-1810
PHILLIPS, Roland	Scout Commissioner	1890-1916
PHILPOT, Sir John	Grocer	died 1384
PIATKOV, Peter (alias SCHTERN)	Political Activist	circa 1910-1911
PLATT, Sir Hugh	Horticulturalist & Pioneer Food Preserver	1552-1608
PLIMSOLL, Samuel	Sailors' Friend	1824-1898
POTTER, Beatrice see WEBB, Martha Beatrice		
POTTER, Henry III	Chemist	1848-1928
PRELLEUR, Pierre or Peter	Organist and Composer	circa 1705-1741
PUDDEFOOT, Sydney Charles	Footballer	1894-1972
RAINE, Henry	Brewer	1679-1738
RALEIGH, Sir Walter	Explorer and Statesman	1552-1618
RAMSEY, Edith MBE	Educationalist and Community Worker	1895-1983
RANDOLPH, Jane	Mother of President Thomas Jefferson	1720-1776
RAVENSCROFT, John	Musician	died 1735-1745(?)
RAVENSDALE, Lady Mary Irene	Social Worker and Philanthropist	1896-1966
REED, Rev. Andrew	Philanthropist	1787-1862
REEVE, Ada	Musical Comedy Actress	1874-1966
REGELOUS, Arthur see BANNISTER, Charles Acres		
RENNIE, John	Engineer	1761-1821
RICARDO, David	Economist	1772-1823
ROBERTS, Dr. Harry	General Practitioner	1871-1946

ROCKER, Rudolf	Political Activist	1873-1958
ROGERS, Frederick	Social Reformer and Journalist	1846-1915
ROSENBERG, Isaac	Poet and Painter	1890-1918
RUSSELL, John Scott	Engineer and Shipbuilder	1808-1882
RUSSELL, William	Organist and Composer	1777-1813
RYDER, Sir William	Deputy Master of Trinity House	died 1669
SALMON, Robert	Merchant	1567-1641
SAMUDA, Joseph D'Aguilar	Engineer and Shipbuilder	1813-1885
SAUNDERS, Thomas Henry	Papermaker	1813-1870
SCURR, John	Labour Leader	1876-1932
SCURR, Julia	Suffragette and Councillor	1871-1927
SHEA, Danny	Footballer	1887-1960
SHEPPARD, Rev. Hugh Richard Lawrie (Dick)	Priest	1880-1937
SHEPPARD, Jack	Highwayman	1702-1724
SHINWELL, Emanuel (Lord 'Manny')	Labour Leader	1884-1986
SILLEY, John Henry	Shipbuilder	1872-1941
SLADE, John see BANNISTER, Charles Acres		
SMITH, George Joseph	Bride Murderer	1872-1915
SMITH, Sir Hubert Llewellyn	Civil Servant	1864-1945
SMITH, Corporal Issy VC	Soldier	1886-1940
SNELL, Hannah	Female Soldier	1723-1792
SOLOMONS, Jack	Boxing Promotor	1902-1979
SOMES, Joseph	Ship Owner	1787-1845
SPERT, Sir Thomas	Founder & First Master of Trinity House	died 1541
STEEVENS, George	Shakespearean Scholar	1736-1800
STEPHENSON, Robert	Civil Engineer	1803-1859
STEPHENSON, Rev. Thomas Bowman	Founder, National Children's Homes	1839-1912
STOTHARD, Thomas	Painter and Book Illustrator	1755-1834
STRYPE, Rev. John	Historian and Biographer	1643-1737
SWAYTHLING, Lord see MONTAGU, Sir Samuel		
SYMINGTON, William	Engineer – Pioneer of Steam Navigation	1763-1831
TATE, Beatrice Lilian	Borough Councillor	1896-1969
TATE, Henry Edward	Borough Councillor	1883-1978
TAWNEY, Richard Henry	Historian	1880-1962
TELFORD, Thomas	Engineer	1757-1834
TILLETT, Benjamin	Labour Leader	1860-1943
TOMLINSON, Henry Major	Writer	1873-1958
TOYNBEE, Arnold	Economic Historian	1852-1883
TRAPNEL, Anna	Prophet	circa 1642-1660
TRAVERS, Nat	Music Hall Singer	1875-1958
TREVES, Sir Frederick	Surgeon	1853-1923
TREVITHICK, Richard	Engineer	1771-1833
TRUMAN, Sir Benjamin	Brewer	1690-1780
TRUMAN, Charles Samuel	Local Historian	1892-1978
TURNER, Merfyn	Youth Worker and Penal Reformer	1915-1991
TYRRELL, H. see CHURCH, Henry Tyrrell		
VALE, George Frederick	Librarian and Local Historian	1890-1960
VALLANCE, William	Poor Law Reformer	1834-1909
VASSALL, John	Sailor	died 1625
VATCHER, Marion	Philanthropist	1850-1933
VOISEY, William (Bill)	Footballer	1891-1964
WAINWRIGHT, Rev. Lincoln Stanhope	Priest	1847-1929
WALEYS, Henry Le	Politician	died 1302
WARDELL, William Wilkinson	Architect and Engineer	1823-1899
WARNER, see WATERS, Horace John		

WATERS, Elsie OBE and WATERS, Doris OBE	Stars of Stage, Film and Radio	
	1896-1990 and circa 1900-1978 respectively	
WATERS Horace John OBE	Actor	1896-1981
WATTS, Dr. Isaac	Hymn Writer	1674-1748
WEBB, George William	Footballer	1888-1915
WEBB, Martha Beatrice	Social Reformer	1858-1943
WEINTROP, Chaim Reeven *see* FLANAGAN, Robert OBE		
WENTWORTH FAMILY	Lords of the Manor	no dates
WESLEY, Rev. John	Founder of Methodism	1703-1791
WESLEY, Susannah	Mother of John and Charles Wesley	1669-1742
WHIFFIN, William Thomas	Photographer	1878-1957
WHISTLER, James Abbott McNeill	Painter	1834-1903
WIDGERY, David MB,BS	Doctor and Campaigner	1947-1992
WIGRAM, Sir Robert	Ship Owner	1743-1830
WILD, Robert	Headmaster	1840-1916
WILLIAMS, John	Scholar	1797-1875
WILLIAMSON,, Father Joseph (Father Joe)	Priest	1895-1988
WINNINGTON-INGRAM, Arthur Foley	Bishop of London	1858-1946
WINTHROP, Robert *see* FLANAGAN, Robert OBE		
WOODIN, William Samuel	Entertainer	1825-1888
WOOLMORE, Sir John	Ship Owner	1755-1837
WYLLIE, George Cameron GC	Royal Engineer	1908-1987
YARROW, Sir Alfred Fernandez	Shipbuilder	1842-1932
YOUNG, Canon Edwyn	Rector of Stepney	1913-1988
YOUNG, George Frederick	Shipbuilder	1792-1870
ZANGWILL, Israel	Writer	1864-1926

Alderman Adams speaking at the opening of Sumner House, Maddams Street, Bromley 28th September 1929

ADAMS, David Morgan 1875-1942
Labour Leader

David Adams was born in Poplar of Welsh parents. He was taken to Wales and worked in a coal mine when he was 12. Some years were spent at sea serving in India during the first World War.

After returning to London, he became a casual labourer in the docks, going on to become an official of the Transport and General Workers' Union.

His public life began as a Guardian of the Poor in 1913 and service lasted seventeen years, From 1919 to 1942 he was on the Poplar Borough Council, became Mayor in 1934 and joined many of his fellow councillors in prison in 1921 in the struggle for rate equalisation. After one year serving as the elected representative to the London County Council he raised his sights again and successfully won the South Poplar Parliamentary Constituency which he held from 1931 to 1942.

A colleague of George LANSBURY, he was a great fighter for the underdog and causes and ideas he felt to be right.

David Adams lived for many years in Southill Street, Poplar, and on most days had a string of callers from all over the country.

During the London air raids he was bombed out and moved to Ilford.

Dave Adams House, Norman Grove, E3, a children's home, is named after him.

DLB

ADAMS, William 1564-1620
Navigator and Merchant

William Adams wa born in Gillingham, Kent, and came to London at the age of 12 to serve as a shipbuilding apprentice with Nicholas Diggins in Limehouse. At the end of his apprenticeship, he entered the Navy as Master and Pilot, and served the Worshipful Company of Barbary Merchants, trading with the Muslim kingdoms of North Africa for ten years.

He was Captain of the *Richard Duffield*, a food and ammunition supply ship for the English battle fleet fighting the Spanish Armada in 1588. The following year he married Mary Hyn at St. Dunstan, Stepney.

In 1598 he then took service with Dutch merchants, and in a voyage with many disasters eventually landed with the cargo of woolen cloth off the Japanese port of Bungo in April 1600. He was the first Englishman to visit Japan.

17

At the instigation of jealous Portuguese traders in Japan, he was cast into prison on a piracy charge, but was released by the intervention of Emperor Iyeyasu, keen to learn his knowledge of shipbuilding, navigation, astronomy and mathematics. He co-operated with the Emporer's wishes and built him two ships and was rewarded with a salary, land and a title of Anjin Sama (Lord Pilot). He revered to this day as the only non-Japanese Samurai.

The Emperor offered to allow him to return to England but Adams decided to remain and married a Japanese girl. During his twenty years in Japan he continued his overseas trading, acting as an agent for the East India Company and establishing an English colony in Japan. Letters between William Adams, James I and the Emperor of Japan in 1611 have survived, and are held at the India Office Library.

His tomb was discovered in 1872 on one of the hills overlooking Yedo (now called Tokyo) harbour and a street in the city called Anjin Cho (Pilot Street) commemorates his links with the country.

His adventures were the subject of James Clavell's novel *Shogun* (1975), which was later made into a TV film of the same title.

Books

Tames, R. *Servant of the Shogan* (Norbury, 1981)
Birdwood, Sir G. and Foster, W. (eds) *The First Letter Book of the East India Company 1600-1619* (Bernard Quaritch, 1893)
Keay, J. *The Honourable Company* (Harper Collins 1991)
Farrington, A. *The English Factory in Japan 1613-23* (British Library, 1991, 2 vols)

DNB

ADAMS, William 1825-1904
Engineer and Inventor

William Adams was born in Limehouse, his father was John Adams, clerk of works to the East India Dock Company. He was educated privately at academies in Margate.

In 1841 he was apprenticed as a machinery fitter with Miller and Ravenhill, shipbuilders at Orchard Wharf, Blackwall. In 1846 he joined Charles Vignoles, civil engineer at Trafalgar Square, Westminster as a draughtsman and two years later was working as a marine engineer in Marseilles and Genoa.

He returned to England in 1852 to plan the North London Railway's locomotive and carriage works, becoming locomotive and carriage superintendent in 1854.

William Adams introduced new high-capacity suburban trains with continuous brakes, probably the first in Britain, to serve the rapidly growing commuter traffic. He was also first in the use of coal gas for train lighting in 1862. William Adams invented a two-axle guiding bogie which greatly improved the engine's negotiation of curves, and enabled speed to be increased.

In 1873 he took up a similar appointment with the Great Eastern Railway, modernising the Stratford works.

William Adams later became locomotive superintendent of the London and South Western Railway in 1878.

A major development patented by William Adams and his nephew in 1885 was the Vortex steam exhaust system which increased efficiency and locomotive power. It was applied to over five hundred locomotives in Britain, France and Austria.

He retired because of ill health in 1895.

William Adams was musically talented with a Fine Base voice and while with the North London Railway, he persuaded its directors to provide suitable accommodation for concerts and evening classes at the Bow and Bromley Institute, Bow Road, Bow.

William Adams was married and had 10 children.

DNB-Missing Persons (1993)

AINSWORTH, Robert 1660-1743
Lexicographer

Robert Ainsworth was born near Manchester and educated in Bolton. He became a master in a boarding school in Bethnal Green, possibly at Bethnal House. The school later removed to Hackney.

He was the compiler of a Latin-English/English-Latin dictionary which was first published in 1736.

Having acquired a small fortune he gave up his school and spent his time privately as a collector of old coins and curios. He was elected a Fellow of the Society of Antiquaries in 1724. Charles Wesley met him and mentioned him in his journal for the 12th May 1738.

Ainsworth is buried in Poplar Chapel (now St. Matthias Church, Poplar) and there is an inscription engraved on a wall in the church.

DNB

Wapping Pierhead, built by D. A. Alexander, photographed in 1975

ALEXANDER, David Asher
1768-1846
Architect

David Alexander was born in London and educated at St. Paul's School. He became a student at the Royal Academy in 1782 where he gained a silver medal.

One of his first jobs was the widening of the bridge over the River Medway at Rochester.

He designed warehouses at London Dock. Today only the Skin Floor Warehouses, Tobacco Dock survive and fine houses at Wapping Pierhead. Examples of work undertaken in the provinces include the lighthouses at Lundy Island and at Harwich as well as prisons at Dartmoor and Maidstone.

DNB

ALEXANDER, Dr. Frederick
1859-1937
Medical Officer of Health

Frederick Alexander was born in London and lived for many years in Stepney Green. He qualified as a doctor at St. Bartholomew's Hospital, West Smithfield, in the City. After becoming assistant medical officer at Mile End Old Town Infirmary, Bancroft Road, he was later appointed Medical Officer of Health for Poplar in 1893. He completed 43 years of public service.

He was a pioneer in many fields of public health, such as the use of artificial sunlight lamps for children needing sunshine treatment. In addition, a system of cleaning swimming baths by the use of chlorine was introduced and many slum properties were demolished. He was responsible for making blindness in infants a notifiable disease. His main interest, which was continued after retirement, was in helping blind adults to lead a more active and purposeful life.

Alexander House, Tiller Road, E14 commemorates his name.

ALLEN, William 1770-1843
Chemist

William Allen was the very delicate child of a silk manufacturer. He was born in Steward Street, Spitalfields. He received very little formal education and when old enough, he entered the silk trade. His heart though, was in science and in 1791 he joined the chemical establishment of Joseph Bevan in Old Plough Court, Lombard Street in the City, famed as the birthplace of Alexander Pope.

In 1803 William Allen was elected President of the Physical Society at Guy's Hospital, later becoming Professor of Experimental Philosophy. In the same year he became a Fellow of the Royal Society.

As a Quaker, he was greatly concerned for the poor and was a leading member of the Spitalfields Soup Society, founded in 1797 to save unemployed weavers from starvation. He was a sponsor of a local school for poor children, a friend of William Wilberforce and an ardent opponent of the slave trade.

By the close of the eighteenth century, he had risen to become proprietor of the firm of Bevan in Old Plough Court. He married, as his second wife, Charlotte Hanbury, and later took her nephews into partnership.

Allen and Hanbury, as the company became known, moved to larger premises in April 1874, to Three Colts Lane, Bethnal Green. The buildings were previously occupied by Letchford, a match manufacturer. William Allen is commemorated locally by Allen Gardens, Buxton Street, E1.

Biographies

Chapman-Huston,D. and Cripps, E.C. *Through a City Archway* (J. Murray, 1954)

Fayle, J. *The Spitalfields Genius* (Hodder and Stoughton, 1884)

AMES, Joseph 1689-1759

Historian of Printing

Joseph Ames was born in Yarmouth, and arrived in Wapping as a boy. After schooling, and apprenticeship to a plane maker he began a life-long business in Wapping near The Hermitage, as a ship's chandler and pattern maker. He also became known for his collection of old books and prints.

His first book on typography, one of the earlist works on printing was published in 1749. Later enlarged and edited by William Herbert, it was published in 1785 from his shop at the 'Sign of the Golden Globe' on London Bridge.

Ames was encouraged in his studies by Rev. John Russell, Vicar of Wapping, Sir Peter Thompson and Rev. John Lewis of Margate,a well known antiquary. Fellowships were gained in 1736 from the Society of Antiquaries and in 1743 from the Royal Society. Examples of his work include *Typographical Antiquaries* (a catalogue of English printers from 1471-1600) as well as an illustrated catalogue of English engraved portraits (1748). Notes for these publications are in the British Library and the Library of the Society of Antiquaries.

Book

Typographical Antiquaries (J. Robinson, 1749)

DNB

ANDERSON, Dr. Elizabeth Garrett 1836-1917

Physician

Elizabeth Garrett, the daughter of a pawnbroker, was born at 1 Commercial Road, Whitechapel (later called Gardiner's Corner) and was baptised in St. George's-in-the-East Church.

As a woman she found it difficult to gain access to medical training and the qualifying examinations, to become a doctor. She lived for a time near the London Hospital at 8 Philpot Street, Whitechapel. One of the tutors, Nathaniel HECKFORD invited her to be a medical officer of the East London Childrens Hospital which he had founded.

In 1871 Elizabeth married J.G.S. Anderson, a partner in the firm Anderson, Thomson and Company which later formed part of the Orient Steam Navigation Company. Anderson died in 1907. She met him while he was Governor of the East London Childrens Hospital.

Dr. Anderson was the first woman to be elected to the School Board for London, the first woman in England to qualify in medicine, the first woman to obtain a degree of Doctor at the Sorbonne University in Paris, the first woman to be appointed warden of a medical school and the founder of the first hospital to be staffed by women. She began a dispensary in 1866 for women and children in Marylebone which developed into a hospital. In 1918 the name changed to Elizabeth Garrett Anderson Hospital, which is now in Euston Road.

In 1908 she was elected Mayor of Aldeburgh, Suffolk, as the first woman mayor in England.

There is a Greater London Council plaque at 20 Upper Berkely Street, W1.

Biography

Manton, J. *Elizabeth Garrett Anderson* (Methuen, 1958)

DNB

ANGELL, Moses 1818-1898
Headmaster

Moses Angell was appointed Head of the Jews' Free School, Bell Lane, Spitalfields in 1839 at the age of 21. He won the respect of Matthew ARNOLD, HM School Inspector, who allowed him to develop the school into a training college for teachers. More Rabbis and Readers were taught by him than were training at Jews' College during his lifetime. He also taught the head teachers of Jewish Day Schools in Birmingham, Manchester, Liverpool and all Jewish Teachers employed by the London School Board. He retired from the Jews' Free School at the age of 79 in 1897.

Moses Angell became Co-Editor of the first series, 1841-42, of *The Jewish Chronicle*, with David Mendola, a minister of Bevis Marks Synagogue, and then decided to join its competitor, the *Voice of Jacob*.

The school building in Bell Lane was destroyed in the second World War. The JFS Secondary School is now in Camden.

Articles
Times Educational Supplement 5th September 1978
Jewish Historical Studies Vol. 32 (1990-92) pp.259-278

APPLETON, Rt. Rev. George
1902-1993
Archbishop in Jerusalem

George Appleton was born in Windsor, the son of a head gardener and a cook. At the age of seven he decided that one day he would be a missionary. From his school he won a scholarship to Selwyn College, Cambridge where he obtained degrees in mathematics and theology. Following a course at St. Augustine's, Canterbury, he came to Stepney as a curate at St. Dunstan's Parish Church. George Appleton's study of Confucianism and Buddhism paved the way for the twenty years he spent in Burma.

He was sent in 1927 to a parish in Rangoon, and was told he was to take no services in English for nine months, during which time he must became proficient in the Burmese language. He would then be able to take over the parish when the incumbent left.

In Burma, George Appleton and his wife, Marjorie lived through some very hard times; with the Japanese invasion, bombings, bubonic plague and eventual exile in India. At the end of the war he returned to Burma as Archdeacon of Rangoon, but felt ill and returned to Britain.

After he recovered he ran a parish near Harrow which was followed with eight years with the Conference of British Missionary Societies. In 1957 he became Rector of St. Botolph's, Aldgate, where he began work for homeless men and women by transforming the tunnels under the Church and making it a place of warmth and welcome. There was also a large youth club meeting in the evenings.

In 1962 George Appleton was appointed Archdeacon of London and was soon invited to be Archbishop of Perth, Australia. When thinking of retiring to concentrate on his writing, he was urged by the Archbishop of Canterbury to become Archbishop in Jerusalem in 1969. This was a very difficult appointment but he worked tirelessly to reconcile conflicting factions.

Autobiography
Unfinished (Collins, 1990)
Obituaries
The Independent 7th September 1993
Church Times 10th September 1993

ARMSBY, Eva 1905-1991
Labour Councillor

Eva Armsby, nee Kelshaw, was born in Swansea. Her father, a Scotsman, was a travelling tinsmith. All the family ultimately worked in the nearby tinworks. Becoming an Evangelical Christian in her early teens, she became concerned for the well-being of her fellow female workers, and acted on their behalf to obtain equal wages and conditions with the men. When her father died she had to care for seven brothers and sisters.

She met her future husband David Armsby, a dock worker, who lodged at her family home after he had transferred from the bomb damaged London Docks to Swansea Docks.

They married in 1945, setting up home in Watts Street Buildings, E1, later moving home to Gosling House, Sutton Street, E1, and finally to Sheridan House, Tarling Street, E1.

She continued her involvement in trade union work whilst employed at an aluminium factory, and this led to her becoming Councillor for Stepney Borough Council, 1949-54, and then for Tower Hamlets Council, 1968-86.

Eva Armsby sat on the International Links, Welfare, Cleansing and Housing Committees and in 1971 was Chair of the Old People's and Welfare Committee. In 1979 she was the first woman to be elected Mayor of Tower Hamlets.

Her great gifts were compassion and conscientiousness. She was an active worker at the Strangers' Rest Mission, The Highway, E1, for over 40 years, she helped many of the young and elderly of the area, and her work is commemorated by the Eva Armsby Family Centre, Glamis Road, E1.

Book

Mellor, J.B. *The Armsby File* (Privately Published, 1995)

ARNOLD, Matthew 1822-1888

Poet

Born at Laleham, Middlesex, Matthew Arnold was the son of Dr. Thomas Arnold, the famous headmaster of Rugby School.

He was educated at Winchester, Rugby and Oxford. After working as secretary to Lord Lansdowne, he was appointed as a Lay Inspector of Schools in 1851 and from 1853 to 1860 was school inspector for Bethnal Green.

In Tower Hamlets Local History Library and Archives there are copies of letters he wrote to Rosella Pitman, headmistress of Abbey Street School, Bethnal Green. Miss Pitman was the sister of Sir Isaac Pitman, inventor of a shorthand system.

Arnold's poem entitled *East London* was published in 1867 and describes a walk through Bethnal Green and Spitalfields. The first verse is:-

> Twas August, and the fierce sun overhead
> Smote on the squalid streets of Bethnal Green
> And the pale weaver, through his windows seen
> In Spitalfields, look'd thrice dispirited

He wrote many poems and about forty books and became Professor of Poetry at Oxford University from 1857 to 1867.

There is a bust of him by Bruce Joy in Westminster Abbey.

Biography

Jump, J.D. *Matthew Arnold* (Longmans, Green, 1955)
Collected Poems

DNB

ASHBEE, Charles Robert
1863-1942

Architect

Charles Ashbee was born at Isleworth and educated at Wellington College and Cambridge. He was articled to G.F.Bodley, an architect who specialised in church work and so was able to study fine handicraft. He later went into private practice.

His main interest was the revival of artistic handicraft and under the influence of John Ruskin and William Morris he established a Guild of Handicraft. This was in Toynbee Art School, Commercial Street, Spitalfields, part of Toynbee Hall, a university settlement. He moved in 1891 to Essex House, Mile End Road, corner of Aberavon Road. Here he collected and trained a body of craftsmen to specialise in furniture making, metal work, jewellery, silver smithing, printing and bookbinding.

In 1902 he moved the Guild, numbering 150 men, women and children to Chipping Campden in Gloucestershire. He bought William Morris' two presses and printed the *King Edward Prayer Book* and the *Essex House Song Book*, both examples of fine printing and binding.

Ashbee founded the London Survey Committee who initiated the *Survey of London* which was taken over by the London County Council and Greater London Council and is now under the aegis of English Heritage.

After the first World War, he was invited by the Governor of Jerusalem to become civil adviser to a society for preserving and safeguarding the buildings of the Holy City. The planning of modern Jerusalem incorporated many of his ideas.

Locally he prepared surveys of St. Dunstan's Church, Stepney and St. Mary's Church, Bromley Saint Leonard.

There is a commemorative plaque at Besso House, Mile End Road, opposite Mile End Station.

Book

McCarthy, F. *The Simple Life* (Lund Humphries, 1981)

DNB, Groves Dictionary of Music

ATKINSON, Dr. Stanley Bean
1873-1910

Doctor and Lawyer

Stanley Atkinson was born in Stepney and his father was pastor of Latimer Congregational Church, Bridge Street (now Ernest Street), Mile End for 50 years. After qualifying as a doctor and barrister he devoted much of his time to public service in Stepney. He was a member of the Stepney Borough Council from 1903-1910, vice chairman of the Board of Guardians and the author of books on medicolegal subjects.

He is commemorated by a bust in the Public Library, Bancroft Road, E1. and a clock tower memorial, originally in Burdett Road and now in Stepney Green, E1.

ATTLEE, Clement Richard, (Earl) 1883-1967
Prime Minister

Clement Attlee was born in Putney and educated at Haileybury School and Oxford. He developed a practical interest in social problems after he came to live at Haileybury House, Durham Row, off Ben Jonson Road, E3, a boys club in Stepney. Soon after, he joined the Limehouse branch of the Independent Labour Party in 1908.

He became secretary of Toynbee Hall, a university settlement in Commercial Street, E1 in 1908 and started lecturing in 1913 at the London School of Economics. This was followed by wartime promotion to the rank of major.

After being elected Mayor of Stepney Borough Council in 1919 he became Labour member of Parliament for Limehouse from 1922 to 1950 and, when the boundaries were changed, for Walthamstow West from 1950 to 1955. He served in the first Labour Government (1924) and the second (1929) under Ramsay MacDonald. In 1931 he was one of the few Labour members to retain his seat and he became Deputy Leader of the Opposition under George LANSBURY, succeeding him as Leader in 1935.

In the second World War, he was Deputy Prime Minister under Sir Winston Churchill from 1942 to 1945 and Prime Minister 1945 to 1951, bringing forward a vigorous programme of reform and nationalisation. The National Health Service was begun in 1946, and independence was granted to India in 1947 and to Burma in 1948.

Clement Attlee received a Companion of Honour in 1945, and the Order of Merit in 1951 and was elevated to the peerage as Earl Attlee in 1955.

He summed up his political career thus:-

Few thought he was even a starter
There were many who thought
    themselves smarter
But he finished PM, CH and OM
An earl and a Knight of the Garter

The Limerick, written by himself was published in the *Daily Telegraph* 18th February 1983.

Attlee, speaking into the microphone at Transport House, Westminster after being elected Chairman of the Labour Party on 8th October 1935 *Whiffin Collection*

His name is commemorated by Attlee House, 28, Commercial Street, E1 and by a statue outside Limehouse Library, Commercial Road, E14.
Autobiography
As it happened (Heinemann, 1948)
Biographies
Jenkins, R. *Mr Attlee* (Heinemann, 1948)
Brome, V. *Clement Attlee* (Lincolns-Praeger, 1949)
DLB, DNB

ATTWELL, Mabel Lucy 1879-1964
Illustrator

Mabel Lucy Attwell was born at 182 Mile End Road, Mile End Old Town, the daughter of Augustus Attwell, a butcher. She was educated at Coopers' School, Tredegar Square, Bow and then attended classes at Regent Street Polytechnic and Heatherly's Art School. In 1909 she married the painter and illustrator Harold Earnshaw.

She contributed drawings to the *Tatler* and *Bystander* magazines, she must enjoyed making sketches and drawings of imaginary subjects arising out of her enjoyment of fairy stories.

She was commissioned to illustrate a series of books in the 'Raphael House Library of Gift

Books'. These included *Mother Goose* (1909), *Alice in Wonderland* (1910), *Hans Andersen's Fairy Tales* (1913), *Water Babies* (1915), *Peter Pan* (1921) and *Grimm's Fairy Tales* (1925), all published by Raphael Tuck.

Mabel Lucy Attwell also designed picture postcards for Valentine and Sons, and her pictures of children figured on all kinds of nursery equipment.

The *Lucie Attwell Annual* was published from 1922-1974, continuing for ten years after her death.

A centenary exhibition of her work was held at the Brighton Museum from December 1979-January 1980.

DNB

ATTWOOD, Edward Lewis 1871-1940
Naval Architect

Edward Attwood was born in Poplar. He was one of the first 12 pupils selected as foundation scholars of the second George Green's School, which was on the corner of East India Dock Road and Kerby Street, Poplar. This was followed by work in the drawing office of R. and H. Green of Blackwall. A further scholarship was then gained to the Royal Naval College, Greenwich.

Later he became Professor of Naval Architecture at the College and a renowned teacher. His *Textbook of Theoretical Naval Architecture* (1899) was regarded as a standard work.

Most of the major battleships built between the first and second World Wars came during his tenure as Director of Naval Construction at the Admiralty.

AYLWARD, Ellen 1894-1988
Labour Councillor

Ellen Aylward followed the tradition of her family in being elected a member of Stepney Borough Council in 1918.

Her father had also been a member, and Aylward Street, E1 was named after him.

A retired Local Government Officer, Ellen Aylward was Mayor 1962-63.
Articles
Step Ahoy June 1962
East London Advertiser 3rd November 1978

BAILEY, Nathan or Nathaniel
died 1742
Lexicographer

Little is known about the early life of Nathan Bailey. He was probably born in Stepney and his father was a Dissenter.

Nathan became a member of the Seventh Day Adventists at Mill Yard, off Leman Street, Whitechapel in 1691.

He kept a boarding school in Stepney which was advertised in the first edition of his dictionary published in 1721. He also wrote the *Antiquities of London* together with a spelling book and English and Latin exercises.

Thirty editions of his dictionary were published, the last in 1802. Samuel Johnson used an inter-leaved folio copy in compiling his own dictionary.

In their book *The English Dictionary from Cawdry to Johnson* (1946) D.T. Sarnes and G.E. Noyes say of Bailey: 'Spanning eighty years, this book may be logically considered the most popular and representative dictionary of the 18th century'.

Bailey's death was reported in the *Gentleman's Magazine* Vol.12 (July 1742).
Source
Mangold, A.J. *The Place of N. Bailey in the Development of the English Dictionary*
(Unpublished dissertation for the degree of M.A. University of Bristol, 1962)

DNB

BAILLIE, Robert 1818-1899
Engineer and Bridge Builder

Robert Baillie was born in Joppa near Edinburgh. He was apprenticed to an engineering firm in Edinburgh and took part in the building of the first steam cars made to the order of John Scott RUSSELL.

Baillie came to London in 1837. He formed a partnership with Robert STEVENSON, building his Britannia tubular bridge over the Menai Straits. On completion of the bridge, Baillie and Westwood became works managers at the firm founded by C.J. MARE.

In 1856, with Westwood and James Campbell he commenced business as Westwood and Baillie at London Yard, Millwall constructing many famous bridges, notably the Sukkur Bridge, parts of which were erected in the yard before shipment to what is now Pakistan. This was the largest cantilever bridge in the world before the Forth Bridge and was designed by Arnold MUSTO. The firm also

built battleships. Westwood and Baillie ceased trading in 1893.
Book
Banbury, P. *Shipbuiders of the Thames and Medway* (David and Charles, 1971)

BANCROFT, Francis 1667-1727
City Officer

Francis Bancroft was born in Spitalfields. He was the son of John Bancroft, Sergeant Carver to the Lord Mayor. He worked for the City Corporation as servant to the Common Crier; his duties included summoning and attending people wanted for certain committees. He later became an under Water Bailiff and then Yeoman at the Waterside, but he returned to his position. He became a Freeman of the Drapers' Company in 1690.

His estate, which was about £28,000 was left to the Drapers' Company in trust to include £4,000/£5,000 for the foundation of almshouses for 24 old men and a school for 100 boys. After some years, a site in Mile End was purchased, near the Jews Burial Ground, now inside the grounds of Queen Mary and Westfield College. Bancroft's Hospital, as the whole site became known, opened in 1737, with a hospital, almshouses and a year later, with a school. The education function was the only part to survive the re-organisation with Bancroft's school moving to Woodford, in 1886.

There is a monument to Francis Bancroft in St. Helen's Church, Bishopsgate. He is also commemorated by Bancroft Road, E1.
Book
Francombe, D.C.R. and Coult, D.E. (eds) *Bancroft's School, 1737-1937* (Privately printed, 1937)

BANNISTER, Charles Acres
1868-1901
Resident

On the 14th October 1901, a severe fire broke out at the premises of Emery and Son, Drapers, 127-131 Bow Road, Bow. The fire was caused by the lighting of a gas burner in a window, by an assistant with a taper. A curtain caught fire and soon the whole building was burning.

Charles Bannister, who lived at Brewery Yard, Bow, worked in auction rooms opposite the drapers. He ran across the road to give what help he could to the 23 assistants who worked there.

The next day two bodies were discovered in the basement of the burnt out premises, Henry Ludlow of Peckham and Charles Bannister. The inquest concluded that Bannister had been helping Ludlow to escape when they were overcome with smoke.

The courageous acts by ordinary Tower Hamlets residents who lost their lives in attempting to save others are also commemorated by tablets in the churchyard of St. Botolph's, Aldersgate, EC1. They are:-

Elizabeth BOXALL, resident of Bethnal Green 1871-1888. Died of injuries received in trying to save a child from a runaway horse, 20th June 1888.

Alice DENMAN, resident 1875-1902 and Arthur REGELOUS, resident 1877-1902. Both died in trying to save Alice Denman's four children from a burning house in Bethnal Green, 20th April 1902.

Solomon GULAMAN, 1890-1901. Died of injuries received after saving his younger brother from being run over in Commercial Street, E1.

Joseph William ONSLOW, lighterman. He drowned at Wapping trying to save a boy's life.

John SLADE, of Stepney. A private in the 4th Battalion Royal Fusiliers, when his house caught fire. After saving one man, he lost his life in going upstairs to save others.

Alice Denman and Arthur Regelous are also commemorated by a drinking fountain in Bethnal Green Gardens.
Source
East London Advertiser 19th October 1901; 26th October 1901

BARLOW, Peter William
1809-1885
Civil Engineer

Peter Barlow was born in Woolwich, the son of a Professor of Mathematics at the Royal Military Academy.

He became assistant to Thomas TELFORD and then an associate of the BRUNELS in the building of the Thames Tunnel from Rotherhithe to Wapping. This was the first tunnel in the world in which the system of the tunnel shield was used.

The first Lambeth Bridge, Tower Subway (1869-70), and Cubitt Town were built whilst he was resident engineer under Sir William CUBITT. He became engineer-in-chief to the London and Dover Railway, 1840, and was responsible for the Tunbridge Wells branch

and other lines in the area. In 1845 he was elected a Fellow of the Royal Society.
Book
Pudney, J. *Crossing London's River* (J.M.Dent, 1972)
DNB

Barlow's Thames Tunnel shield

BARNARDO, Dr. Thomas John
1845-1905
Founder of Homes for Destitute Children

Thomas Barnardo was born in Dublin. In 1866 he came to the London Hospital as a student with the idea of becoming a medical missionary. Going about Stepney he was greatly troubled by the large number of homeless children that he found in the street.

In his spare time he taught in a number of local 'ragged schools' from which he learned much about local conditions. He later claimed that this work had influenced his 'rescue mission'.

He founded his East End Juvenile Mission in 1868 in two small cottages at the end of a blind alley called Hope Place, Limehouse, off the south side of Ben Jonson Road.

A house at 18 Stepney Causeway was rented in 1870 as the first lodging place and a notice was placed above the door that,

> No destitute boy or girl (later, child) ever refused admission

Soon it became the headquarters of the operations of 'Dr. Barnardo's Homes' organisation and in 1887, a major extension took place, with the conversion of other properties in the street into the infirmary. In 1970 Dr. Barnardo's Homes left Stepney and moved to Barkingside.

The Homes still provide residential and non-residential care for over 9,000 children in need. Branches have been opened in Eire, Australia and New Zealand.

There is a Greater London Council Blue Plaque, erected in 1952, near the original site of Hope Place.

He is commemorated in the borough by Barnardo Street, E1, and Barnardo Gardens, a housing estate in Cable Street, E1. A commemorative plaque exists at 30 Coborn Street where he lodged on first coming to London in 1866.

Biographies
Wagner G.   *Barnardo* (Weidenfeld and Nicolson, 1979)
Williams, G.   *Barnardo; the Extraordinary Doctor* (Macmillan, 1966)
Pamphlet
Ridge, T.S.   *Dr. Barnardo and the Copperfield Road Ragged Schools* (Ragged School Museum Trust, 1993)

DNB

Wax figure of Dr. Barnardo

BARNATO, Barney 1852-1897
Financier

Barney Barnato was born, Barnett Isaacs, in Whitechapel. His grandfather was Rabbi of a synagogue in Aldgate, and his father, a general dealer. He attended the Jews' Free School in Bell Lane, Spitalfields.

In 1871 his elder brother, Henry, went to the diamond fields in Kimberley, South Africa, as a conjurer and entertainer. On arriving, he obtained employment as a diamond dealer and he invited Barney to join him.

Barney arrived in 1873 with fifty pounds in his pocket; he began business as a diamond dealer and by 1876 had amassed three thousand pounds.

He bought up mines that were thought to be exhausted, and discovered that the blue subsoil was richer in diamonds than the surface yellow.

He returned to London and established the firm of Barnato Brothers, financiers and diamond dealers. Later, there was great competition with Cecil Rhodes for control of the gold mining firm of de Beers.

Barnato was elected to the South African Assembly and was re-elected for a second term.

In 1897, his health began to fail, and on his way home to England, he threw himself overboard near Madeira. His body was recovered and he was buried in Willesden Cemetery.

Although he had great financial aptitude, he was almost illiterate, he read nothing, spending his time at horse racing and prize fighting.

DNB

BARNETT, Henrietta Octavia Weston DBE 1851-1936
Social Reformer

Henrietta Barnett was born in Clapham, Henrietta Rowland. She met her husband, Samual BARNETT through Octavia Hill, a housing pioneer. They were married in 1873 and shared their work for forty years.

She was the first nominated woman Guardian of the Poor in 1875. Her appointment to a government committee on the conditions of Poor Law children, led in 1896 to the State Children's Association, of which she became Honorary Secretary. In 1884 she was a joint founder with her husband of the Children's Country Holiday Fund and also at that time became President of the London Pupil Teachers' Association.

An advocate of the settlement ideal in America, in 1920 she was invited to become President of the 480 strong American Federation of Settlements.

After leaving East London her work was mainly in Hampstead. She raised £43,000 to

Rev. S.A. and Mrs Barnett at the time of their marriage in 1873

save 80 acres of Hampstead Heath for the public and in 1903 formed the Hampstead Garden Suburb Trust to purchase a further 240 acres for houses and grounds, the work beginning in 1907. She also founded the Dame Henrietta Barnett School and was active in many organisations for women and children.

In 1918 she wrote the biography of her husband, and when she was 72 she began painting and had a picture accepted for the Royal Academy exhibition of 1923.

Appointed CBE in 1917 and DBE in 1924.

DNB

BARNETT, Rev. Samuel Augustus 1844-1913
Founder of Toynbee Hall

Samuel Barnett was born in Bristol and educated at Oxford. In 1873 he was appointed Vicar of St. Jude's Church, Commercial Street, Whitechapel. He was greatly disturbed by the conditions under which many people had to live and he wanted to do something practical to help them.

After long discussions the historian Arnold TOYNBEE, who died at an early age, Barnett founded Toynbee Hall in his memory in 1884. It was the first university settlement to be established and was modelled on the lines of an Oxford College, where men from Oxford and Cambridge could live in contact with their neighbours to learn of their problems and give practical help. Many people who became famous began their work here.

Among many things that Samuel Barnett began with his wife Henrietta BARNETT were the Children's Country Holiday Fund and the Whitechapel Art Gallery, opened in 1901. Samuel was a Guardian of the Poor for Whitechapel for 29 years.

In 1894 he became a Canon of Bristol Cathedral and in 1906 a Canon of Westminster.

There is a memorial tablet to him in Westminster Abbey and he is commemorated in the Borough by Canon Barnett Junior School, Commercial Street, E1.

Biography
Barnett, H. *Canon Barnett* (J.Murray, 1918)
Book
Pimlott, J.A.R. *Toynbee Hall* (J.M.Dent, 1935)
Briggs, A. and Macartney, A. *Toynbee Hall* (Routledge and Kegan Paul, 1984)

DNB

BARON, Bernhard 1850-1929
Philanthropist

Born in Russia, as a boy Bernhard Baron emigrated to America and began work in a cigarette factory. Later he began a cigar making business in Baltimore. He invented a machine for making cigarettes, settled in England and purchased the tobacco business of J.J. Carreras which became very succesful under him.

The generous contributions of £2 million to hospitals, including the former Poplar Hospital and to homes for crippled children stemmed from a sympathy he held from his early life towards the needs of poor people. Some money also went to help fund the Bernhard Baron St. George's Jewish Settlement, formerly in Henriques Street, E1 of which Sir Basil HENRIQUES and his wife Lady Rose HENRIQUES were Wardens.

When he died his estate was worth nearly £5 million.

DNB

Ernest James Bartlett

BARTLETT, Ernest James
1870-1942
Antiquary

Ernest Bartlett was born in Bow. His family moved to Bethnal Green when he was a few months old and he lived there for the rest of his life. Education took place at Olga Street School, and Haberdashers Askes School, which was then followed by work in the office of a marine insurance broker.

He remained a bachelor, and became an ardent collector of prints and other materials relating to Bethnal Green.

Pamphlet
Snaith, S. *The Bartlett Bequest* (Bethnal Green Public Libraries, 1947)

Rev. Philip Mandeville Bartlett

BARTLETT, Rev. Philip Mandeville
1885-1958
Priest

Philip Bartlett was the son of a wealthy baronet whose firm were the builders of Tower Bridge and Waterloo Station. He went to Westminster School and Oxford, where he obtained a rowing blue.

In 1906 he made his first visit to Poplar's Christ Church Mission and following His Ordination in 1910, he became its curate. Nine years later he became Vicar of St. Saviour's Church, Northumberland Street, Poplar and was there for nearly forty years.

He frequently went hop-picking with his parishioners and bought a large house in Herne Bay to enable children from St. Saviour's School to go on holiday.

In 1951 he was appointed Rural Dean of Poplar. His name is commemorated by Bartlett Park, E14.

BEAUMONT, John Thomas Barber
1774-1841
Philanthropist

Barber Beaumont was born in Marylebone. He attended the Royal Academy School and began as an artist, specialising in miniature portrait painting. He was appointed painter to the Duke of Kent and to the Duke of York.

In 1806 he became the founder and manager of the County Fire Office, an insurance company, and of the Provident Life Institute and Bank of Savings. This was the first properly constituted friendly society and workman's savings bank.

Shortly before his death he founded the New Philosophical Institute in Beaumont Square, Mile End and left money in his will for its continuation. His trustees collaborated with the Drapers' Company to found the People's Palace and the East London Technical College which were opened by Queen Victoria in May 1887. Queen Mary and Westfield College now occupies the site.

His memorial stone can be seen in the entrance to the Queens Building of Queen Mary and Westfield College. He is also commemorated by Beaumont Grove, Beaumont Square and Barber Beaumont House, Bancroft Road, E1.

Book
Beaumont, W.S. *A Brief Account of the Beaumont Trust* (Charles and Edwin Lawton, 1887)

DNB

BEDFORD, Peter 1780-1864
Silk Merchant and Reformer

Peter Bedford was born at Old Sampford, Essex. His parents were Quakers who owned a farm and a draper's shop. On leaving school he entered the silk weaving business of Joseph Allen, the father of William ALLEN, in Steward Street, Spitalfields. When Joseph Allen died, Peter Bedford became the proprietor of the business.

Interested in the social conditions of the area, he became involved in starting a number of charitable societies to assist people who were very poor. In 1797 the Spitalfields Soup Society was formed, serving some 1,000 people each day. A school and working men's club was started in Spicer Street, an association for relief of the poor in Spitalfields and a night shelter in Hoxton.

He is best remembered for his interest in delinquency and its causes. He earned the respect and affection of many criminals, as well as those who worked with him. After his death an association of centres for social work was formed by his fellow Quakers, who decided to call it the Bedford Institute Association. The building which housed the first Bedford Institute can still be seen in Wheler Street, E1. There were other centres in Ratcliff, Bethnal Green and Hoxton. The work of the Bedford Institute continues to the present day.

He is commemorated locally by Bedford House, Ford Square, E1.

Biographies
Tallack, W. *Peter Bedford; the Spitalfields Philanthropist* (S.W.Partridge, 1865)
Friends Education Council *Peter Bedford* (Friends Education Council, 1973)

BEKE, Dr. Charles Tilstone 1800-1874
Explorer

Charles Beke was born in Stepney and educated at a private school in Hackney. On leaving, he began a business career which took him for a time to Genoa and Naples. On his return he decided to study law and entered Lincoln's Inn.

While undertaking legal studies he published *Researches in Primeval History* in 1834. It was the first attempt to reconstruct history on the principles of what was then the young science of geology. In this work he theorized on the tripartite division of the origins of mankind, from which had arisen all existing languages and dialects. Tubingen University, Germany, honoured him with a doctorate.

In 1840 he made his first journey to Abyssinia to open up commercial relations, to explore the extent of the slave trade and to discover the source of the Nile. He mapped 70,000 square miles and collected vocabularies of 14 languages and dialects.

In 1873 he led an expedition to discover the true location of Mount Sinai and the route taken by Israelites in their escape from Egypt. A book *The Late Dr. Charles Beke's Discoveries of Sinai in Arabia and of Midan* was published in 1878 by his wife after his death but the book caused much controversy.

DNB

BELL, Edward 1860-1954
Labour Leader

Edward Bell was born in Bethnal Green and became a natural leader from the beginning. His life was inextricably bound up with the growth of the Labour movement. He began work as a pot boy for a gang of workmen. Brought up in a depression, his early life was shadowed by the spectre of unemployment and his life was devoted to the defeat of poverty. He was a fine public speaker and a widely read man.

He was one of the organisers of 'Bloody Sunday', as the 13th November 1887 became known, when a march of working people from all over London demonstrated in Trafalgar Square for the right of free speech. The marchers were attacked by police and Life Guards and over 200 people were injured and three died. The demonstrations lasted another two weeks.

Two leaders, John Burns and R.B. Cunninghame-Graham, MP were wounded badly and arrested. Two months later, when they were tried, both were found innocent of riot, but guilty of unlawful assault and sent to prison for six weeks.

In 1890 Edward Bell became a founder member of the Socialist Democratic Federation. He formed the first local branch, holding meetings in his front parlour, continuing until its dissolution in 1930, when he joined the Labour Party.

He worked for the Gas, Light and Coke Company until his retirement in 1925 and then worked as a roadman for Walthamstow Council until he was 73.

BENN, Sir John Williams
1850-1922
Publisher

John Benn was born in Hyde, Cheshire, the eldest son of Julius BENN. He came to Stepney with his parents when they took over 'The Star in the East' in Stepney Causeway, a home for destitute children. In the 1870s and 1880s he lived at 119 Stepney Green, Mile End.

At the age of eleven, John Benn began work in a city office. Taking up drawing, he made sketch plans of furniture. From junior draughtsman he rose to become chief designer in 1868. Three years later he began an independent career as a draughtsman in the furniture trade.

He joined a debating society in his spare time and became a proficient speaker and organiser, giving help to his father's church and social work. In 1880 he entered the world of trade journalism with a magazine he began, called the *Cabinet Maker*. As a part-time lecturer at evening classes he gained wide experience and extra money. He also wrote several plays.

The London County Council began in 1889 and he was one of its first members, being elected for East Finsbury. He became secretary and whip of the Progressive Party and held many important positions. He was Chairman of the Highways Committee which introduced the tramways system in 1903. He became Leader of the Council, holding the office for thirty-three years, and was Chairman, 1904-1905.

He was elected Liberal Member of Parliament for St. George's-in-the-East and later for Devonport.

His sons were Ernest, later Sir Ernest Benn (1875-1954) a publisher, and William Wedgewood Benn, later Viscount Stansgate (1877-1960) who was the father of Tony Benn, MP.

Biography
Gardiner, A.G. *John Benn and the Progressive Movement* (Ernest Benn, 1825)

BENN, Rev. Julius 1824-1883
Dissenting Minister

Julius Benn began work as an assistant in a draper's business in Limerick. He then came to England and with his wife began a school at Hyde near Manchester. This was the start of a career in educating and caring for children. It was followed by an appointment as master of 'The Star of the East', a home for destitute children, situated in an old rope factory in Stepney Causeway. Charles DICKENS is said to have visited the home. After a period as master of a reformatory school in Northamptonshire he returned to East London as missionary for St. George's-in-the-East district.

In 1874 he became Minister of the Independent Meeting House in Old Gravel Lane, Wapping, founded in 1736 by Isaac WATTS. The chapel became known as 'Benn's Chapel'.

Benn was responsible for the suggestion to Nathaniel HECKFORD that an old warehouse in Butcher Row be converted into a children's hospital.

Julius was the father of Sir John Williams BENN.

At a boarding house in Matlock Julius was tragically killed by his third son William on holiday with his father. The boy had previously been confined to an asylum and had been considered to have greatly improved.

'Benn's Chapel' closed temporarily on his death and was re-opened by the London Congregational Union in 1885 as a mission hall.

Book
Higgins, S. *The Benn Inheritance* (Weidenfeld, 1984)

BENTHAM, Jeremy 1748-1832
Philosopher and Legal Reformer

Jeremy Bentham was born in Red Lion Street, Spitalfields, now part of Commercial Street. He was the son of an attorney.

He entered Lincoln's Inn to begin legal studies, but he had no real interest in becoming a lawyer, and abandoned it in favour of chemistry and physical sciences. He travelled in Italy, Turkey and Russia. Subsequently he turned his attention to the study of legal, political and economic systems. Jeremy Bentham became one of the most influential radical thinkers of his time. His ideas substantially affected the government reform of the Poor Laws in 1834, and many nineteenth century reforms of the English legal system.

In his *Introduction to the Principles of Morals and Legislation* (1789), he advanced the philosophical theory of unitarianism which underlay much of the social reform of the nineteenth century.

Throughout his life, Jeremy Bentham was pre-occupied with issues of prison reform, and the ideas put forward in *The Principles of Penal Law* influenced later reforms.

In 1823 Jeremy Bentham was one of the founders of the radical *Westminster Review*, and he was amongst the founders also of University College, London. He bequeathed his body for dissection by medical students, and his skeleton is preserved at University College, Gower Street, WC.

DNB

BERG, Jack (Kid) 1909-1991
Boxer

Judah Bergman was born in Cable Street, St. George's-in-the-East, and became an outstanding lightweight boxer. He lived to be the oldest British Champion.

He was apprenticed as a lather boy in a barber's shop and began his boxing career at the Premierland, Back Church Lane, Whitechapel when he was fourteen.

Between 1923 and 1936 he had 192 professional fights, winning 157 of them.

A large number of his fights were in America where he won 64 out of 76.

He moved to America and in 1930 he beat Mushy Callahan, to win the Junior Welterweight title but lost it to Tony Canzoneri in 1931. In 1934 he became British Lightweight Champion.

In his retirement he became a film stunt man.

He is commemorated by a plaque unveiled in 1993 on Noble Court, Cable Street, E1, close to the place where he was born.
Source
Morrison, I. *Boxing Who's Who* (Guinness Publishing, 2nd edn, 1993)
Autobiography
Harding, J. with Berg, J.K. *Jack Kidd Berg* (Robson, 1987)

BESANT, Annie 1847-1933
Social Reformer

Annie Besant was born in London of Irish parents and brought up in Harrow. She was a friend of Charles BRADLAUGH, becoming, a co-defendant with him in the famous birth control trial of 1877. In 1885 she joined the Fabian Society and the Social Democratic Federation.

She became a public speaker; Bernard Shaw regarded her in the 1880s as 'the greatest orator in England, possibly Europe'. She was also a prolific writer on a wide variety of topics including euthenasia, the French Revolution, prostitution, and women's rights.

Annie Besant helped to found the Law and Liberty League, which published a weekly

Annie Besant speaking to the strike committee of the Matchmakers' Union

journal called *The Link*. In this journal she waged her famous campaign leading to the strike of the East London match girls in 1888. In an article entitled *The White Slavery in London* she attacked the employers, BRYANT and MAY for paying a dividend of 23 per cent to shareholders, while the girl workers were grossly underpaid, receiving 4/6d and 5/- a week; only four women in the firm earned 13/- a week. After a girl was dismissed for insubordination the strike began on 5th July.

Mrs Besant was invited to be the strike leader and *The Link* became the strike paper. The strike lasted a fortnight with victory for the girls. Annie became secretary of the Matchmakers' Union which by September had over 600 members. This was the first strike in the history of the Labour movement involving a large number of women. The protest gained wide interest and much sympathy.

Annie Besant was elected a member of the School Board for London from 1888-91. In 1890 she moved a resolution for the abolition of school fees, which played an important part in the Government's introduction of free schools in 1891.

Her other main interest was Indian nationalism, and she drafted a Bill seeking Dominion status for India within the Empire. The Bill was introduced in the House of Commons by George LANSBURY in 1925.

She was married in 1867 to Rev. Frank Besant, brother of Sir Walter BESANT but they were legally separated and lived apart for many years.

Annie is commemorated locally by Annie Besant Close, E3.

There is a Greater London Council Blue Plaque at 39, Colby Road, SE5

Biography
Nethercot, A. *The First Five Lives of Annie Besant* (Rupert Hart-Davis, 1961)

DLB, DNB

BESANT, Sir Walter 1836-1901
Historian and Writer

Walter Besant was born in Portsmouth. He was educated at Stockwell Grammar School, King's College, London and Cambridge. After a period as a schoolmaster in England and a Professor in Mauritius, he devoted himself to writing.

His early novels were written in partnership with James Rice, editor of the magazine *Once a Week* to which Besant contributed. When Rice died, Besant continued writing and in 1882 published *All Sorts and Conditions of Men*, a novel about East London. The book encouraged interest in the idea of the People's Palace, opened in 1887, founded with the assistance from the Beaumont Trust and the Drapers' Company. The foundation eventually led to the establishment of Queen Mary College and many evening schools for adults throughout England.

In addition to his many novels, Walter Besant is remembered for his *History of London* (1893).

He had many interests, and between 1868 and 1886 he was secretary to the Palestine Exploration Fund and first Chairman of the Incorporated Society of Authors, 1889 to 1892.

There is a memorial to him by Sir George Frampton in St. Paul's Cathedral entitled 'Historian of London', with a replica on the Victoria Embankment.

Locally he is commemorated by Walter Besant House, Bancroft Road, E1.

BEVERIDGE, Lord William
1879-1963
Economist

William Beveridge was born in India and educated at Charterhouse School and Oxford. He became a resident at Toynbee Hall, a university settlement, from 1903 to 1906, and was its Sub-Warden from 1903 to 1905 with responsibilities for educational activities.

A leading authority on unemployment insurance, he became the Director of Labour Exchanges, 1909 to 1916. Eighteen years were served as Director of the London School of Economics from 1919, followed by eight years as Master of University College, Oxford, from 1937.

He became well known for his report on *Social Insurance and Allied Services*, produced during the second World War. The *Beveridge Report* (1942) proposed a comprehensive scheme of social insurance covering the whole community without income limit.

The Labour Government of 1945 to 1951 under Clement ATTLEE implemented a similar scheme.

William Beveridge was knighted in 1919 and was raised to the peerage in 1946.

Biography
Harris, J. *William Beveridge* (Clarendon Press, 1977)

DNB

BHOWNAGGREE, Sir Mancherjee Merwanjee 1851-1933
Barrister and Member of Parliament

Mancherjee Bhownaggree was born in Bombay and educated at Elphinstone College, Bombay and Bombay University. As a student he won a prize for the best English essay of the year, entitled *The Constitution of the East India Company*, which later formed the basis of a book.

He always intended to be a lawyer, but he commenced his working life as a journalist on the Indian newspaper *The Statesman*. On the death of his father in 1875, he succeeded him as head of the State Agency Office of the Bhavnagar territory for which he became Judicial Councillor. He was also a translator of English books into Gujerati.

In 1882 he paid his first visit to England to read for the Bar at Lincoln's Inn, and qualified in 1885. On his return to India he played a prominent part in tracking down and prosecuting a gang of blackmailing journalists. He acted as secretary to the Rukhmibai Committee which successfully upheld the rights and dignity of Indian women, and became an authority on their education.

He founded the Ave Bhownaggree Nurses Home in Bombay in memory of his only sister.

In 1895 he was adopted as Conservative candidate for North East Bethnal Green Constituency and was elected a year later, beating George Howell by 160 votes. In Parliament, his advocacy of the civil rights of Indians in working as indentured labourers in South Africa and other parts of the British Empire won him many friends. He continued as Member of Parliament until 1906.

He was created a Baronet in 1897.

For many years he was the leading Indian permanently resident in Britain.
Article
The Eastern Argus and Borough of Hackney Times
15th April 1895
Who Was Who 1929-1940, DNB

BILLIG, Hannah, MBE, GM, FRCGP, MBBS 1901-1987
General Practitioner

Hannah Billig was born at 41 Hanbury Street, Mile End New Town, the daughter of Russian refugees, Barnett and Millie Billig. In 1912 Hannah Billig won a scholarship to Myrdle Street Central School and later trained to become a doctor.

She was a resident doctor at the Jewish Maternity Hospital in Underwood Street, now Underwood Road, and in 1927 she moved to Watney Street, St. George's-in-the-East to establish a clinic. By 1935 the clinic opened at 198 Cable Street, St. George's-in-the-East.

During the Blitz she helped in rescue work. Although injured on the 13th March 1941 she selflessly continued to look after the other casualties. The bravery she displayed during the air raids in Wapping were recognised with an award to her of the George Medal in June 1941.

She was awarded the MBE in 1945 for her famine relief work in Bengal and Assam.

After the War she returned to her practice in Cable Street and worked there until her retirement in 1964. Hannah Billig was a member of the Jewish Medical Society and the Jewish Infants' Welfare Centre, and worked for the Society for the Protection of Women and Girls.

Following her emigration to Israel she worked in the Arab villages and Jewish settlements, and in 1975 received an Honorary Fellowship of the Royal College of General Practitioners.
Pamphlets
Brooks, M.H. *Dr. Hannah Billig 1901-1987; the 'Angel of Cable Street'* (Privately Published, 1993)
Taylor, R. *Hannah Billig* (The Author, 1996)

BIRCH, Canon John Godfrey 1880-1965
Priest

John Birch was educated at Oxford. He was ordained in 1907 and came as a curate to St. Barnabus Church, Bethnal Green from 1907 to 1911. He then went to St. George's Church, Hanover Square, Westminster.

In 1920 he became Rector of St. Anne's Church, Limehouse and worked there for thirty five years. For many years he was governor of the Hamlet of Ratcliff School (Greencoat) when this eighteenth century establishment changed its status to a Church of England Central School (1929). He devoted much time to the British Sailors' Society and to the welfare of his parishioners young and old.

In 1930 he wrote a history of the parish entitled *Limehouse through five centuries*.
Crockford's Directory 1963-64

BISHOP, Sidney Macdonald
1900-1949
Footballer

Sidney Bishop was born in Stepney. He played for Ilford before joining West Ham Football Club in 1920.

He was in the West Ham team that lost to Bolton Wanderers in the first F.A. Cup Final to be played at Wembley. He was later capped for England.

BLIZARD, Sir William 1743-1835
Surgeon

William Blizard was born at Barn Elms, Surrey, the son of an auctioneer. He was apprenticed to an apothecary in Mortlake and then became assistant to a surgeon in Crutched Friars, in the City, attending lectures at St. George's, St. Bartholomew's and Guy's Hospitals. He was appointed surgeon at Magdalen Hospital in Prescot Street, Whitechapel, the buildings formerly occupied by the London Hospital.

He was appointed surgeon to the London Hospital in 1780, and founded the London Hospital Medical School in 1785, a new building in Turner Street opened in 1854.

The Samaritan Society was also founded by him, and still functions, its purpose to give assistance to patients after they had been discharged. The motto of the Samaritan Society is 'Take Care of Him', words from St. Luke's Gospel.

Blizard was also largely responsible for the formation of the Royal College of Surgeons and became its President in 1814. One of the functions of the President was to supervise the handover of bodies from Newgate Prison, there being a rule that bodies had to be dissected within a certain distance of the prison. Blizard would appear in his ceremonial gown providing a sharp contrast to the seedy and gloomy surroundings. There is a portrait of him by John Opie in the Royal College of Surgeons.

Book
Clark-Kennedy, A.E. *The London* (Pitman-Medical, 1962)
DNB

BOLT, Daniel 1873-1946
Deputy Borough Surveyor, Poplar

Daniel Bolt was born in Stepney. His father, Captain Bolt was well known at the Riverside and on sailing ships; the ship he commanded, Holmsdale, is commemorated by Holmsdale House, Poplar High Street.

On leaving school Daniel accompanied his father on a voyage round the world in the *Harbinger*. The experience aroused in him a life-long interest in the sea, and he was recognised as an authority on sailing ships, and was consulted by individuals and groups all over the world.

He presented to Poplar Borough Council a unique collection of house flags flown by vessels trading in Poplar. In 1934 part of the collection was exhibited at the Centenary Maritime Exhibition in Melbourne, Australia. Other valuable material passed to the Library in 1942. The 'Bolt Collection' is now in Tower Hamlets Local History Library.

Daniel Bolt served Poplar Borough Council for 50 years, entering their service in 1887 as a junior and working his way up to Deputy Borough Surveyor. For a time, he acted as Borough Surveyor. In 1938 Poplar Borough Council published a list of streets, places and subsidiary names, compiled by Bolt, giving the origin of many street names. He is commemorated by Daniel Bolt Close, E14.

BOMBERG, David Garshen
1890-1957
Painter

David Bomberg was born in Birmingham, the son of a leather worker who emigrated from Warsaw to the East End in the 1880s, but was forced to move about the country in search of work. In 1895 the family came to Brushfield Street, Spitalfields. After several more moves they settled at 20 Tenter Buildings, St. Mark Street, Whitechapel. Apprenticed to a lithographer, he broke his indentures in 1908 to enable him to devote all his time to art.

He attended evening classes for two years and studied under W.R. Sickert. From 1911 13 he was a full-time student at the Slade School, winning a prize for drawing in his second year. In 1913 he went to Paris and met Picasso, and during that year he became a founder-member of the London Group.

Among pictures exhibited at his first exhibition in 1914 was *Ju-Jitsu* which is now in the Tate Gallery. He served with the Royal Engineers in France and in 1918, was commissioned by the Canadian Government to assist in the Canadian War Memorial. His picture *Sappers at Work* is in the National Gallery in Ottawa.

He then travelled extensively and many of his pictures are in galleries in this country and abroad. He died in obscure poverty. The Arts Council organised a retrospective exhibition in 1958 and in 1967 there was an exhibition of his paintings at the Tate Gallery. There is a portrait of him by Gerald Summers and a self-portrait in the Slade Collection.
Biography
Lipke, W. *David Bomberg* (Evelyn Adams, 1967)
DNB

BONNER, Bishop Edmund
1500(?)-1569
Bishop of London

Edmund Bonner was born in Cheshire. He was educated at Oxford. He became Chaplain to Cardinal Wolsey and was promoted after Wolsey's death. As a Catholic Bishop he was deposed in 1549 and committed to Marshalsea Prison. Restored in the reign of Mary Tudor, his persecution of Protestants made him unpopular.

In 1559 he refused to take the Oath of Supremacy making Elizabeth I head of the Church of England and was again deposed and imprisoned in Marshalsea where he died. He was replaced as Bishop of London by Nicholas Ridley.

Since medieval times Bishops of London were lords of the Mayor of Stepney, which included most of present day Tower Hamlets and Hackney. The title was surrendered to the Crown when Bonner was deprived of his Diocese by Edward VI in 1549, and it was given to Thomas WENTWORTH.

Bonner was buried at the Church of St. George-the-Martyr, Southwark. A monument to several of Bonner's victims is in front of the Church in Stratford Broadway, E15.

He is commemorated by Bonner Road, E2 and Bonner Street, E2.
DNB

BOOTH, Catherine 1829-1890
Mother of the Salvation Army

Catherine Booth was born at Ashbourne, Derbyshire, the daughter of John Munford, a Clapham coachbuilder. In 1844 she became a member of the Wesleyan Methodist Chapel in Brixton, South London. Her radical views led her, and others, to leave the Methodist church and joined a Reformer's Chapel. William BOOTH preached there occasionally and in 1855 Catherine and William were married. William became a pastor of a church in Gateshead, and in 1860 Catherine began preaching there.

William Booth's revivalist style led to a conflict with the Wesleyans and when asked to conform, he walked out.

William Booth visited Whitechapel on 2nd July 1865 and spoke outside the *Blind Beggar* public house, Whitechapel Road. He held services in a tent in Bakers Row (now Vallance) Gardens, Whitechapel, until a storm blew it down and decided to open the first indoor meeting place in September 1865 at 23 New Street, Whitechapel, where a commemorative plaque has now been unveiled. In this way he began the East London Christian Mission which in 1878 was re-named the Salvation Army. Although there was a family of eight children Catherine Booth played a full part in the development of the Salvation Army. She became a very able speaker and organiser of the Army's work for women. She would conduct large meetings single handed and wrote many pamphlets, describing the work and purpose of the Salvation Army, together with printed sermons.

She died in Clacton and her funeral at the London Olympia was said to have been attended by some 31,000 people.
Book
Booth Tucker, F. de L. *Life of Catherine Booth* (The Salvation Army, 1892) 2 vols.
DNB

BOOTH, Charles 1840-1916
Ship Owner and Social Reformer

Charles Booth was born in Liverpool. He was educated at the Royal Institution School. After some training in a shipping office, at the age of 22, in partnership with his brother, he founded the Booth Line Steamship Company. He came to London in 1875.

Interested in social research, he began a pioneer study into the lives of working people. Between 1891 and 1903 he published seventeen volumes of his monumental work *Life and Labour of the People of London*. Much of the information was based on inquiries made in East London. He found that 90% of the inhabitants questioned lived on or below the poverty line.

The object of the survey was to show the numerical relation which poverty, misery and depravity bear to regular earnings and comparative comfort, and also to describe the conditions in which people lived. The work was based on the records of the School Board visitors, the Charity Organisation Society and his own findings.

One of his assistants was his cousin Beatrice POTTER who became the wife of Sidney Webb.

The survey was the prototype of the modern social survey. The passing of the Old Age Pensions Act in 1908, was largely due to Booth's advocacy of the reform.

Biography
Simey, T.S. and M.B. *Charles Booth* (Oxford University Press,1960)

Book
Fried, A. and Elman, R.M. *Charles Booth's London* (Hutchinson, 1969)

DNB

A Salvation Army service held by General Booth at the headquarters in Whitechapel Road in 1865

BOOTH, William 1829-1912
Founder of the Salvation Army

William Booth was born in Nottingham, the son of a builder. He began work as an apprentice to a pawnbroker. When he was fifteen, he became a Christian and joined a chapel of the Methodist New Connexion. He became a good preacher and was in great demand as a visiting missioner. He occasionally preached at a Reformer's Chapel when Catherine Munford was a member and in 1855 they were married.

William Booth became a pastor of a church in Gateshead and in 1860 Catherine Booth began preaching there. His revivalist style led to a conflict with the Wesleyans and when asked to conform he walked out.

On 2nd July 1865 he visited Whitechapel and spoke outside the *Blind Beggar* public house, Whitechapel Road. He held services in a tent in Bakers Row (now Vallance) Gardens, Whitechapel, until a storm blew it down and he decided to open the first indoor meeting place in September 1865 at 23 New Street, Whitechapel, where a commemorative plaque has now been unveiled. In this way he began the East London Christian Mission which in 1878 was re-named the Salvation Army.

Catherine Booth greatly assisted his work. She became a very able speaker and organiser of the Army's work for women. William Booth devoted his life to the salvation of and the social work for, the 'submerged classes', as he called those whose conditions at the time were so deplorable that even religious organisations were often unwilling to provide help. He gave help to all, without distinction of nationality, social class, colour, and creed.

His Salvation Army meetings had a great impact and he involved converts immediately, by asking them to speak and visit the sick. *The War Cry,* the Salvation Army's newspaper, was first issued in 1879. In 1890 General Booth, as he became known, wrote *In Darkest England and the Way Out* which detailed the horrors of poverty and offered a comprehensive rescue plan. In the same year he set up a Labour Exchange in London, 20 years before the Government. He opened a missing persons' bureau. Later he introduced a legal aid scheme for the poor. He attempted nothing more than an assault on the basic prejudices of society.

William Booth was also concerned about match making factory girls working with yellow phosphorus, which caused a bone disease called 'Phossy Jaw' and in 1891 he opened his own factory in Lamprell Street, Bow from which six million boxes of safety matches a year were produced.

When William Booth died in 1912 the Salvation Army had spread to 58 countries. Women were working side by side with men in the organisation one hundred years before the Equal Opportunities Commission was set up. The work which began and continues in Tower Hamlets, is now established in more than 80 countries.

He was buried at Abney Park Cemetery in Stoke Newington, large crowds attending his funeral.

He is commemorated by Booth House, Whitechapel Road, E1. A life size statue in Mile End Road, E1, was erected to mark the centenary of the beginning of his work. In 1993 the Salvation Army organisation was given an honorary freemanship by Tower Hamlets Borough in recognition of their long established local welfare services.

Biographies
Bishop, E. *Blood and Fire!* (Longmans, 1964)
Collier, R. *The General Next to God* (Collins, 1965)
DNB

BOROUGH or BURROUGH, Sir William 1536-1599
Navigator

William Borough or Burrough was born at Northam in Devon. He lived in Limehouse in 1579 and was a member of the Stepney Vestry.

He sailed as seaman with his elder brother Stephen to Russia several times. In 1587 he was second in command to Sir Francis Drake on the expedition to Cadiz. On that voyage he was put under arrest for questioning Drake about the wisdom of attacking Lagos.

In 1588 he commanded a small ship, *The Bonavolia* in the fleet against the the Spanish Armada. Later he became Comptroller of the Queen's Navy. On one of his expeditions he captured a number of pirates, ten of whom were executed at Wapping in 1583.

He wrote a number of articles on navigation, the principal being *A Discours of the Variation of the Cumpas or Magneticall Needle* (1581). There are a number of charts and accounts of his voyages preserved in the manuscript room of the British Library.

He is commemorated by Sir William Burrough Junior School, Dalgleish Street,
DNB

BOTTOMLEY, Horatio William
1860-1933
Journalist and Financier

Horatio Bottomley was born in St. Peter's Street, Bethnal Green, the son of a tailor's foreman. Both his parents died before he was five years old and he was placed in an orphanage at Erdington. He ran away when he was fourteen, coming to London and working first as an errand boy and then in a solicitor's office. He later became a shorthand writer in the Law Courts. He met Charles BRADLAUGH who introduced him to the world of books.

He married in 1880 and lived at Clapham, going into the printing business. In 1884 he started the *Hackney Hansard* which became successful, leading to the establishment of other papers. In 1889 he promoted the Hansard Publishing Company with a capital of £500,000. The Company failed in 1891, leaving him bankrupt. He was charged with conspiracy to defraud and following BRADLAUGH'S example he defended himself and was acquitted. The judge was so impressed with Bottomley's defence that he advised him to study law, but he instead plunged into finance. In about two years he had promoted 50 companies and it was estimated that he had made some £3 million. He started a racing stable and for a time was very successful, winning a number of major races.

Bottomley was a journalist and a speaker of great ability. He bought *The Sun* in 1898 and founded *John Bull* in 1906. When the *Sunday Pictorial* was begun, in 1915 he was engaged to write at £100 an article. He was elected Liberal Member of Parliament for South Hackney in 1906.

In 1909 he was charged again with fraud, but was acquitted. In 1911 his financial position was desperate and he presented a petition in bankruptcy.

The outbreak of war in 1914 gave him a new opportunity; he spent much of his time recruiting and making patriotic speeches, his articles in the *Sunday Pictorial* giving him a national reputation.

He paid off his debts and recovered his old seat in Parliament in 1918.

However in 1922 he was charged with fraudulent conversion of funds and at his trial he was found guilty and sentenced to seven years penal servitude. He was formally expelled from the House of Commons. An acquaintance finding him stitching mail bags in prison, said:-

"Ah Bottomley, sewing?"
Bottomley replied, "No, reaping"

Released in 1927, his efforts to re-establish himself failed and he died in obscurity.
Autobiography
Bottomley's Book (Odhams, 1909)
Biography
Hyman,A. *The Rise and Fall of Horatio Bottomley* (Cassell, 1972)
DNB

BOWKETT, Dr. Thomas Edward
1805-1874
Building Society Pioneer

Thomas Bowkett was born in Bermondsey. He qualified as a doctor and began practising in East India Dock Road, Poplar.

Through his work with local people he developed radical opinions, and wrote in one letter about low wages that '... the only effect of men working for little is that it enables masters or capitalists to grow rich while the men are continually getting more poor'. He became an early supporter of trade unions, the co-operative movement and was involved in the Chartist movement. He wanted working people to make use of democratic liberties to assist them in emancipating themselves. Much of his attention was directed towards the creation of societies which would enable working people to purchase their own homes. In 1843 he explained his ideas at the Poplar Literary Institution, of which he was a founder. Considerable attention was attracted and three building societies were formed in Poplar. Several pamphlets on the subject were published.

By 1915 there were eighteen societies formed. Thomas Bowkett regarded the basis of his plan as the same as that of the Rochdale Pioneers and their imitators in the sphere of co-operative stores.
Article
History Workshop Journal Vol.9 (Spring 1980) pp.143-148

BRABAZON, Reginald, Lord Meath 1841-1929
Pioneer of Public Open Spaces

Reginald Brabazon was born in London and educated at Eton, He then served in the diplomatic service in Europe. In 1877 he moved on to devote time to social and philanthropic work. In 1880 he founded the Metropolitan Public Gardens Society and became its Chairman.

Londoners are indebted to him for his initiative and energetic action in preserving many open spaces and the formation of parks and gardens. As Alderman of the London County Council he became the first Chairman of the Parks Committee.

In 1894 the disused Victoria Park Cemetery was turned into a public open space, inaugurated by the Duke of York and named Meath Gardens; Brabazon was created Lord

Meath in 1887. The scheme was a joint venture between the London County Council and the Metropolitan Public Gardens Society.

Lord Meath was the originator in 1893 of 'Empire Day' to celebrate the birthday of Queen Victoria on 24th May. There is a memorial to him in Lancaster Gate, W2 showing a medallion portrait in relief. He is commemorated locally by Brabazon Street, E14.

Autobiographies
Memories of Nineteenth Century (J.Murray, 1923)
Memories of Twentieth Century (J.Murray, 1924)

Charles Bradlaugh

BRADLAUGH, Charles 1833-1891
Social Reformer

Charles Bradlaugh was born in Hoxton. His parents moved to Columbia Road and then to Warner Street, Bethnal Green. He attended Abbey Street School, Bethnal Green. After various jobs he became a busy lecturer and pamphleteer under the name of 'Iconoclast'. He also edited a paper called the *National Reformer*.

When elected in 1880 as Member of Parliament for Northampton he claimed the right to make an affirmation rather than to take the usual parliamentary oath. The House of Commons refused to allow him to do this. Three re-elections took place and in 1886, having been allowed to make an affirmation, he took his seat in Parliament. Great respect was gained for his debating powers in Parliament. Speeches were also often made in Victoria Park, Bow and his agitation about 'perpetual' pensions made him popular in the country. He was a fine speaker and with Annie BESANT he wrote the preface to a new edition of Charles Knowlton's *The Fruits of Philosophy; an Essay on the Population Question* which was considered an 'obscene' publication on birth control. He was prosecuted in 1876 and received a sentence of six months imprisonment and a fine of £200 but the conviction was quashed on appeal.

A Greater London Council Blue Plaque was erected at his house at 29 Turner Street, E1 in 1961.

Biographies
Centenary Committee *Champion of Liberty* (Watts; Pioneer, 1933)
Bonner, H.   *Charles Bradlaugh* (Fisher Unwin, 1894)
Arnstein, W.L.   *The Bradlaugh Case* (Oxford University Press, 1965)

BRANDON, Richard died 1649
Executioner

Richard Brandon lived in Rosemary Lane, now Royal Mint Street, Whitechapel.

Gregory Brandon, his father, was also an executioner and Richard claimed the right by heredity. He is popularly regarded as the 'unwilling' executioner of Charles I in 1649, for which he said he was paid, within the hour, thirty pounds all in half crowns. He told his wife "it was the 'deerst' money he had ever earned in his life". He was also said to be the executioner of the Earl of Strafford and Archbishop Laud.

He was greatly troubled about the King's execution and wrote his 'confession' on his deathbed. He was buried in Whitechapel churchyard and a great hostile crowd attended his funeral.

Biography
Sidney, P. *The Headsmen of Whitehall* (Simpkin, Marshall, 1905)

DNB

BRAY, Rev. Dr. Thomas 1656-1730
Philanthropist

Thomas Bray was born at Marton in Shropshire and was educated at Oswestry School and Oxford.

Bray was responsible for establishing 80 parochial libraries in England and 39 in America, where he lived from 1699-1706.

Out of his Library scheme grew two great national institutions – The Society for Promoting Christian Knowledge (SPCK) and the Society for the Propagation of the Gospel (SPG).

The SPCK had great influence on the Charity School movement and there were many of these schools in East London.

From 1706 until his death he was Rector of St. Botolph's Church, Aldgate.

DNB

BRESSLAW Bernard 1934-1993
Actor

Bernard Bresslaw was born in Stepney, the son of a tailor's cutter. His English teacher was impressed by his acting potential and persuaded him to try for a scholarship at the Royal Academy of Dramatic Art. He was to win the Academy's Emile Littler Award as the 'Most Promising Actor'.

He gained practical experience by touring hospitals, army camps and prisons as 'Lachie' in John Patrick's play *The Hasty Heart*, and made his London West End stage debut in 1953.

Bernard Bresslaw began making films in 1954 and appeared with Norman Wisdom in *Up in the World*. When the writer Sid Colin saw the film he immediately decided to give him a key role in Granada Television's new comedy *The Army Game* in which he became a great success as 'Private "Popeye" Popplewell'. The feature film that followed took its title from his catchphrase *I only Arsked!* In 1958 Bernard Bresslaw starred with Bruce Forsyth and Charlie Drake in *Sleeping Beauty* at the London Palladium where he met one of the dancers whom he later married.

Returning to the theatre he appeared in Shakespeare's *Twelfth Night* as Sir Toby Belch, and had a part in *Taming of the Shrew*. He also began a long association with the Regent's Park Open Air Theatre.

He acted in fourteen *Carry On* films and worked with the English Stage Company, The Royal Shakespeare Company, The Young Vic and the Chichester Festival Theatre where he appeared in *Arsenic and Old Lace*. His most impressive film role was as 'Rell' in the 1983 science fiction *Krull*.

He was 6ft. 7in. tall and was instantly recognisable.

He collapsed in his dressing room before a performance of *The Taming of the Shrew*.

Obituary
The Independent 12th June 1993

BRIDGEMAN, William Walter 1883-1947
Footballer

Bill Bridgeman was born at Devas Street, Bromley-by-Bow. He attended Marner Street School where he gained a reputation for his athletic and footballing abilities.

After success in junior football he was signed by West Ham, but sold to Chelsea in 1906. At Chelsea he played alongside his former school team mate, George HILSDON, as inside forward. He retained his position fairly regularly in Chelsea's first team until the 1914-15 season, missing out on the team for the F.A. Cup final in 1915, when Chelsea lost to Sheffield United.

BRINSON, William 1894-1984
Labour Councillor

William Brinson was born in Millwall and lived in Portree Street, E14, for over seventy five years.

He worked for the London Electricity Board.

William Brinson met his wife, Edith when she was selling *The Suffragette* newspaper at East India Dock Gates.

Elected to Poplar Borough Council in 1949, in an unusually short time he was made Mayor in 1952. He was also Leader of the Council.

The William Brinson Centre, Arnold Road, E3, where people with learning difficulties are cared for, was named after him.

He was made a Freeman of the Borough by Tower Hamlets Council in 1979.

Article
East London Advertiser 28th September 1979
Obituary
East London Advertiser 9th March 1984

BRODETSKY, Professor Selig
1888-1954
Mathematician

Selig Brodetsky was born in Russia. He came with his family to Whitechapel in 1893. His father got a job as a beadle in a local synagogue.

He attended Hanbury Street School and the Jews' Free School in Spitalfields. By achieving first place in all England in the Cambridge junior local examinations in 1905 a sensation was caused. The mathematical scholarship to Trinity College, Cambridge followed, and he obtained the degree of Ph.D. in mathematical astronomy there. Later he became a lecturer at Bristol University and President of the Association of University Teachers.

Brodetsky became involved in work for the Jewish Community, especially the Zionist movement, and in 1940 President of the Board of Deputies of British Jews. After his election as President of the Hebrew University in Jerusalem in May 1949 the administration was much improved.

Autobiography
Memoirs (Weidenfeld and Nicholson, 1960)
Article
'Selig Brodetsky' I. Finestein in *Jewish East End* edited by A. Newman (Jewish Historical Society of England, 1981)

DNB

BRONOWSKI, Dr. Jacob 1908-1974
Scientist

Jacob Bronowski was born at Lodz in Poland. He came to England in 1920 hardly able to speak a word of English. He lived at 22 Commercial Street, Whitechapel and attended Canon Barnett and Davenant Schools, going on to Jesus College, Cambridge where he read mathematics. He became lecturer in mathematics at Hull University.

For a time he was Director of Research at the National Coal Board and in 1962 he went to America to become senior fellow and trustee of the Institute of Biological Science in California.

A gifted poet, playwright and author, he became well known as a member of the television Brains Trust and later presented the series on *The Ascent of Man*.

When he was elected President of the Library Association, in his inaugaural address he paid tribute to the help he had received as a boy in the Whitechapel library.
Book
The Ascent of Man (BBC,1973)

BROOKS, Thomas JP 1886-1954
Chimney Sweep

Thomas Brooks was born in East London. He began chimney sweeping as a boy of 12. He lived in Brick Lane, Bethnal Green and had the sign of a sweep's broom over his front door.

He was a Member of Bethnal Green Borough Council for 34 years, and was elected Mayor for 1931-32. When he was elected Mayor it was said that he was 'well sooted' to the task.

Invited to attend the Buckingham Palace Garden Party, he swept chimneys in the morning, and returned to his work again in the evening.

On 15th February 1936 he gave a talk on the radio about his work.

BROWN, Georgia 1933-1992
Singer

Born Lillie Klot in Whitechapel, as a teenager she joined the Brady Club, which helped her to develop as a singer. She performed at youth clubs while learning the rag trade by day.

At seventeen she was working at the Stork Club in London and appeared on television. Her stage name was taken from one of her songs *Sweet Georgia Brown*. Her early influences were jazz singers, but became equally at home with 'music hall' in the Marie Lloyd tradition.

In 1965 she was cast as Lucy in *The Threepenny Opera* at the Royal Court Theatre and in 1960 she was playing Nancy in *Oliver*, having great success which was later repeated in the Broadway production, New York.

Georgia Brown settled permanently in Los Angeles, performing in a number of productions in America. She returned to London to star in *42nd Street* and other musicals.

She recorded *Oliver* and *Carmelina* and many other songs.

Her last show was *Georgia Brown and Friends* and she came to London for an appearance in a charity tribute to the singer, Sammy Davis Junior.

BROWNFIELD, Dr. Matthew
1825-1908
Doctor

Qualified in 1854, Matthew Brownfield became a medical practitioner in Poplar, living at 171 East India Dock Road, Poplar. He was Police Surgeon for 'K' Division of the Metropolitan Police and Public Vaccinator for Bromley-by-Bow. He was the first Hon. Surgeon to Poplar Hospital for Accidents, and a well known East London figure.

Matthew Brownfield also owned several tugs on the Thames. Three of these, the *Athlete*, the *Expert* and the *Rescue* competed against several other towage firms at Gravesend. On one time, the financial position of the doctor was so low that he decided to lay his tugs up. But the skipper of the *Expert* persuaded the doctor to let his tug make just one more trip to find work. The doctor reluctantly agreed and the trip secured one of the estuary's biggest salvage jobs. The Doctor's finances were restored. An oil painting, the *British Tar*, which completely covered the Gravesend tavern, commemorated the episode.

Brownfield Street, E14, was named after him.

Source
P.L.A. *Monthly* July 1955 p.147

BRUNE, Walter and Rosea
active circa 1190

Walter and Rosea Brune founded a religious house on the edge of the City of London towards the end of the twelfth century. It was re-founded as a hospital in 1235 and acquired the name of St. Mary Spital, which in turn gave the name Spitalfields to the surrounding area.

They were commemorated locally in the twentieth century by Brune Street, E1, and Brune House, Toynbee Street, E1.

BRUNEL, Isambard Kingdom
1806-1859
Civil and Marine Engineer

Isambard Brunel was born in Portsmouth and educated in Paris. He was the son of Sir Marc Isambard BRUNEL. At the age of 17 he entered his father's office, helping him plan the Thames Tunnel from Rotherhithe to Wapping, later becoming resident engineer. Building the tunnel was a hazardous venture

I.K. Brunel, third from the left, with J.S. Russell, first from the left, at the launch of the Great Eastern
Brunel University Library

43

in which many lost their lives, and he was a great help to his father in meeting the various crises that occurred. During the construction he gained valuable experience and personally saved the life of one man from drowning.

Brunel designed the Clifton Suspension Bridge over the river Avon at Bristol, the work began in 1836 but owing to lack of funds was not completed during his lifetime. He also designed the old Hungerford Bridge over the Thames at Charing Cross.

In marine engineering Brunel designed the *Great Western*, the first steamship to be in service across the Atlantic, crossing in the then unprecedented time of 15 days; the *Great Britain*, the first ocean-going screw steamer; and, with John Scott RUSSELL, the *Great Eastern*, the largest iron vessel ever built at that time. The ship was launched from Napier's Yard, West Ferry Road, Millwall in 1858.

In 1833 Brunel was appointed Engineer to the Great Western Railway and constructed all the tunnels, bridges and viaducts on that line.

Brunel is commemorated by a statue erected in 1877 on Victoria Embankment, SW1; a plaque by Wapping Station and a Greater London Blue Plaque in West Ferry Road, Isle of Dogs, E14 marking the launch of the *Great Eastern*.

Biographies
Noble, C.B. *The Brunels; father and son* (Cobden-Sanderson, 1938).
Rolt, L.T.C. *Isambard Kingdom Brunel* (Longmans, 1957).

DNB

BRUNEL, Sir Marc Isambard
1769-1849
Civil Engineer

Marc Brunel was born in Normandy, France and educated at Rouen. His parents intended him to enter the priesthood, however, he developed interests in mathematics and mechanics and qualified for the Navy in hydrography. He served in the West Indies for six years. Returning to France he found himself out of sympathy with the Revolution and escaped to America in 1793.

Working as an engineer and architect in America he was engaged on survey work and became Chief Engineer to New York Council.

Brunel returned to settle in England in 1799 and designed works for the government at Woolwich Arsenal and Chatham Dockyard.

He also conducted experiments in steam navigation but the Admiralty did not take up his proposals.

His greatest achievement was the building of the Thames Tunnel from Rotherhithe to Wapping. Financial and engineering difficulties extended the construction period from 1825-43. It was taken over in 1865 by the East London Railway Company as the use by pedestrians did not create the vast profits originally envisaged, and it is still in use by the East London line of the London Underground. In this venture Brunel was greatly helped by his son Isambard Kingdom BRUNEL. Sir Marc Brunel was made a Fellow of the Royal Society in 1814 and knighted in 1841.

There is a plaque to commemorate Sir Marc Isambard Brunel and Isambard Kingdom Brunel at Wapping Station, Wapping High Street, E1.

Biography
Beamish, R. *Memoir of the Life of Sir Marc Isambard Brunel* (Longmans, 1862).

DNB

BRYANT, William 1804-1874
Match Manufacturer

William Bryant was born into a Methodist family in Tiverton, Devon. He joined the Society of Friends in 1832.

After leaving school, he began work in the Excise Service but in 1833 he set up in partnership with Edward James as soap and grease makers and refiners of sugar.

William Bryant became associated with Francis May and by 1844, May's grocery business was trading under the name of Bryant and May, with premises at Philpot Lane, in the City, and Tooley Street, Southwark.

In July 1861, they opened their factory in Fairfield Road, Bow. The buildings had been used previously for making candles and crinolines. For some time they had imported matches from Sweden. The first 'safety matches', which could only be ignited by striking across a specially prepared surface were first patented by Bryant and May, 1855. They began manufacturing matches themselves six years later.

Phosphorous friction matches began to be commercially produced in 1833. The match workers suffered for eighty years from tissue damage called phosphorous necrosis or as it was known 'phossy jaw', mainly caused by the penetration of fumes of yellow phosphorous into the jaw bone through cavities in decayed teeth. In 1898 came the discovery of a non-poisonous substance to replace yellow phosphorous, and in 1900 Bryant and May acquired the British patent rights.

William Bryant's son, Wilberforce, turned the business into a public company in 1884 and became its first Chairman. The match girl's strike led by Annie BESANT occurred in 1888.

The firm is still famous but no longer in East London, having moved to High Wycombe in 1979-80.

Book

Beaver, P. *The Matchmakers* (Henry Melland, 1985)

BURDETT-COUTTS, Baroness Angela Georgina 1814-1906

Philanthropist

Angela Burdett-Coutts was the daughter of Sir Francis Burdett, Member of Parliament. At the age of 23 she inherited great wealth from her grandfather Thomas Coutts, the banker. In her time she was considered to be one of the richest women in the world, and as a wealthy heiress she received many marriage proposals. Angela Burdett-Coutts chose to remain single for most of her life (she married William Bartlett in 1881) and, spurred on to good works by her strong evangelical faith, she used her wealth for social provision, education and reform.

She was an astute business woman and took an active part in the affairs of Coutts Bank, whilst her interests and the extent of her influence in projects for social reform were widespread.

She set up charities which embraced the provision of housing for the poor, education, childcare, the development of work for women, animal welfare, and financed many welfare projects run by the Church of England. She was a close friend of Charles DICKENS, who encouraged her in her schemes for social improvement, and with his help she set up a house of rescue for young prostitutes. Dickens's novel *Martin Chuzzlewit* (1844) is dedicated to her.

Angela Burdett-Coutts was very active in East London schemes. The church of St. John's, Vincent Street (later Halley Street), Limehouse (consecrated 1853) was built with funds supplied by her. In 1860 she set up a 'sewing school' in Brown's Lane, Spitalfields where women were taught skills and could receive medical care and food. The scheme was so successful that the women were able to obtain government contracts for their products.

A team of nursing sisters was employed to work in the Spitalfields district.

After 1860, when the silk industry declined in the area, Angela Burdett-Coutts founded the East End Weavers Association which looked after the welfare of out of work weavers and aimed to help them find other employment. A night school for boys and young men founded in Shoreditch in 1875 later became Burdett-Coutts Club.

Animal welfare was an abiding concern, and she financed the building of stables on the Columbia Estate, Bethnal Green for the donkeys of costermongers.

She was one of the leading figures in the founding of the RSPCA, and paid for the horse and cattle drinking troughs, and a public fountain, in Victoria Park, at a cost of £5,000.

On a site at Nova Scotia Gardens, Bethnal Green, in 1862, she financed the building of four blocks of model tenements, to house 1,000 people. This was re-named Columbia Square. Her architect, H.A. DARBISHIRE also designed Columbia Market (opened 1869) which began as a project 'to supply the poor with wholesome food at a fair rate'. Other markets in London were subject to tolls, which increased the retail price of the foods. The Columbia Market Scheme was an attempt to break the monopoly and toll system, and to supply the East End with cheap food. The covered market which provided room for 400 stalls, and cost £20,000 to build, was a complete failure. By 1871 the management was transferred to the City Corporation; unable to make it pay, it was transferred back to Angela Burdett-Coutts in 1874. Various attempts to run it as a fish market in conjunction with the railways and an East coast fishing fleet also failed. It was closed in 1886.

During the second World War the market cellars were used as air-raid shelters but they were not safe enough and many people were killed there. The building was demolished in 1960.

The first woman to be raised to the peerage in her own right (1871) she was also the first woman 'freeman' of the City of London.

Angela Burdett-Coutts is buried in Westminster Abbey, and commemorated locally by Angela Street, Baroness Road, E2, Burdett Road, E3, and E14.

Biographies

Orton, D.   *Made of Gold* (Hamish Hamilton, 1980)
Healey, E.   *Lady Unknown* (Sidgwick and Jackson, 1978)

DNB

BURKE, Thomas 1886-1945
Writer

Thomas Burke was born in London. His father died when he was a few months old and he came to live with his uncle in Gill Street, Limehouse until he was nine. For some years he was in the Hardcress Home for Orphans which stood outside a village in the West Country.

Leaving school when he was 15 he began work in an office later becoming an assistant to a secondhand bookseller.

He sold his first story when he was 16 and attracted the attention of a literary agent for whom he later worked.

Commissioned by a publisher to write two novels he produced *Nights in Town* (1915) and *Limehouse Nights* (1917) which were instantly successful and enabled him to devote his time to writing full-time. He wrote altogether about 30 books, some of them about the Chinese community in Limehouse.

Autobiography
The Wind and the Rain (Thornton Butterworth, 1924)

BURMAN, William, VC 1897-1974
Soldier

William Burman was born at 5 Baker Street, Mile End Old Town and attended Stepney Redcoat School. He joined the 16th Battalion Rifle Brigade in March 1915.

Promoted sergeant in the field in April 1916, he was awarded the Victoria Cross for gallantry in a machine gun action at Ypres, 20th September 1917.

The Mayor of Stepney, Councillor Jerome Reidy, presented him with a bayonet of honour and £200 in War Bonds, in August 1918, the money for which had been collected by public subscription.

Books
The Register of the Victoria Cross (This England Books, 1981)
Creagh, Sir O'M. and Humphries, E.M. (eds) *The V.C. and D.S.O.* (Standard Art Book, 1924)

Article
Eastern Post 3rd August 1918

BUXTON, Sydney Charles, (Earl) 1853-1934
Liberal Statesman

Sydney Buxton was born in London and educated at Clifton School and Cambridge, the grandson of Sir Thomas Fowell BUXTON. He served on the London School Board from 1876-1882 and later became Liberal Member of Parliament for Poplar from 1886-1914.

During his parliamentary career he served the the governments of Sir Henry Campbell-Bannerman and Herbert Asquith as Postmaster-General and he introduced the penny post between England and America. He also served as Under-Secretary for the Colonies and as President of the Board of Trade.

Buxton was present at the meeting in 1889 when the Dock Strike was settled through the intervention of Cardinal MANNING. He was also actively involved with the 1911 Unemployment Act, the settlement of the Dock Strike, 1912, the building of the Blackwall Tunnel, the setting up of the Port of London Authority, the Woolwich Free Ferry and the Poplar Free Public Library.

In 1914 he was appointed Governor-General of South Africa and created an Earl.

DNB

BUXTON, Sir Thomas Fowell
1786-1845
Brewer and Social Reformer

Born at Earls Colne, Essex, Thomas Fowell was educated at Trinity College, Dublin. He became a director of the brewery firm, Truman, Hanbury and Buxton in 1808.

Elected Member of Parliament for Weymouth 1818-1837, Buxton worked for the modification of the criminal law, prison reform and abolition of the slave trade.

In 1824 he succeeded William Wilberforce as leader of the anti-slavery movement in Parliament which persuaded the government to introduce a Bill to abolish slavery in 1833.

Greatly concerned about the needy in Spitalfields he gave much support to philanthropic causes bringing relief. He was a great friend of William ALLEN.

A statue of Buxton by Frederick Thrupp is situated near to that of William Wilberforce in the north transept of Westminster Abbey.

He is commemorated locally by Thomas Buxton Junior and Infants' Schools and Buxton Street, E1.

Biography
Buxton, C. (ed) *Memoirs of Sir Thomas Fowell Buxton, Baronet* (John Murray, 1848)

DNB

CASLON William 1692-1766
Typefounder

Born at Cradley, Worcestershire, William Caslon set up in business as a gun engraver and tool maker in 1716 at Vine Street, Minories. He soon began cutting type for printers. His skill was widely acknowledged and his 'Old Face' types were extensively used in Europe and America, until the end of the 18th century when they went out of fashion. They were revived 50 years later and have continued their popularity until the present day.

From 1758 until his death, Caslon lived in retirement at his country house in Bethnal Green. This was probably in Victoria Park Square, near Sugar Loaf Walk.

He was buried in St. Luke's Churchyard, Finsbury, where there is a monument to him. There is a Greater London Council Blue Plaque at 23 Chiswell Street, EC1.

Locally he is commemorated by William Caslon House, Patriot Square, E2, and Caslon Place, Cudworth Street, E1.

Biography
Ball, J. *William Caslon* (Roundwood Press, 1973)

DNB

CASS, Sir John 1666-1718
Merchant

The son of an architect for the Admiralty, John Cass was Master of the Carpenters' Company 1712 and Sheriff of the City of London the same year. An Alderman for the Portsoken ward, he was Member of Parliament for the

City of London 1710 and 1713. He left money in trust for educational and social purposes.

In July 1718, John Cass, realizing he was at the point of death began to make a new will. He died with only two pages of the document signed, having burst a blood vessel whereby his quill was stained red. For this reason the girls of the school wear a red quill in their berets. There is a memorial window in St. Botolph's Church, Aldgate.

He is commemorated by a Primary School, Duke's Place, EC3, and Sir John Cass Secondary School, Stepney Way, E1. The Sir John Cass Technical College and Art School later formed part of the London Guildhall University.

Pamphlets
A Short Account of Sir John Cass and His Foundation (Typescript, unpublished, 1955)
Barrell, G.R. *Sir John Cass's Foundation and Red Coat Secondary School; a Description* (Typescript, 1966)

DNB

CATCHPOOL, Egerton St. John (Jack) 1891-1971

Founder Member of the Youth Hostels Association

Educated at Sidcot School, Woodbrooke College and Birmingham University, Catchpool was associated with the Toynbee Hall, an educational settlement for fifty years.

In the first World War he served with a Friends Ambulance Unit in Russia, China and Japan, having many adventures.

From 1920 to 1930 he was Sub-Warden of Toynbee Hall and a pioneer in establishing prison libraries and the voluntary prison visitors' scheme.

A founder member of the Youth Hostels Association, he became General Secretary in 1930. Twenty one years later there were 300 hostels accommodating 14,000 young people overnight. Becoming President of the International YHA, he played an important part in establishing youth hostels throughout the world.

He returned to Toynbee Hall from 1963-64 to act temporarily as Warden.

Autobiography
Candles in the Darkness (Bannisdale Press, 1966)

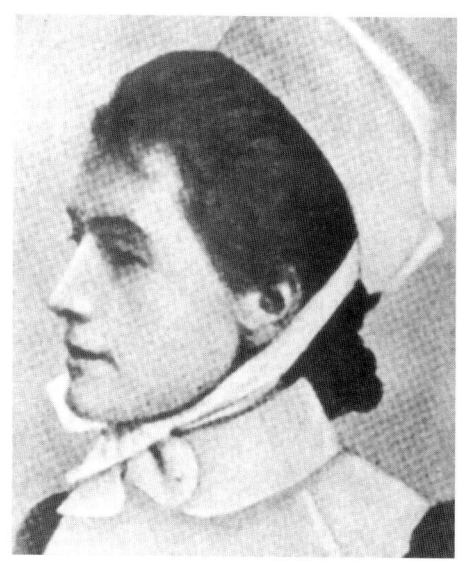

Edith Cavell at the time she was at the London Hospital, 1899
Royal London Hospital Trust Archives

CAVELL, Edith 1865-1915

Nurse

Edith Cavell was born at Swardeston in Norfolk, where her father was the Rector. She went to school in Somerset and then in Brussels.

In 1895 she entered the London Hospital for training and qualified as a staff nurse. After district nursing in Highgate and Shoreditch in 1906 she went to Brussels to establish with Dr. Depage a training centre for nurses on the English system.

After the outbreak of the first World War she continued to work in Brussels, tending all who needed care irrespective of nationality.

In October 1915 she was tried and executed by the Germans for allegedly helping Belgian and Allied fugitives.

She is commemorated by a Sir George Frampton statue in St. Martin's Place, WC2, unveiled in 1920 by Queen Alexandra. The inscription added in 1924 was:-

Patriotism is not enough, I must have no hatred or bitterness for for anyone

Cavell Street, E1 is commemorated for her.
Biographies
Clarke-Kennedy, A.E. *Edith Cavell* (Faber, 1965)
Ryder, R. *Edith Cavell* (Hamish Hamilton, 1975)

DNB

Frederick Nicholas Charrington

CHARRINGTON, Frederick Nicholas 1850-1936
Missioner

Frederick Nicholas Charrington's abode on the day of his baptism at St. Dunstan, Stepney, was 3 Tredegar Place, later renumbered 87 Bow Road, Bow. He was the son of Frederick Charrington, brewer, and Louisa Elizabeth. He was educated at Marlborough School and Brighton College. Passing *Rising Sun* public house in Cambridge Road, Bethnal Green, one day, he saw a poor woman with three children pleading with her husband for money to feed them. The man struck the woman, and Charrington, going to remonstrate, saw his own name over the door.

He renounced his share in the family brewing business, reputedly worth one and a quarter million pounds, and bought a house at 41 Stepney Green from which he raised money to build the Great Assembly Hall in Mile End Road. The Hall was opened in 1886 to hold 5,000 people. It was burned down during the second World War and a new mission was opened in January 1959.

In addition to his opposition to drink, Charrington also campaigned against music halls, particularly 'Lusby's', a short distance from the Great Assembly Hall. He also campaigned against prostitution and the exploitation of women.

The Mission was the centre of evangelism and social work. In 1910, 850 families were supplied with Christmas dinner and coal was distributed to many needy families.

Charrington was a member of the London County Council from 1889-1895.

He is commemorated by Frederick Charrington House, Wickford Street, E1.

Biographies
Thorne, G. *The Great Acceptance* (Hodder and Stoughton, 1913)
Fishman, W.J. *The Streets of East London* (Duckworth, 1979)

DNB

CHAUCER, Geoffrey 1340(?)-1400
Poet and Chronicler

The son of John Chaucer, Vintner, Geoffrey Chaucer studied law at the Temple.

A friend of John of Gaunt, he was appointed a Commissioner of Customs in the Port of London. Needing to reside near his work from 1374 he rented rooms over Aldgate. Here he lived for about twelve years during which time many of his poems were written.

He went on the Canterbury pilgrimage in 1388 and his *Canterbury Tales* were first printed by William Caxton probably in 1478.

Appointed Clerk of Works at Westminster Abbey, he lived in a house that was pulled down to make room for the Henry Vll chapel.

Chaucer was buried in Westminster Abbey and his monument was erected in 1555. There is also a memorial window.

DNB

CHESWORTH, Donald Piers OBE 1923-1991
Warden of Toynbee Hall

Donald Chesworth came to Toynbee Hall as Warden in 1977, with a wealth of experience of voluntary and public service in this country and overseas.

He was elected to the London County Council as member for North Kensington in 1952, and served as a member of the Inner London Education Authority. His interests were in child care and race relations.

As Chairman of the Notting Hill Social Council, he was able to play a large part in re-building the local community after the race riots in the 1950s. He was also involved in achieving the downfall of the notorious landlord Peter Rachman in his exploitation of tenants.

Donald Chesworth was appointed Chairman of a Royal Commission by the Mauritius Government to set levels of pay and working conditions. He worked in Tanzania and Bangladesh where he was a labour adviser. He also served on the Economics Board of the International Labour Office in Geneva.

On his return to Britain he became Chairman of the charity 'War on Want'.

As Warden of Toynbee Hall he worked to increase the number of residents and develop voluntary involvement in the community. He was active in attempts to get the Children's Beach re-opened at Tower Bridge, he also established a Heritage Centre in Spitalfields and was greatly involved with the Bangladesh community providing educational and social facilities for them.

He was awarded an OBE in 1987.

Book

Briggs, A. and Macartney, A. *Toynbee Hall; the first hundred years* (Routledge and Kegan Paul, 1984)

CHEYNEY, Peter 1896-1951

Writer of Crime Novels

Peter Cheyney was the pseudonym of Reginald Evelyn Peter Southhouse-Cheyney, who was born at 92 Whitechapel High Street where his mother had a corset manufacturers shop. He was educated at Davenant School, Mercers School and London University.

Initially he became an actor and then a journalist. He was also a part-time policeman. Cheyney took up writing novels, and his first success was *This Man is Dangerous* (1936).

Biography

Harrison, M. *Peter Cheyney, Prince of Hokum* (Neville Spearman, 1954)

CHICKEN, George Bell, VC

died 1860

Mercantile Marine Officer

George Chicken lived in King David Lane, Shadwell, and served with the Indian Naval Brigade during the Indian Mutiny 1857-1859.

He was awarded the Victoria Cross for an act of bravery at Suhejnee near Peroo in Uttar Pradesh state in September 1858. He escaped with a severe wound. The award was gazetted 27th April 1860.

Chicken lost his life in the sinking of the ship *Emily* in the Bay of Bengal.

The medal was sent to his father, George Chicken, master mariner of Shadwell.

The Victoria Cross was the last to be awarded under the terms of the 1858 Warrant, which had extended the V.C. to 'Non-Military Persons' who had served in the Mutiny as volunteers.

Book

Creagh, Sir O'M. and Humphries, E.M. (eds) *The VC and DSO* (Standard Art Book, 1924)

CHUDLEIGH, Rev. Frederick William 1878-1932

Methodist Preacher

Frederick Chudleigh was born in Bristol, the son of a draper. He developed an early interest in music and obtained a Licentiate of the Royal Academy of Music. He trained for the Methodist Ministry in Manchester, and worked at St. George's Chapel in Cable Street from 1906-1911. After a five year period in South London he returned to the Lycett Chapel, situated on the corner of Mile End Road and White Horse Lane, in 1916. He became Superintendent of the East End Mission, Commercial Road, E1, in 1919.

During the first World War, Frederick Chudleigh was responsible for setting up the first wartime community canteen. Soup, stews and puddings were all sold at two pence a portion, and volunteers were soon serving 2,000 meals a day. Frederick Chudleigh's idea was taken up by the wartime Ministry of Food and such canteens were set up in other cities.

After the war, and throughout the Depression of the 1930s, children on their way to school were able to get a free breakfast at the East End Mission.

One of Frederick Chudleigh's most successful ventures was the introduction of the 'penny pictures'. In order to keep children off the streets, he ran cinema shows after Sunday evening service. Often, as many as 1,000 children attended at a time.

Biography

Burnett, R.G. *Chudleigh* (Epworth Press, 1932)

CHURCH, Henry Tyrrell

(Known as H. Tyrrell) 1821-1859

Secularist

Born in Spital Square, Norton Folgate, the son of a solicitor, Henry Church was educated at Southgate. On leaving school he was apprenticed to a lithographer and later became an actor, but as the work was spasmodic, he took up writing.

Among his publications were *The Practical Elocutionist*, a *History of England for the Young* and the *Complete Works of Shakespeare ... (The Doubtful Plays, with introduction and notes)*.

He came to regard the Bible, of which he had made a study, as a superstition and became a leading secularist.

When he became seriously ill, his family ceased to care for him on account of his unbelief. He had to rely on his wife's brother for comforts and necessities of a long illness. He died at his parents' home; they buried him privately without telling his wife, who was not even told his burial place. She learned of his death on receiving her husband's clothes.

Article
The Reasoner 7th August 1859

CIBBER, Caius Gabriel 1630-1700
Architect and Sculptor

Caius Gabriel Cibber was born in Flensburg, Denmark. He was sent to Rome when young, to develop his talent for sculpture. He became foreman stonemason to an English architect, John Stone, and accompanied Stone to London, where he made his home. Caius Cibber became 'Carver to the King's Closet' which did not make him much money, but established his reputation.

Caius Cibber was the architect of the Danish Church, Wellclose Square, Whitechapel, consecrated in 1696, and he was buried there in 1700. The church was pulled down in 1869, and two of Cibber's wooden statues are now at the Danish Church, St. Katherine's Precincts, Regents Park, NW1.

Other sculptures that can be seen include the Phoenix over the south porch of St. Paul's Cathedral, and the relief on the western side of the base of the Monument set up to commemorate the Great Fire of London.

DNB

CLARK-KENNEDY, Archibald Edmund 1893-1985
Physician and Author

Educated at Wellington College, Corpus Christi, Cambridge, and London Hospital Medical School, Archibald Clark-Kennedy served in the Army in India and Mesopotamia from 1914-1917. He returned to England to qualify in medicine.

Dr. Clark-Kennedy became a member of the Royal College of Physicians in 1922 and was elected Fellow in 1930. He took his MD. in 1923 and became Physician to the London Hospital in 1928.

He became Dean of the London Hospital Medical College in 1937, holding the appointment for sixteen years.

Clark-Kennedy wrote a number of books, some on medical subjects on which he held advanced views, protesting against too much specialisation and advocating the bringing of branches of medicine closer together. He also wrote a biography of Edith CAVELL and a two-volume history of the London Hospital.

As a young man he was a keen cross-country runner and continued his interest in this all his life. He also gave great support to his old college boat club, which named a boat *Archie C-K* in his honour.

Book
Collins, Sheila M. *The Royal London Hospital; a brief history* (Royal London Hospital Archives and Museum, 1995)

CLORE, Sir Charles (Charlie) 1904-1979
Businessman

Sir Charles Clore was born at 15 Casson Street, Mile End New Town and his birth was registered as Charlie Clore, the son of Israel Clore, a master tailor, and his wife Yetta.

Charlie Clore attended Rochelle Street School, Bethnal Green. He started his business life with £1,000 given to him by his father and later became one of the country's richest men, with a fortune estimated at £30 million. At one time he controlled the British Shoe Corporation, Selfridges, the Lewis group, and William Hill organisation. He was said to be the originator of the 'Takeover'.

DNB

COBORN, Priscilla or Prisca 1622-1701
Founder of Coborn School

Daughter of the Curate-in-Charge of St. Mary's Church, Bow, in 1675 Priscilla became the second wife of Thomas Coborn, a wealthy brewer. On her death she left money to establish a charity school for girls. A school was built soon after 1701. In 1814 a new school was opened in Fairfield Road, Bow and in 1880 the school moved to Tredegar Square, Bow. After an agreement between the

Coopers' Company Trust and the Coborn Trust to rationalise educational provision in the area Coborn School for Girls moved into the old Coopers' Company School for Boys premises at 86 Bow Road in 1892.

In 1973 the school amalgamated with the Coopers' Company School and moved to Upminster.

Priscilla Coborn was buried at St. Mary's Church and is commemorated in the borough by Coborn Road, Coborn Street and Priscilla Road, E3.

A copy of her will and codicil may be seen in the Tower Hamlets Local History Library.

COHEN, General Morris Abraham   1887-1970
Soldier

Morris Cohen was born in Poland and grew up in Umberston Street, St. George's-in-the-East, off Commercial Road, and attended the Jews' Free School, Bell Lane, Spitalfields. At the age of 12 he was arrested for picking pockets and sent to the Hayes Industrial School. When Morris Cohen graduated he was sent to Canada to work on a farm.

During his 17 years in Canada he became friendly with the expatriate Chinese community. Morris Cohen fought for their political and legal rights, and joined Dr. Sun Yat-sen's nationalist group, which advocated the overthrow of the Manchu empire and the establishment of a Chinese republic (1911).

In the first World War Morris Cohen joined the Edmonton Irish Guards. During his time in France he helped supervise a Chinese labour corps. Following the War he went to China to work as a bodyguard for Dr. Sun. Morris Cohen earned the nickname 'Two Gun' Cohen because he always carried a set of pistols.

Captured in Hong Kong in 1941, he spent 21 months in a Japanese internment camp. He was then repatriated to Canada as part of a prisoner of war exchange.
Biography
Drage, C. *'Two-Gun' Cohen* (Jonathan Cape, 1954)

COLET, Dame Christian   circa 1466
Mother of John COLET

Christian was the daughter of Sir John Knevet of Ashwellthorpe, Sheriff of Norfolk and Suffolk. She married Henry Colet (later Sir Henry Colet, Lord Mayor of London) in 1465. Henry was one of the wealthiest members of the Mercers' Company, who later conveyed his lands in trust to that Company.

Christian gave birth to 22 children, the first and only surviving one was the Rev. John COLET, who became Rector of St. Dunstan's Church, Stepney, and Dean of St. Paul's, London.

Living to her 90th year, Christian stayed in Stepney after her husband's death in 1505 and entertained many of his friends including ERASMUS, the Dutch humanist and scholar.
Articles
East London Observer 6th April and 26th October 1912
Book
Lupton, J.H. *A Life of John Colet, D.D.* (George Bell & Sons, 1887)

COLET, Sir Henry   died 1505
Mercer

A wealthy member of the Mercer's Company, Henry Colet lived in Stepney. The father of twenty-two children, eleven boys and eleven girls, only his son John COLET survived.

Sir Henry Colet was buried in St. Dunstan's Churchyard and his monument is maintained by the Mercer's Company.

He was twice Lord Mayor of London, in 1486 and 1495, and was knighted in 1487.

His wife, Christian COLET, nee Knevet, lived to her 90th year in Stepney.

Sir Henry Colet is commemorated locally by Colet Flats, Whitehorse Road, E1.

DNB

COLET, Rev. John   1467(?)-1519
Scholar and Preacher

The son of Sir Henry COLET, John Colet was born in Stepney. He was educated locally and at Oxford. In a tour of Europe and Italy he was greatly influenced by the Italian preacher Savonarola, and on his return to England he was ordained.

He became Rector of St. Dunstan's Church, Stepney and was a friend of Erasmus and Sir Thomas More. He was appointed Dean of St. Paul's Cathedral in 1504 and while there founded, in 1510, St. Paul's School for 153 boys. He was a great Bible scholar and the number of boys was determined by the account in the New Testament of the miraculous draught of fishes.

The school moved to Hammersmith in 1884, and the building was used as General Montgomery's headquarters before the Normandy Landing in 1944.

Rev. Dean Colet's House, Stepney in 1797

Colet was buried in the old St. Paul's Cathedral which was destroyed by the Great Fire of London in 1666.
There is a statue to him in the forecourt of St. Paul's School.

Biography

Lupton, J.H. *A Life of John Colet, D.D.* (George Bell and Sons, 1887)

DNB

COLLINS, Brenda M. 1946-1990

Liberal Democrat Councillor

Brenda Allchurch was originally from Bermondsey and married William P. Collins in 1968. Whilst living in the Lefevre Walk Estate in Bow, E3, in 1978 she stood for election to the Council for the Liberal Focus Team. She and her sister Gwen Lee were among the first seven Liberal Councillors to be elected in that year. She lived at 233 Brick Lane, Spitalfields, E1, from 1980 until her death.

In 1986 Brenda Collins was elected to represent St. Peter's Ward in Bethnal Green. She was a leading member of the Liberal Focus Team Group which controlled the Council by a narrow margin, and implemented a radical policy of decentralisation of political power and Council services to seven neighbourhoods in Tower Hamlets.

She took a special interest in social services where, as Chair and Vice-Chair of the Social Services Committee, she tackled long-standing problems particularly in children's and old people's homes.

In 1988 Brenda Collins was elected Leader of the Council, dealing with the complex issues relating to the Canary Warf development, the housing of large numbers of homeless families and the introduction of the controversial Poll Tax, imposed by the Conservative government of the day. For most of the time the Liberals controlled the Council only by the Mayor's casting vote.

In 1990 she was re-elected with one of the highest totals of votes cast for an individual councillor, but died shortly afterwards.

Brenda Collins was buried in the family grave in Eltham Cemetery.

COLQUHOUN, Patrick 1745-1820
Magistrate

Born at Dumbarton, where his father was Registrar, Patrick Colquhoun was educated at the local grammar school. He went to work in Virginia, USA for a time before returning to Scotland.

He was elected Lord Provost of Glasgow in 1782 and founded the Glasgow Chamber of Commerce, becoming its first Chairman.

He moved to London in 1789 and was appointed one of the new justices when the police system was reconstructed in 1792. With Peter BEDFORD and William ALLEN, he was one of the founders of the Spitalfields Soup Society, the first of its kind.

Colquhoun wrote *A Treatise on the Police of the Metropolis* (1800), explaining various crimes and suggesting remedies for their treatment. He suggested a public prosecutor, the extension of stipendiary magistrates and the employment of convicts in productive labour. He also proposed a board of commissioners of police for the whole of London.

It was largely due to him that the Thames Police were established in 1800, with headquarters at Wapping, to deal with theft from ships in the Thames.

Colquhoun also proposed that wealthy parishes should be called upon to mitigate the pressure of rates on poor parishes, an idea that was later advocated locally by William NEWTON, and in the present century by the Poplar Councillors' protest.

DNB

CONRAD, Joseph 1857-1924
Writer

Born in the Ukraine of Polish parents, Joseph Conrad joined an English merchant ship in 1878 and became a naturalised British subject when he gained his Master's certificate in 1886.

He was with the *Duke of Sutherland* when he first stayed at the Sailors' Home and Red Ensign club in Dock Street, Whitechapel. He continually used the Home when he was in London and while he was the second mate on the *Narcissus*.

He left the sea in 1894 to devote his time to writing, his best known book being *Lord Jim*.

There are two drawings of him in the National Portrait Gallery, by Percy Anderson and Sir William Rothenstein.

Biographies

Conrad, J. *Joseph Conrad As I Knew Him* (Heinemann, 1926)
Curle, R.H.P. *Joseph Conrad and His Character* (Heinemann, 1957)

DNB

Noticeboard outside St. Paul's Church, Shadwell with details of the Cook family connection with the parish

COOK, Captain James 1728-1779
Navigator

James Cook was born at Marton, Cleveland, the son of an agricultural labourer. He was apprenticed to Whitby shipowners. He came to London in 1746 as apprentice to John Walker, a Quaker shipowner, and lived in Ratcliffe or Wapping, where in 1755 he volunteered for the Navy. He married Elizabeth Batts, at Barking in 1762 where he is registered as living in the parish of St. Paul, Shadwell.

At the end of 1765 James Cook moved with his family to Mutton Lane, Mile End Old Town, now Assembly Passage, E1. The rate book for 1776 shows he lived at 7 Assembly Row, which was re-designated 88 Mile End Road in 1863.

In 1759 he spent about eight years surveying the St. Lawrence River and Newfoundland. From 1768-71, he commanded the *Endeavour* which rounded Cape Horn to Tahiti, circumnavigating and charting New Zealand.

The east coast of Australia was also surveyed and declared British territory. He returned to England by way of the Cape of Good Hope, thus circumnavigating the globe.

In 1772 James Cook sailed again in the *Resolution* to see how far the lands of the Antarctic stretched northwards. His voyage, 1776-79, was to discover a north-west passage round the north coast of America from the

Pacific, sailing east by way of the Cape of Good Hope, Tasmania, New Zealand and the Pacific Islands. He was killed by natives in Hawaii in January 1779.

James Cook did more than any other navigator to add to our knowledge of the Pacific and Southern Oceans. He also discovered a successful treatment for scurvy, a disease then rampant among seamen. He ordered food rations with anti-scorbutic properties such as evaporated malt in the form of beer, called 'wort', and pickled cabbage, or 'sauerkraut'.

There is a Greater London Council plaque at the site of 88 Mile End Road, E1, and an History of Wapping Trust Plaque at Free Trade Wharf, a few yards from his residence in Shadwell, 1763-65, and a statue of him by Sir Thomas Brock (1914) in the Mall, SW1.

Biographies
Beaglehole, J.C.   *The Life of Captain James Cook* (A. & C. Black, 1974)
Hunt, J.   *From Whitby to Wapping* (Stepney Historical Trust, 1991)

DNB

CORNER, Dr. Edred Moss
1873-1950
Surgeon

Edred Corner was born at the Manor House, Poplar, situated between Hale Street and Wade Street, Poplar. He came from a family of doctors. His father, as well as his cousin Dr. Matthew Cursham CORNER's father, were brothers who were born near Whitby in Yorkshire.

He trained at St. Thomas's Hospital and was unique in coming first in both parts of the M.B. qualifying examination.

He became Consultant Surgeon at St. Thomas's Hospital and Great Ormond Street Hospital for Sick Children.

Interested in every part of surgery, he specialised in orthopaedics and was a pioneer in the use of light metal artificial limbs.

CORNER, Dr. Matthew Cursham 1860-1928
Physician and Surgeon

A life long inhabitant of Mile End, Stepney, Dr Matthew Cursham Corner was born at 5 Ireland Row, Mile End Road in the family home where he lived all his life. The property is now 113 Mile End Road, part of an early eighteenth century terrace restored by English Heritage.

Like his father before him he trained at the London Hospital and succeeded him in his medical practice.

Matthew Corner was identified with the best maternity work that modern skill and science could supply. For 42 years he was Medical Officer to the East End Mothers' Lying-In Home, 396 Commercial Road, Stepney. When he retired from this position in 1924 he remarked that he hoped the word 'Home' would never be deleted from the title. It was however later renamed the East End Maternity Hospital.

He held many public appointments in the field of medicine and social welfare and was a well-known local figure being easily recognised, as he stood 6' 3" tall. Dr. Corner probably knew more about East End family life than any other medical practitioner and could be seen daily making calls in the streets of East London with his horse Pendo and a gig. Latterly he became one of the first professional men in East London to use a motor car for his rounds, accompanied at the wheel by his wife Maudie, an accomplished driver.

His little book entitled *Brief Instructions to Mothers and Nurses upon the Feeding, General Management and Treatment of Children* (1886) was for a long time recognised as a textbook and distributed to medical students as the authority on the subject.

He lived a very active life and gave practical support to many local organisations and causes. Dr. Matthew Corner was the cousin of Dr. Edred Moss CORNER.

COTTON, William 1786-1866
Philanthropist

William Cotton was born at Leyton and educated at Chigwell Grammar School. His family wanted him to enter the Church, but he was more interested in business. He became a partner in Huddart's Rope Works, Limehouse, founded by Sir Robert WIGRAM.

In 1821 he became a Director of the Bank of England and from 1843-45 was Governor. He invented an automatic weighing machine for sovereigns.

Throughout his life, William Cotton had a recurring inclination to take holy orders, and with his early associations with Limehouse, later took an interest in the St. Anne's Schools, Limehouse. He was also one of the founders of the 'National Society for Promoting the Education of the Poor in the Principles of the Established Church' in 1811,

William Cotton was also on the committee of the London Hospital.

As a result of collaboration between William Cotton and Sir H. Dukinfield, Vicar of St. Martin's-in-the-Field, Westminster and others, an Act of Parliament was passed in 1847 enabling public authorities to build baths and wash houses at the expense of the ratepayers. Goulston Square (later Street) Baths, Whitechapel, begun in 1846 was extended and officially opened in 1851.

William Cotton was a prime mover in the erection of ten churches in Bethnal Green, and of St. Paul's, Bow Common, and St. Peter's, Stepney.

There is a painted window memorial in St. Paul's Cathedral, paid for by public subscription.

He is commemorated locally by Cotton Street, E14.

DNB

CRAB, Roger 1621(?)-1680
Hermit

A native of Buckinghamshire, Roger Crab was 6' 7" tall and very strong. While serving in the Parliamentary army (1642-1649) he received a blow on the head from a Royalist Trooper. This led to his discharge and he began business as a hatter at Chesham, but after a short while he sold the business and gave the money to the poor.

He began a different life as a hermit near Uxbridge, dabbling in astrology and physic. His asceticism was connected with a kind of mystical revolt against notions of religion.

He lived in a tree house on three farthings a week, eating bran, dock leaves, mallow and grass.

He came to East London and ultimately tranferred his hermitage to Bethnal Green. In his later days he acquired a reputation for sanctity and prophecy, fortelling the Restoration of the Monarchy of 1660 and succession in 1689 of William of Orange to the throne. On his tomb in St. Dunstan's Church, Stepney, is inscribed an epitaph:-

> Through good and ill Reports he past;
> oft censur'd, yet approv'd at last.
> ...
> A Friend to ev'ry Thing that's good.

His life was recorded by John STRYPE.

Pamphlet

The English Hermite or Wonder of this Age (London, 1655)

DNB

CRESSALL, George, OBE
1880-1951
Labour Councillor

Born in Stepney, George Cressall was educated at Dalgleish Street (now Sir William Burrough) School, Limehouse. He worked at Hubbuck's Paint Works, 44-48 Broad Street, later 368 The Highway, Ratcliff.

In 1907 he became a founder member of the Limehouse branch of the Independent Labour Party. About that time he received a visit from C.R. ATTLEE, then a resident at Toynbee Hall, a university settlement, and George Cressall enrolled Clement Attlee as a member of the Party.

On his marriage to Nellie CRESSALL he moved to Poplar and in 1918 was appointed full-time Labour agent and secretary of the South Poplar Labour Party.

He was elected member of the Poplar Board of Guardians 1922-1925 and 1928-1930 and became a member of Poplar Borough Council from 1919 to 1949. He was Mayor in 1931-32.

With other Poplar Councillors he was imprisoned in Brixton in 1921 for refusing to levy Poplar's share of the London County Council's Police and Metropolitan Asylum contributions on the grounds that local rate payers were already impoverished with high levels of unemployment. He was created an OBE in 1949.

Book

Branson, N. *Poplarism, 1918-1925* (Lawrence & Wishart, 1979)

CRESSALL, Nellie Frances
1882-1973
Labour Councillor

Born Nellie Wilson, in Stepney, she had her first introduction to politics when she was eight years old by helping her father on a horse and cart electioneering tour. For a time she worked in a laundry in Whitechapel Road.

She met her husband George CRESSALL at a cricket match. They were married in 1904 and had a family of eight children.

In 1912 she joined the Suffragette movement and became a friend and colleague of Sylvia PANKHURST.

Elected to Poplar Borough Council in 1919, she was a member until 1965, becoming Mayor in 1943-1944. She was one of five women councillors sent to Holloway Prison in 1921 for refusing to levy Poplar's share of the

Earl Attlee, far right, congratulates Councillor Cressall on her receiving the Freedom of the Borough of Poplar on the 8th April 1959

London County Council's Police and Metropolitan Asylum contributions on the grounds that local rate payers were already impoverished with high levels of unemployment.

In 1946 Nellie Cressall was appointed a member of the Lord Chancellor's committee on divorce. A fine orator, at the Labour Party conference of 1951 she made a spirited speech, which was described by Aneurin Bevan as 'the finest address he had ever heard on any platform'.
Book
Branson, N. *Poplarism, 1919-1925* (Lawrence and Wishart, 1979)

CROMWELL, Thomas
circa 1485-1540
Statesman
The son of a Putney blacksmith, Thomas Cromwell was a soldier, fighting in many cities in Europe. On his return to England in 1513 he began practising as a lawyer. He was employed by Cardinal Wolsey as his chief agent in suppressing the monasteries. He later became Wolsey's secretary, and thus became known to Henry Vlll. As an adviser to Henry Vlll, he persuaded him to abolish papal authority, break the power of the Church and make the power of the King absolute, by the Act of Supremacy 1534.

He was successively Chancellor of the Exchequer and Lord Privy Seal, he was created Earl of Essex 1540. He lived at the 'Great Place', Stepney Green near St. Dunstan's Church.

Falling out of favour with the King, he was beheaded on Tower Hill in 1540.
Biographies
Merriman, R.B. *Life and Letters of Thomas Cromwell* (Clarendon Press, 1902)
Wilding, P.   *Thomas Cromwell* (Heinemann, 1935)

CROOK, Lillian 1914-1986
Labour Councillor
Born in Bethnal Green, Lillian Crook was just thirteen when she joined the local Labour Party, where her parents Fred and Rose Hayman were founder members. She also met her husband William Crook there.

Lillian Crook was a member of Tower Hamlets Council for eighteen years on the Social Services and Amenities Committees. She was also Mayor in 1980-81.
Article
East London Advertiser 7th March 1986

Thomas Cromwell

Will Crooks, on the left, and Sir Alfred Yeo, Poplar's MP, seeing off mothers and children for a country holiday in 1917
Whiffin Collection

CROOKS, William 1852-1921
Labour Leader

Born at Shirbutt Street, Poplar, William Crooks spent his early years in deep poverty, his father having lost an arm at work. The family were unable to maintain themselves and William Crooks was sent to the workhouse. Through hard work, Mrs Crooks enabled them to be re-united, but the harsh experience made a lasting mark on his character.

His first job on leaving school was as an apprentice to a cooper, but he also worked as a casual labourer in the docks, experiencing the daily struggle of men to obtain work.

William Crooks became an eloquent speaker and held regular Sunday morning meetings outside East India Dock gates, during which many relevant social questions were discussed. The meetings became known as 'Crooks' College', and from these meetings came successful campaigns for free public libraries, a footway tunnel under the Thames and the operation of the Poor Law under more humane principles. He was one of the leaders of the Dock Strike 1889 although he was working at his own trade as a cooper. Another outcome of 'Crooks' College' was the formation of the Poplar Electoral Committee which later became Poplar Labour League.

Early in the 1890s, William Crooks was able to give up his job and devote all his time to public work. He was elected to the London County Council in 1892, serving until 1910. A member of the Poplar Borough Council, he was elected Mayor in 1901, the first Labour Mayor in London. He was also elected to the Board of Guardians and campaigned for improved workhouse conditions. With George LANSBURY he was associated with 'Poplarism' – which sought to administer the Poor Law more humanely with emphasis on rehabilitation. He was elected to Parliament for Woolwich in 1903.

He lived in Poplar all his life in a small terraced house in Gough Street, and was always available for advice and support for those in need. His ideas sprang from deep religious humanitarianism.

Large numbers of people attended his funeral in Tower Hamlets Cemetery, Bow. His epitaph reads 'He lived and died a servant of the people'.

He is commemorated by William Crooks Estate, Poplar High Street, E14.

Biography
Haw, G. *From Workhouse to Westminster* (Cassell, 1907)

DNB

CUBITT, Sir William 1791-1863
Builder and Politician

Born at Buxton, Norfolk, William Cubitt entered the Navy and served for 4 years. He then went into partnership with his brother, Thomas Cubitt, builder and landlord.

When Thomas Cubitt decided to concentrate on house building, William continued the business as a general contractor. He developed Cubitt Town and built Christ Church, Manchester Road, Isle of Dogs, the foundation stone being laid in 1852.

William Cubitt was Lord Mayor of London 1860-61 and unusually, was re-elected for 1861-62. During his time as Lord Mayor he raised large sums for charity.

He was Member of Parliament for Andover 1847-61 and President of St. Bartholomew's Hospital from 1861 until his death in 1863.

He is commemorated by Cubitt Town, E14.

CULPEPER, Nicholas 1616-1654
Herbalist and Writer

Born in London, Nicholas Culpeper was educated at Cambridge and then apprenticed to an apothecary in Bishopsgate.

He came to live at Red Lion Street, Spitalfields and wrote books in simple language explaining how readers could cure their illnesses by means of herbs. He was always ready to give personal advice to poor people, much to the opposition of physicians.

His best known books are *The English Physician Enlarged* (1653) and *A Physical Directory, or a Translation of the London Dispensatory* (1649) which was an English translation from the Latin of the College of Physicians' Pharmacopoeia. *The Complete Herbal* is still published.

He is commemorated in the Borough by Culpeper House, Blount Street, E14.

DNB

CURRIE, Sir Edmund Hay
1834-1913
Philanthropist

Edmund Currie was the son of the proprietor of the Bromley Distillery in St. Leonard Street, Bromley-by-Bow. At an early age he decided to take up religious and social work in East London.

He established St. Michael's School, which became Byron Street School in 1878 under the London School Board, was re-named Hay Currie in 1908 and later called Langdon Park School. The headmaster from 1862 to 1906 was Robert WILD.

The school buildings were used in the evenings for boys' clubs and adult education classes. Currie was also responsible for building St. Michael's and All Angels Church, Bromley-by-Bow.

Currie lived in Bromley and was a member of the local Board of Guardians. He was one of the first members elected to the School Board of London in 1870 and became its Vice-Chairman. He was Chairman of the Beaumont Trustees, who were responsible for opening of the People's Palace, Mile End, and he received a knighthood in 1876 for this.

He was a pioneer in providing camping holidays for young people.

He became secretary to the Metropolitan Hospital Sunday Fund and Chairman of the London Hospital for 12 years, during which time a new wing was built.

He is commemorated by Hay Currie Street, E14 and Currie House in Abbott Road, E14.

CUTNER, Samuel CBE 1902-1988
Concert Pianist

Solomon, as he was always professionally known, was born at 29 Fournier Street, Spitalfields. He was the youngest of seven children of a music loving Polish immigrant tailor.

He first attracted attention at the age of six by playing a piano arrangement of Tchaikovsky's 1812 overture. At the age of seven he began to study with Matthilde Verne, a pupil of Clara Schumann. He made his debut in 1909 by playing Mozart's B. flat concerto and the slow movement of Tchaikovsky's first concerto at the Queen's Hall. He played again there under Sir Henry Wood and made his 'Prom' debut in 1914. Soon he appeared with many of the world's most famous conductors and orchestras.

At the age of sixteen, Solomon grew tired of performing, and took the advice of Sir Henry Wood to retire from the platform and continue studying. In 1921, armed with a more powerful technique, he began a second concert career and for the next thirty five years became one of the most sought after players with a large repertory. He made his American debut in 1926 and was greatly admired there.

He became one of the twentieth century's most distinguished concert pianists, best known for his playing of the Mozart,

Nicholas Culpepper

Beethoven and Brahms sonatas and concertos. His flourishing career was cut short by a severe stroke in 1956. Many of his performances are recorded.
He was created CBE in 1946.

DANCE, George (The Elder)
1700-1768
Architect

George Dance was Clerk of City Works for the Corporation of London for 33 years from 1735.

Although the Commissioners for the Building of the Fifty New Churches bought two and a half acres of land in Bethnal Green, it was only in 1742 that a petition for the building of a church was finally presented to the House of Commons by representatives of the recently growing hamlet of 15,000. An Act of Parliament was passed enabling money to be borrowed for the construction of St. Matthew's. The Church was opened in 1746.

George Dance was responsible for the rebuilding of St. Botolph's, Aldgate between 1741-1744, and was architect of St. Leonard's Church, Shoreditch, 1736-1740. The builder he employed provoked a riot by employing cut price labour and armed forces had to be called from the Tower of London.

George Dance also designed the Mansion House for the Corporation of London from 1739-1753.

Books
Clarke, B.F.L.   *Parish Churches of London*
   (Batsford, 1966)
Young, E. and W.   *Old London Churches* (Faber and Faber, 1956)

DNB

DARBISHIRE, Henry Astley
1838-1908
Architect

Henry Darbishire, a London-based architect and Fellow of the Royal Institute of British Architects was employed by the wealthy philanthropist Baroness Angela BURDETT-COUTTS to design dwellings for the working classes in East London.

Financed by the Baroness, Henry Darbishire designed the Columbia Square flats in Bethnal Green which were built 1860-62. The development comprised four grim blocks arranged around courtyards.

Henry Darbishire later designed the Columbia Market 1866-68, which stood at the centre of the Baroness's dwellings for the poor.

In contrast to the architecturally gloomy blocks, the Market was a very ornate Gothic extravaganza with innumerable pinnacles and a clock tower. The whole complex represented a major feat of philanthropic patronage but the Market failed within six months.

He was also employed by the Peabody Trust which had been set up in 1862 by George Peabody to 'ameliorate the condition and augment the comforts of the poor ... of London'. In the next year, with Darbishire as its architect, the Trust started work in a block in Commercial Street, Spitalfields which was opened in 1864 as a prototype block of dwellings for the Peabody Trust.

Although best known as the designer of serviceable but dismal blocks of working class tenements, an example of Darbishire's elaborate architecture still survives locally in Victoria Park, Bow. In 1861 he designed and supervised the erection of a drinking fountain in the park, made of granite and marble which was formally presented to the park by its benefactor Baroness Burdett-Coutts on 30th June 1862.

Columbia Square and Columbia Market were demolished between 1958 and 1966 by the London County Council.

Henry Darbishire retired in 1894.

Books
Tarn, J.N.   *Five Per Cent Philanthropy*
   (Cambridge University Press, 1973)
Poulsen, C.   *Victoria Park* (Stepney Books, 1976)

DASH, Jack   1906-1989
Dockers' Leader

Jack Dash was born in South London near to the Elephant and Castle. He described his early years and his family's poverty and hardship through unemployment in his autobiography *Good Morning Brothers*.

He left school at fourteen and said "having been taught the three 'Rs', reading, writing and arithmetic, I entered the 'University of Life', my college 'The College of Industry'". He began work at Lyons Corner House in Coventry Street, W1, later he became a hod carrier for bricklayers, building a cinema in Brixton.

He married in 1931, later moving to a house in what is now Timothy Road, E14, becoming a member of the Communist Party in 1936. He was actively involved in the stand against Sir Oswald Mosley's march through Stepney in 1937.

His trade union convictions and activities

made it difficult for him to hold jobs for very long. While working at the Odeon Cinema in Bow Road, he led his first strike. This was a campaign by hod carriers climbing ladders over forty feet being entitled to receive 'height' or 'danger' money at the rate of 2d. an hour. This was refused at first, but after a short strike and discussion the rate was agreed and paid retrospectively.

During the second World War he volunteered for the Royal Navy, but was told he would have to wait, so he joined the London Fire Brigade and served during the heavy air raids on East London, later volunteering for a Commando division to serve with troops on the Second Front.

In 1946 he obtained work with the National Dock Labour Board and from that time until 1970 he brought Communism and Trade Union activity to open air meetings. He opposed not only the London and Liverpool dock employers but also the leadership of the Transport and General Workers Union. The Devlin Report ended dock casual labouring and weakened his power on the Royal Docks Liaison Committee. Jack Dash took an active part in every major dock strike.

He was a gifted person with a talent for painting and writing poetry. He was a good public speaker and was often asked to take part in University debates. He also gave lectures on the history and problems of the docks.

In his retirement he became a London tourist guide. He was active in a campaign for better old age pensions and spoke to pensioners groups at Dame Colet House, Ben Jonson Road, E1, the Dockers Club, Boulcott Street, E1, and many other venues.

He was a colourful and charismatic person.

He is commemorated by Jack Dash House, Lawn House Close, E14.
Autobiography
Good Morning Brothers! (Wapping Standing Neighbourhood Committee, 1987)

DAVENANT, Rev. Ralph   died 1680
Rector of Whitechapel

Ralph Davenant was born in Gillingham, Dorset. As a young man he was a favourite in the court of Charles II, and this brought a remarkable rise in his life. The King obliged Cambridge University to give young Davenant the degree of Master of Arts and make him a Fellow of Trinity College, 'notwithstanding any statutes to the contrary'.

The same influence of royal writ was exerted to appoint him to be Rector of St. Mary Matfelon, Whitechapel. During his years at Whitechapel, the church was pulled down and re-built. In the 1670s the fields around Whitechapel were being built over, and Davenant provided schooling for the poor children of the parish, educating them in 'the principles of religion and to read and write and cost accounts'.

On his death he left a legacy to educate 40 boys and 30 girls of the parish which was the beginning of Davenant School, formerly in Whitechapel Road. The school moved to Loughton, Essex in 1965.

He is commemorated locally by Davenant Street, E1, and by the Davenant Centre, 179-181 Whitechapel Road, E1, and by the Davenant Trust.
Book
Reynolds, R. *History of Davenant School* (Leach, 1967)

DAVIES, Micky   1910-1954
Youth Worker

Micky Davies was a Shelter Marshall in Spitalfields during the second World War, and organised a large shelter which became known as 'Micky's shelter'. He persuaded the users to elect a shelter committee and when Wendell Willkie, President Roosevelt's Republican rival, visited London, he was taken to Micky's shelter as a showplace of British democracy.

After the war, he kept in touch with many lads who had been fire service messengers, and started the Vallance Club, becoming its full-time leader.

He represented the Spitalfields West ward on Stepney Council 1949-53.

Micky Davies is mentioned in *The People's War* by Angus Calder (Jonathan Cape, 1969).
Pamphlet
Powley, T, *A brief history of the Vallance Youth Club* (Vallance Youth Club, c.1973)

DAY, Thomas   1748-1789
Writer

Thomas Day was born in Wellclose Square, Whitechapel and educated at Charterhouse School and Oxford. His father, who worked at the Custom House, left him a fortune of £1,200 a year.

Having acquired a new philosophy of education based on the principles of Rousseau, he decided that his wife-to-be should be educated in these principles. He chose two young girls from orphanages and took them to France to discover and discipline their characters.

Neither could meet his qualifications and they returned, one to school and the other to be apprenticed to a milliner. He became attracted to a Miss Esther Milnes of Wakefield, a woman of considerable culture who had herself written poems and appreciated Day's writings. He was deterred from offering himself by her possession of a fortune and his doubt of her willingness to submit to his conditions. She loved him devotedly however, and after two years they came to an understanding. She was to live as strictly as he wished and her fortune was placed beyond his control, so that she might retreat from the experiment if it proved too painful, and they were married in 1778.

He wrote poetry and prose against the American War of Independence 1775-1783.

His main work was the *History of Sandford and Merton* (1783-89), a succession of episodes in which the rich Merton is contrasted with the virtuous Sandford.

DNB

de BLANK, Rev. Joost 1908-1968

Bishop of Stepney

Born in Holland, Joost de Blank came to England in 1909. Ordained in 1931, as a Chaplain to the forces, he had links with St. James-the-Less Church, Bethnal Green.

He was Bishop of Stepney 1952-1957, a time of great change in church life. Some churches were being closed; others were rebuilt and restored.

In 1957 he was appointed Archbishop of Capetown and proved to be a fearless opponent of apartheid. He returned after a period of ill health to be a Canon of Westminster in 1963.

Throughout his life he was involved in activities for human rights and community relations.

A memorial tablet in Westminster Abbey reads 'An indomitable fighter for human rights'.

Biography
de Blank, B. *Joost de Blank* (Boydell, 1977)

Sir Wyndham Henry Deedes

DEEDES, Sir Wyndham Henry
1883-1956

Soldier and Community Worker

Born in London, after finishing his education at Eton, William Deedes joined the Rifle Brigade and served mainly in the Middle East.

In 1920 he was appointed Chief Secretary to the Governor of Palestine, Sir Henry, later Lord Samuel. He resigned the post in 1923 and came to Bethnal Green to do social work.

He lived at Oxford House University Settlement, Mape Street, Bethnal Green, becoming Head in 1936 and then going on to University House, a community centre in Victoria Park Square, Bethnal Green.

He was Labour member for North East Bethnal Green on the London County Council from 1941-1946, serving on the Education Committee. He also became Chairman of the London Council of Social Service.

During the second World War he was Chief Air Raid Warden for the borough. He led a relief mission into Turkey following some severe earthquakes. He was a fluent speaker of the Turkish language and helped found a Turkish Centre in London. He also had great interest in Zionism.

Wyndham Deedes was keen to encourage Bethnal Green residents to have flowering window boxes and gardens. Forced to retire through ill health in 1950, he went to live in Hythe.

There is a memorial plaque to him on the housing development which has replaced University House, Victoria Park Square, E2., and he is also commemorated by Wyndham Deedes House, Hackney Road, E2.

Biographies

Presland, J. *Deedes Bey* (Macmillan, 1942)
Elath, E. et al. *Memories of Sir Wyndham Deedes* (Gollancz, 1958)

DNB

DENNIS, Harold Escott OBE
1880-1973
Town Clerk of Poplar

Harold Dennis was appointed to the staff of the Poplar Board of Guardians in 1896. Through some trying times immediately after the end of the first World War, the policies of the Board of Guardians were pursued with administrative skills, vision and initiative, providing humane treatment in relief for the unemployed and destitute of the Borough. His steady and determined pressure upon the Ministry of Health and the Treasury enabled the policies to be funded. He was not the originator of the 'Poplarism' movement, but the architect of its achievement.

On leaving the Board of Guardians in 1926 he became Town Clerk to the Borough of Poplar. He continued beyond retirement age through a sense of duty and through his organisational expertise thousands of children survived and were fed. In 1941 he was awarded an OBE for outstanding public service and in 1945 became the first Freeman of the Borough of Poplar after completing 49 years of public service in the Borough.

DENT, Joseph Malaby 1849-1926
Publisher

Born in Darlington, the tenth child of a house painter. Joseph Dent left school when he was 12 and was apprenticed first to a printer and then to a bookbinder, from which he derived a love of beautiful books.

Three Freemen of the Borough of Poplar,from left to right; Nellie Cressall, Charles Key, and Harold Dennis, on 8th April 1959

He came to London in 1867 and secured work with a bookbinder in Bucklersbury, in the City. He enrolled at Toynbee Hall as a student. He made a habit of looking in the windows of the City booksellers and so admired the small gift volumes bound in leather, that he decided to set up in business as a publisher on his own account.

He never forgot his lack of education and resolved to help those who were similarly handicapped. First he produced the *Temple Shakespeare* and *Temple Classics*. His great ambition was to produce a library of 1,000 books, the finest and most helpful ever written, obtainable at one shilling each, giving a working man a collection for a total of £50.

In 1906 the first 50 titles were produced and the name 'Everyman's Library' taken from the old morality play:-

Everyman I will go with thee and be thy guide
In thy most need to go by thy side.

Autobiography
The Memoirs of J.M. Dent (Dent, 1928)

DNB

DIAMOND, Alfred 1902-1978
Businessman and Community Worker

Born in Wapping, Alfred Diamond became a successful businessman. Associated with Sir Basil HENRIQUES and the Bernhard Baron Settlement, he was a manager of the boys' club for nearly 50 years. A member of the Jewish Board of Deputies for 27 years, he was Chairman of the 'Bridge in Britain' movement, designed to foster understanding between Britain and Israel and Jews and non-Jews.

DICKENS, Charles 1812-1870
Writer

Charles Dickens was born in Portsmouth. When he was very young his family moved to Chatham and then to London, his father working in the dockyards. Charles Dickens had many homes but none in East London, although he knew parts intimately from his childhood visits to Christopher HUFFAM his godfather, who lived in Church Row, now Newell Street, Limehouse.

His books contain many allusions to East London life, its characters and settings. Whilst writing his last novel, *Edwin Drood*, Charles Dickens frequented opium dens in Shadwell, and visits to Limehouse, Wapping and Mile End are described in *The Uncommercial Traveller*. 'The Grapes' Public House in Narrow Street, Limehouse, is said to be the original of 'The Six Jolly Fellowship Porters' referred to in *Our Mutual Friend*, and Limehouse is also the residence of various characters in this novel.

The Nickleby family in *Nicholas Nickleby* rented a 'little cottage at Bow'; David Copperfield arrived in London at an inn in Aldgate; and Bill Sikes' household in *Oliver Twist* was in Bethnal Green. Well-known film versions of these latter three novels – George Cukor's *David Copperfield* made in Hollywood in 1934 starring W.C. Fields, and the British films, both starring Alec Guiness, *Oliver Twist* (directed by David LEAN in 1948) and *Nicholas Nickleby* of 1947, together with the musical *Oliver!*, filmed in 1968, have helped extend the popularity of Dickens' work.

He was consulted by Angela BURDETT-COUTTS about her plan for Columbia Market and flats. Following his visit to Nathaniel HECKFORD at his East London Children's Hospital, Charles Dickens wrote an article in *McMillan's Magazine* in 1870 which brought in much money from the public and enabled Heckford to build a new hospital in Glamis Road, Shadwell.

Charles Dickens was buried in Westminster Abbey and he is commemorated locally by Charles Dickens House, Mansford Street, E2.

Biographies
Wilson, A.   *The World of Charles Dickens* (Penguin, 1972)
Mackenzie, N. and J. *Dickens, A Life* (Oxford University Press, 1973)

DNB

DICKIN, Maria Elizabeth
1870-1951
Founder of P.D.S.A. (People's Dispensary for Sick Animals)

The daughter of Rev. W.G.Dickin, Maria Dickin became a social worker in Whitechapel. She married her first cousin Arnold Francis Dickin of Clapham in 1899 in Westminster.

Maria Dickin possibly began a free dispensary in the crypt of St. Mary's Church, Whitechapel, in November 1917, or in Fulbourne Street, Whitechapel or Vallance Road, Whitechapel. After two months the dispensary moved to Harford Street, Mile End and then a small hospital was opened at 542 Commercial Road, Ratcliff. The headquarters is now in Whitechapel Way, Priorslee, nr. Telford.

It soon became evident that it was necessary to open further treatment centres, and Maria began by paying for the first five herself, setting about the task of raising £80,000 to fund the project.

The People's Dispensary for Sick Animals has 50 animal treatment centres now, entirely supported by Voluntary contributions. The treatment centres are supplemented by an auxiliary service provided by local veterinary services where there is no Society centre. Over one million pets are treated annually. The Society has branches in Morocco, Egypt and South Africa.

After her death, the PDSA instituted the Maria Dickin medal to be awarded to animals for brave conduct.

On 19th November 1985, Tower Hamlets Council arranged for a tree to be planted, together with a plaque to commemorate Mrs Dickin's first dispensary, at St. Mary's Open Space, Whitechapel, now Altab Ali Park.
Article
The Times 3rd March 1951
Who Was Who 1951-60, PDSA Annual Reports

DITCHBURN, Joseph 1801-1870
Engineer

Born in Chatham, Joseph Ditchburn became manager to Fletcher and Fearnall, shipbuilders in Limehouse. He lived at Palm Cottage, 153 East India Dock Road, Poplar.

In 1837, with C.J. MARE he set up the iron shipbuilding yard at Blackwall where they built over 400 vessels. The Recruit was the first and only iron sailing warship. The Warrior was the first sea-going iron frigate built for the Royal Navy.

Ditchburn also built Fairy, the favourite yacht of Queen Victoria, pronounced at the time to be 'the most perfect gem that ever floated on the water'. He retired from the partnership with Mare in 1846.

He was churchwarden at All Saints, Poplar.

He is commemorated in the borough by Ditchburn House and Ditchburn Street, E14.
Book
Banbury, P. *Shipbuilders of the Thames and Medway* (David & Charles, 1971)

DODD, Robert 1748-1816(?)
Marine Artist and Engraver

Robert Dodd began his professional life as a landscape painter, but through living close to the Thames at 33 Wapping Wall, near St. James's Stairs, Shadwell he became interested in ships and the water. His pictures first appeared in the Society of Artists' Exhibition in Spring Gardens, Westminster in 1780.

He was a constant exhibitor at the Royal Academy, with pictures of the great sailing ships of his day. Eight pictures are in the collection of the Port of London Authority and his painting of the *Glorious First of June* is in the National Maritime Museum, Greenwich, together with a series of five paintings of the sinking of the *Romillies*. Some of his engravings are in the Print Room of the British Museum.

He also lived in Redman's Road, Mile End Old Town, and at Charing Cross. He is buried in St. Dunstan's Church, Stepney.
Book
Chatterton, E.K. *Old Sea Paintings* (John Lane, 1928)

DNB

DOLLOND, John 1706-1761
Optician and Mathematician

John Dolland was born in Spitalfields of French Protestant parents who came with other refugees following the revocation of the Edict of Nantes, 1685. For a time he earned his living as a weaver but his spare time was taken up with mathematics and natural philosophy.

His first contribution to science was the improvement of the telescope: he developed the achromatic or colourless telescope for which he was awarded the Copley Medal 1758 and elected a Fellow of the Royal Society 1761. He also improved the micrometer. He corrected an error of Isaac NEWTON asserting an important law of optics.

His son Peter Dollond and his nephew George were also noted opticians, and the firm continues until this day.

John Dollond is commemorated by Dollond House, Maroon Street, E14.
Book
King, H.C. *The History of the Telescope* (Griffin, 1955)

DNB

DORÉ, Gustave 1832-1883
Painter and Illustrator

Gustave Doré was born in Strasbourg where his father was a government engineer of bridges and highways. He was supporting himself as an artist in Paris at the age of 16. By the age of 20 he had achieved an international reputation.

He settled in London and opened the Doré Gallery at 35 New Bond Street, Westminster in 1867, where he exhibited his work. The gallery survived until the present century and is now occupied by Sothebys.

He made his name by illustrating Milton's *Paradise Lost* (1866), Tennysons *Idylls of the King* (1868) and Dante's *L'Inferno* (1861). Doré's illustrations for Jarrold's *London; A Pilgrimage* (1872) contain many graphic scenes of East End poverty, contrasted with the fashionable and wealthy life of the West End.

Books

Jarrold, B. *London; A Pilgrimage* (Grant, 1872)
de Mare, E. *The London Doré Saw* (Allen Lane, 1973)
Rose, M. *Gustave Doré* (Pleiades Books, 1946)

DOREE, George 1844-1916
Weaver

Of Huguenot descent, George Doree lived in Spitalfields for a time, then moved to Globe Road, Bethnal Green.

He became well known as a weaver of velvet cloth and in 1860 was superintendent of 250 weavers working for a firm in Trump Street, in the City.

He was awarded the silver medal of the Weavers' Company in 1893.

George Doree wove the velvet for the coronation robe of Edward VII. He was asked to do the same for the coronation of George V but had to decline owing to failing eyesight.

Article

Manchee, W.H. 'George Doree, Citizen and Weaver of London' in *Huguenot Society of London Proceedings* Vol. 11 (no 3) (1918)

DOWNHAM, Rev. Denis 1921-1979
Rector of Spitalfields

Denis Downham was born and brought up in Liverpool. He became a Christian while serving in the army and for a time worked as a layman with the London City Mission before going to Clifton College to train for the Ministry. After working in Lancashire he became Rector of Christ Church, Spitalfields in 1961.

Following the experience of trying to help a friend who had become alcoholic, he decided to open the church crypt as a rehabilitation centre for alcohol addicted men who had no home of their own. The work began in 1965, and was financed by a Trust which enabled the Crypt to be opened at all times. It continues with grants from public funds and voluntary gifts.

In 1969 Downham became Warden of the Mayflower Settlement in Canning Town, E16.

DRAKE, Corporal Alfred George, VC 1893-1915
Soldier

Alfred Drake was born in Skidmore Street, Mile End Old Town. He later lived at Copley Street and attended Ben Jonson School, Harford Street, Mile End Old Town. As a soldier in the first World War he showed conspicuous bravery, when in November 1915, He was in a patrol of four near LeBrique, France when they were attacked. Corporal Drake remained with his officer after the other two men were taken back and he was last seen kneeling and bandaging the officer's wounds regardless of enemy fire. A rescue party found the officer unconscious but alive and bandaged. Alfred Drake had given his life but saved his officer.

The Victoria Cross was awarded posthumously and gazetted 22nd January 1916.

Book

O'M. Creagh and Humphries, E.M. (eds) *The VC and DSO* (Standard Art Book, 1924)

DRIFFIELD, Rev. George 1817-1901
Priest

George Driffield was born in Prescot, Lancashire. He studied at Oxford and was ordained in 1840. He came to be a curate at St. Philip's Church, Newark Street, Stepney, and was Rector of St. Mary's Church, Bow, 1844-1880. He was energetic in the foundation of St. Stephen's Church, Tredegar Road, Bow, opened 1857; destroyed by enemy action 1942,

He was appointed to the local Board of Guardians, and became President of Sion College, an ecclesiastical library for the Church of England clergy.

He is commemorated by Driffield Road, E3.

DRUCE, Joseph 1777-1819
Maori Chief

Born in Shadwell, the son of a Limehouse distillery worker, Joseph Druce was baptised at St. Paul's Church, Shadwell. After leaving school he worked for a time in Bellamy's rope works and on a fishing smack.

Druce was arrested for housebreaking and stealing in March 1791 and convicted at the Old Bailey. Sentenced to death, he was recommended for mercy because of his youth, and was transported to New South Wales in 1792.

He was pardoned about 1801, finding various jobs as a bushranger, a policeman and then as a sailor. On a ship going to and from New Zealand he met a Maori chief, who became ill. Druce nursed him and married one of his daughters, so becoming a Maori chief himself. About this time he changed his name to George Bruce. When his wife died, his baby daughter was put into an orphanage and Bruce joined HMS *Porpoise* for a journey to England. In 1815 he spent some time in Shadwell Workhouse, where he was helped by the Church Missionary Society. He was admitted to Greenwich Seamen's Hospital in 1817 where he produced a 19,000 word manuscript entitled *The Life of a Greenwich Pensioner*.

Article
Bodle, R. 'The Road to Transportation' in *East London Record* No.4 (1981)

DUCKETT, Sir George 1777-1856
Canal Builder

Son of Sir George Jackson M.P. for Colchester and Weymouth who had changed his name to Duckett in order to claim a family fortune. George Duckett the younger was for many years Member of Parliament for Colchester and Weymouth, becoming Secretary to the Admiralty, and Judge Advocate. He was a friend and patron of Captain James COOK who named Port Jackson in Australia after him.

George Duckett was Member of Parliament for Lymington 1807-1812 and succeeded to the baronetcy in 1822. He claimed he could trace his ancestry back through his mother to Gundreda, daughter of William the Conqueror. A classical scholar and linguist, he translated many books into English.

He was builder of the Hertford Union Canal, cut through land south of what is now Victoria Park, Bow. Its purpose was to provide a link between the River Lea and the Regent's Canal. An Act of Parliament in 1824 provided the authority and the canal was opened in 1830. It failed to make a profit and Duckett was bankrupted in 1832.

The canal was put up for sale in May 1851 but no buyer could be found until the Regent's Canal Company purchased it in 1857. It has since operated as part of the Regent's Canal, but is often called 'Duckett's Canal'.

He is commemorated by Duckett Street, E1.

Book
Boyes, J. and Russell, R. *The Canals of Eastern England* (David and Charles, 1977)

Obituary
Illustrated London News 5th July 1856

DUNBAR, Duncan 1790-1862
Ship Owner

Born at Ropemaker's Fields, Limehouse, Duncan Dunbar became one of London's wealthiest shipping magnates and owner of Dunbar Wharf, Limehouse.

He built a handsome residence on the north side of East India Dock Road between Pekin Street and Upper North Street and named it 'Howrah House' after his dockyard at Moulmein, Burma.

The house was afterwards occupied by Sisters of Mercy and known as Howrah House Convent. It was demolished in 1951 to make way for the new Lansbury Estate.

Dunbar was buried in St. Anne's, Limehouse churchyard.

DUTCH SAM (ELIAS, Samuel)
1775-1816
Bare Knuckle Fighter

Born in Whitechapel of Jewish parents, as a bare knuckle fighter Samuel Elias (Dutch Sam) was feared as the deadliest puncher of the London prize ring. He was reputed to be the inventor of the 'Upper Cut', attracting much attention after he had knocked out heavier men. Samuel Elias was 5'6" tall and weighed only 133 pounds, but was deep chested and muscular. His son, 'Young Dutch Sam' was English welterweight champion in 1825.

Books
Fleischer, N. and Andre, S. *Pictorial History of Boxing* (Hamlyn, 1977)
Downes, H.D. *Pugilistica* Vol 1. (Weldon, 1880)

DYCHE, Rev. Thomas died 1727
Lexicographer

Thomas Dyche was born and educated in Ashbourne, Derbyshire. He was ordained and came to London in 1708 to be a schoolmaster, in Fetter Lane, in the City.

He became a curate and schoolmaster of the free school at Stratford Bow. He wrote a number of books, but his most popular was a *Spelling Dictionary, or a Collection of All the Common Words and Proper Names in the English Tongue* (1725). It went into many editions and was translated into French.

DNB

EAST, Mary 1715-1780
Publican

Mary East was born in Limehouse. In her youth she became the victim of an unfortunate love affair. Her boy friend was tried at the Old Bailey for highway robbery and was sentenced to transportation. She then decided to live with a woman friend as 'man and wife' calling herself James Howes.

They took on the tenancy of a tavern in Epping and one evening a local resident assaulted 'James', resulting in the loss of 'his' right hand.

There followed a claim from which they received £500, which they used to purchase a licensed house in Limehouse. After some years they moved on to the *White Horse* in Poplar High Street. There, a woman recognised them both and blackmailed them for varying sums of money. Eventually the blackmailer and her companions were committed to Bridewell Prison and later to Newgate. Mary then retired to the country. Her 'wife' died while visiting a brother in Essex.

Mary East and her friend always lived in good credit. When she died she left bequests to individuals ard local charities.

Book
Lemoine, H. (ed) *The Eccentric Magazine* Vol 1.
  (G.Smeeton, 1813)

EDWARDS, Walter 1900-1964
Member of Parliament

Walter Edwards was born in Whitechapel, the son of a dock labourer. On leaving school he went to sea for five years. In 1937 he became a full-time worker for the Transport and General Workers' Union. He was a Stepney Councillor from 1934 and elected Mayor 1944-45.

Always known as 'Stoker Edwards' he was called up at the beginning of the second World War and in 1942 was given leave to fight a by-election in Whitechapel, which he won. He held the seat until 1950 when there were boundary changes and he became M.P. for Stepney. He was appointed Civil Lord of the Admiralty in C.R. ATTLEE's government, 1945.

He was the first man to enter Parliament from the 'lower deck' and the only Civil Lord with experience as a stoker in the Royal Navy and as a casual labourer in the docks.

ELBOZ, Annie 1899-1985
Labour Councillor

Born Annie Delew, she lived with her parents and eleven brothers and sisters in Wentworth Street, Spitalfields. She lived all her life in the same area and in her childhood began helping people.

She joined the Labour Party when she was seventeen and represented the Whitechapel Middle Ward on Stepney Borough Council from 1935 to 1964. She served as a Councillor for Spitalfields until her death. She was Mayor of Stepney in 1961 and made a Freeman of the Borough in 1963.

During the second World War she was an ARP warden. Annie Elboz served on numerous committees, was a governor of local schools and gave much of her time to voluntary work for all the people in the community in need. She was on the Board of the Mile End Hospital as a Governor and visited patients who had no visitors.

Obituary
East London Advertiser 7th June 1985
Article
Jewish Chronicle 26th October 1984

ENSOR, Sir Robert Charles Kirkwood 1877-1958
Journalist and Historian

Born at Milborne Port, Somerset, Robert Ensor was educated at Winchester and Oxford.

He joined the *Manchester Guardian* as a leader writer in 1901, later working on the the *Daily News* and *Daily Chronicle*.

After he came to live in Poplar, he became active in Labour politics. From 1907-1919 he was on the executive committee of the Fabian Society and from 1909 on the National Council of the Independent Labour Party. He was elected to the London County Council as member for Poplar 1910-13, although he had moved to High Wycombe during 1910. From 1931 he lectured at the London School of Economics and worked as a free-lance journalist.

He deputised for the Oxford Professor of Political Theory and Institutions in 1933 and again from 1940-1944.

He became a Senior Research Fellow at Corpus Christi College, Oxford and wrote Volume 14 of the Oxford History of England, *England 1870-1914* (1936).

From 1941 onwards he published a regular series of articles in the *Sunday Times*. He was knighted in 1955.

DNB

ENTICK, Rev. John 1703(?)-1773
Schoolmaster and Writer

John Entick was curate of St. Dunstan's Church, Stepney and a joint master of Bancroft School, Mile End Road, first with Thomas Downes (1736-1744) and then with Joseph Fisher from 1745.

Entick was the compiler of several dictionaries and wrote a *History of London- A New and Accurate History and Survey of London, Westminster, Southwark and Places Adjacent* (1766)

He also edited Maitland's *The History of London*, to which he added a continuation. This was published posthumously in 1775.

He was buried in St. Dunstan's Churchyard.

Books
Francombe, D.C.R. and Coult, D.E. (Eds) *Bancroft's School, 1737-1937* (Privately Printed, 1937)
Lysons, D. *The Environs of London* (W.Davies, 1792-6)

DNB

ERASMUS, Desiderius
circa 1469-1536
Dutch Humanist

Desiderius Erasmus was born in Gouda. Holland and became a Catholic reformer and classical scholar. In all, he visited England six times.

On the first of these visits he met and became friends of John COLET and Thomas More, the leading English humanists. Though probably more attached to More, Erasmus was increasingly influenced by Colet, whose lectures on St. Paul strengthened his own

Rev. John Entick

resolve to apply himself to biblical and patristic studies.

In 1505 he returned to England, renewing his contacts with Colet and More. Dean Colet's mother, Dame Christian COLET, took great pleasure from their meetings, when he displayed his vast general knowledge and witty entertaining style.

Articles
East London Observer 26th October 1912
Encyclopaedia Americana

FAIRBAIRN, Sir William
1789-1874
Engineer and Shipbuilder

Born in Kelso in Scotland, William Fairbairn was apprenticed in North Shields And there met George and Robert STEPHENSON. He was a pioneer in building iron ships at his yard in Millwall 1835-1849.

Robert Stephenson consulted him about the design of the Britannia Bridge over the Menai Straits and Fairbairn invented the system of the 'rectangular tube' which was used in the construction. Fairbairn superintended the bridge building. In 1846 he took out a patent for the wrought iron girder, in which STEPHENSON shared, and Fairbairn claimed that he had erected a thousand bridges on this principle.

He was President of the Institution of Mechanical Engineers in 1854, and of the British Association in 1861. Created baronet 1874.

Biography

Pole, W. (ed) *The Life of Sir W. Fairbairn* (David and Charles, 1970)

DNB

FELS, Joseph 1854-1914

Soap Manufacturer

Joseph Fels was born in Virginia, U.S.A. In 1874 he went into partnership with a Philadelphia soap manufacturer. He built up the huge Fels-Naptha plant which sold its products all over the world.

Coming to England in 1901 he became friendly with Keir Hardie and George LANSBURY. He bought 1,300 acres of land at Hollesley Bay, Suffolk, for the settlement of the unemployed from Poplar as agricultural workers. He gave generously to many social causes.

Biography

Fels, M. *Joseph Fels* (George Allen and Unwin, 1920)

FISHER, Dorothea Kate E.M.W., OBE 1894-1974

Barge Owner

Dorothea Evans was born in Edmonton to a middle class family, and educated at Cheltenham Ladies College. In 1916 she married a lighterman, Billie Woodward Fisher who was born in Mellish Street, Poplar.

Together they set up a successful lighterage business in Limehouse and bought their first barge for £20. The company later owned 80 barges and 12 tugs and wharves on the Thames. When her husband died in 1964 she continued to run the firm. Their barge building company at 94 Narrow Street, E14 ran for 20 years from 1958.

In 1911 Billie Woodward Fisher, a member of the Poplar, Blackwall and District Rowing Club since 1908, won Doggett's Coat and Badge. These were annual prizes originally given by Thomas Doggett from 1715 to celebrate the August 1st anniversary accession of George I in 1714. Newly qualified tideway watermen and lightermen raced between London and Chelsea Bridges.

Dorothea Woodward Fisher was President of the Poplar, Blackwall and District Rowing Club for the last 10 years of her life, following on from her husband's long Presidency. She raised £65,000 to build a new boathouse in Ferry Street, E14, which was opened in 1970.

She belonged to many organisations and involved herself in social work and in raising money for charitable funds throughout her life.

An OBE was given to her in 1961 for public and political work in Lewisham where she lived.

A memorial plaque to her was unveiled on the boathouse in Ferry Street, E14 in 1975. She was a familiar figure on all river occasions.

Articles

East London Advertiser 19th November 1948, 16th June 1961, 15th May 1964

Read, H. *50 Years at Poplar and Blackwall; a Brief History* (Unpublished, 1995)

FITZGERALD, Canon Thomas 1895-1968

Priest

Born in South London, Thomas Fitzgerald trained for the priesthood and was ordained when he was 23. From 1941-1964 he was Parish Priest at St. Mary and St. Michael's Church, Commercial Road, E1. Working through the war years, he was injured when a V2 rocket damaged the church in 1944.

After the war he was responsible for restoring the church and building a new presbytery and a new primary school adjacent to the site. He retired in 1964.

He is commemorated by Fitzgerald Lodge, a home for old people in Sutton Street, E1.

FLANAGAN, Bud OBE 1896-1968

Comedian

Bud Flanagan was registered at birth as Reuben Weintrop and was also known as Chaim Reeven Weintrop and Robert Winthrop. He was born at 12 Hanbury Street, Spitalfields where his parents, who were refugees from Poland, kept a fried fish shop and a barber's.

He joined the Brady Street Club for Working Boys which was established in

Durward Street, Whitechapel in 1896, and began entertaining children in a local backyard.

'Bud Flanagan' was the name he adopted from a sergeant who made his life a misery in the first World War. He became famous as the singing partner of Chesney Allen and a member of the 'Crazy Gang' at the London Palladium.

His best known songs were, *Underneath the Arches*, *'The Umbrella man*, and *We're Gonna Hang Out the Washing on the Siegfried Line* and the theme song from 'Dad's Army'. He was awarded OBE in 1959.

He is commemorated with an English Heritage Plaque at 12 Hanbury Street, E1.

Article
Jewish Chronicle Colour Magazine 30th September 1983
Autobiography
My Crazy Life (Frederick Muller, 1961)

FOXE, Rev. Richard 1448(?)-1528
Bishop

Richard Foxe was born at Ropesley, near Grantham, Lincs, and educated at Grantham School and Oxford.

He was instituted Vicar of St. Dunstan's, Stepney, 1485 and later became founder of Corpus Christi College, Oxford, Chancellor of Cambridge University and successively Bishop of Exeter, Bath and Wells, Durham and Winchester.

Book
Fowler, T. *The History of Corpus Christi College* (Oxford Historical Society, 1893)

DNB

FRANKEL, Daniel 1900-1988
Member of Parliament

Dan Frankel was born in Mile End, the son of a tailor, becoming a tailor himself when he left school.

In 1925 he was elected to the Stepney Board of Guardians and also as a Labour member for Stepney Borough Council. In 1929, he was chosen as the borough's youngest ever Mayor.

Elected to the London County Council in 1931, he became Chairman of the hospital and management services committee, where he helped to transform antiquated medical conditions and established a 48-hour week for nurses.

He became Labour Member of Parliament for Mile End from 1935 to 1945, when he was defeated by the Communist candidate, Phil Piratin.

He campaigned vigorously in and out of Parliament in defence of his Jewish constituents facing violence from Sir Oswald Mosley's Fascist movement.

His home and business were destroyed by air raids in 1944, and he worked hard for the restoration of the area and re-housing for local people.

FRANKLIN, Sydney 1887-1970
Merchant Banker

Sydney Franklin was one of the first voluntary helpers at the Oxford and St. George's Club, Cannon Street Road, St. George-in-the-East founded by Sir Basil HENRIQUES in 1914.

A partner in the merchant banking firm of Samuel MONTAGU, Franklin lived at the settlement for about thirty years and devoted the whole of his leisure to voluntary work in the club, amateur boxing, the committees of the London Federation of Boy's Clubs and the British Legion.

Portrait of Barnett Freedman by Rothenstein

FREEDMAN, Barnett CBE
1901-1958
Artist

Barnett Freedman was born in Stepney. As a child he had a great deal of illness and taught himself to draw to relieve the boredom. He later attended St. Martin's School of Art part-time, and from there won a scholarship to the Royal College of Art.

Freedman produced a number of posters for London Transport. He worked for the BBC and the Post Office, designed the stamp to celebrate the Silver Jubilee in 1935. His paintings are hung in the Tate Gallery and Victoria and Albert Museum.

During the war Freedman was invited to be an official War Artist and was among those rescued from Dunkirk.

Appointed CBE in 1946, he received the highest award from the Royal Society of Arts in 1949, an inscribed certificate, 'Royal Designer for Industry'.

A portrait of Freedman by Sir William Rothenstein is in the Tate Gallery.

DNB

FROBISHER, Sir Martin
circa 1535-1594
Navigator

Martin Frobisher lived in Ratcliff and was sent to sea as a boy. For many years he thought there must be a north-west passage to Cathay, the ancient name for China and East Tartary, and he determined to find it.

On 7th June 1576 he sailed from Ratcliff Cross with the *Gabriel* and the *Michael* – 20 tons each, together with a pinnace, a small two-masted ship, having a total complement of 35 men. The pinnace foundered and the crew of the *Michael* deserted and Frobisher, who was on the *Gabriel* almost became lost off the coast of Greenland, and reached Labrador on the 28th July.

He brought home rock that was at first thought to be gold, but was later declared to be 'fool's gold'. He declared that he had attempted to found a colony in Canada.

In 1585 he commanded a vessel in Drake's expedition to the West Indies. He was knighted for his services against the Spanish Armada. He married a daughter of Lord WENTWORTH.

At the siege of Crozen, near Brest, he received a wound from which he died at Plymouth in November 1594. He was buried in St. Giles' Church, Cripplegate, EC.

He is commemorated locally by a Greater London Council Blue Plaque in King Edward VII Memorial Park, Shadwell, E1, and Frobisher House, Watts Street, E1.

Biography
Dawlish, P. *Martin Frobisher* (Oxford University Press, 1956)

DNB

FROST, Samuel 1879-1926
Footballer

Sammy Frost was born in Poplar and was one of the first East Londoners to gain success as a professional footballer. His career with Millwall earned him a transfer to Manchester City. He won an FA Cup winners medal when City beat Bolton Wanderers at Crystal Palace in 1904.

He returned to Millwall in 1907 and retired from football because of an injury shortly before the first World War.

He committed suicide at his home in Grundy Street in 1926.

FRYE, Thomas 1710-1762
Founder of Bow Porcelain

Thomas Frye was born in Dublin, and came to London in about 1734 having achieved some distinction as a painter. He painted a portrait of the Prince of Wales for the Saddlers' Company when he was 28. He also specialised in mezzotint, miniature painting, engraving and enamels.

He was the inventor and first manufacturer in England of porcelain. In 1744 a patent was taken out by Thomas Frye and Edward Heylyn for the production of 'artificial' soft paste porcelain mixed with a high proportion of bone-ash to give great strength and durability. He called his products 'New Canton'. He intended to compete with the imports from China as well as European brands such as Meissen.

The Court Book of 1744 shows that Edward Heylyn acquired a property on the London side of the River Lea at Bow and that an insurance policy was taken out on 7th July 1749 for a purpose-built 'Bow factory of New Canton' on the Essex side of Bow Bridge on the north of Stratford Causeway.

The business was in an expanding trading position by 1750 when Frye and Heylyn's partnership included John Wetherby and John Crowther both of whom had a wholesale pottery business at St. Katherine by the Tower.

The strenuous efforts Thomas Frye made at the Bow China manufactory contributed to his ill health and he retired in 1759. The last year of manufacture was probably 1775.

Examples of Bow Porcelain are in the Fitzwilliam Museum, Cambridge, the Victoria and Albert Museum, the British Museum and the Bethnal Green Museum.

He is commemorated locally by Frye Court, Benworth Street, E3.

Book

Adams, E. and Redstone, D. *Bow Porcelain* (Faber and Faber, 1981)

GANDHI, Mohandas Karamchand 1869-1948

Indian Political Leader

Born in Porbandar, India, at the age of 19, Gandhi came to London to study law. He was entered at Inner Temple and called to the Bar in 1891.

He returned to India but in 1893 accepted an appointment as legal adviser to a business firm in Natal, South Africa.

In 1901 he returned to Bombay, but almost immediately went back to Johannesburg and became the recognised leader of Indians in South Africa. He led a massive resistance campaign against the government requirement for all Asians to carry registration cards. He spent 249 days in prison. He remained in South Africa until 1914.

After the first World War the demand for Indian independence from Britain increased. Gandhi played a leading role in the formation of the India National Congress. He advocated civil disobedience and non-violent resistance to British rule such as fasting. During the struggle for independence, Gandhi was imprisoned several times.

He adopted a simple way of life and a very personal style of dress – white loin cloth, white shawl and sandals, becoming a very popular character for the political cartoonists.

Widely known as Mahatma (Great Soul) he came to London in 1931 for the Round Table Conference on Indian constitutional reform. Because of his friendship with Doris and Murial LESTER he rejected arranged government accommodation and stayed at Kingsley Hall, Powis Road, E3.

Widely respected internationally as a great moral teacher, he did much to improve the plight of India's 'untouchables'.

He was assassinated in Delhi on 30th January 1948 by a Hindu fanatic.

He is commemorated with a plaque at Kingsley Hall.

Biography

Payne, R.B. *Gandhi* (Bodley Head, 1969)

DNB

GARFORD, James 1772-1850

Magistrate

James Garford was a local philanthropist and magistrate who did much to highlight the problems of poverty and overcrowding in Poplar resulting from the influx of labour from the newly established East and West India Docks. Garford House, Milligan Street, E14, and Garford Street, E14, are named after him.

GARRICK, David 1717-1779

Actor, Manager and Dramatist

David Garrick was born at the Angel Inn, Hereford. He attended Lichfield Grammar School and in 1736, with his brother George, he became a pupil of Samuel Johnson in his school at Edial, near Lichfield.

Johnson and Garrick travelled to London in 1737 and David was entered as a pupil at Lincoln's Inn. His uncle having left him a legacy of £1000, he began a wine business with his brother Peter near the Adelphi. The partnership was dissolved in 1740.

David's love of the stage led him to take part in amateur performances at St. John's Gate, Clerkenwell. He also began writing verse and theatrical criticism, of which some was published in the *Gentleman's Magazine*.

In 1741 he made his first professional appearance at the Goodman's Fields theatre, which stood south of what is now Alie Street, E1. His success was immediate and after favourable reviews in the newspapers, all fashionable London was journeying to see the brilliant new actor.

When Garrick left Goodman's Fields, the theatre was closed following objections from the rival Drury Lane and Covent Garden managements.

Moving to Drury Lane, he was there for many years as actor and manager, becoming joint patentee in 1747. He was a most versatile actor, equally at home in tragedy, comedy or farce.

Garrick was buried in Westminster Abbey and there is a monument to him there by Webber.

Biography
Oman, C. *David Garrick* (Hodder and Stoughton, 1958)
Book
Wilson, A.E. *East End Entertainment* (Arthur Barker, 1954)

DNB

GARTHWAITE, Anna Maria
1690-1763
Silk Designer

Anna Maria Garthwaite was one of the foremost designers in the English silk industry in the eighteenth century.

She was the daughter of a wealthy Lincolnshire Rector, and lived with her married sister in Yorkshire, where she produced her first designs.

When the married sister lost her second husband, the two women came to Spitalfields, setting up home with their ward, the daughter of a Lincolnshire friend.

Anna Garthwaite worked on a freelance basis supplying designs to the leading figures in the silk industry. Each year she produced two volumes of designs, neatly bound, with an index containing the names of the weavers and mercers, and the dates they had bought her patterns. The type of silk for which the patterns were intended were also noted. Miraculously the greater part of her work has survived, and some eight hundred of her designs are in the Victoria and Albert Museum.

Anna Garthwaite was credited by Postlethwayt in his *Universal Dictionary of Trade and Commerce* (1751) as being one of three designers who 'attempted to introduce the principles of painting into the loom'. As a result, according to Postlethwayt and the Customs statistics of the time, the sale of English silks at home was greatly increased and a considerable number were exported to Ireland, Northern Europe, Scandinavia and particularly to America.

Books
Postlethwayt, M. *The Universal Dictionary of Trade and Commerce* (London, 1751) [article on engraving]
Rothstein, N. *Spitalfields Silks* (Victoria and Albert Museum, 1975)

GASCOYNE, Joel died 1705
Cartographer

Born into a seafaring family in Hull, Joel Gascoyne moved to London in 1668 and lived in Ratcliff.

He was apprenticed to John Thornton and became skilled in surveying, engraving and chart making. Gascoyne earned his living mainly as a land surveyor.

For six years he worked in the West country and on his return to London was asked by the Vicar and Churchwardens of St. Dunstan's, Stepney, to survey and describe the parish.

The parish was one of ten parishes in the County of Middlesex adjoining the City of London. Gascoyne produced eight sheets describing the bounds of the eight hamlets contained in the parish for which Gascoyne and the engraver John Harris were paid jointly.

Their work provides an early example of an urban survey, and the first detailed and reliable maps of the borough.

Articles
'Joel Gascoyne, a pioneer of large scale county mapping' in *Imago Mundi* Vol. 26 (Amsterdam, 1972)
'Joel Gascoyne's Stepney; his last years in pastures old yet new' in *Guildhall Studies in London History* Vol. 2 (April 1977)

GAVIN, Dr. Hector 1816-1855
Surgeon and Pioneer in Public Health

Hector Gavin qualified as a doctor at Edinburgh University in 1836, obtaining FRCS in 1838. He won a prize for an essay *On the Feigned and Factitious Diseases of Soldiers and Seamen* (1833).

He came to London and had his practice at 5 Thurlow Place, Hackney Road, now 367 Hackney Road, Bethnal Green.

From 1844-1851 he was joint lecturer in Forensic Medicine and Public Health at Charing Cross Hospital Medical School, and he was also surgeon to the London Orphan Asylum, founded by Dr. Andrew REED. Whilst holding these posts he also visited the West Indies as a Medical Inspector.

In 1848 Hector Gavin wrote *Sanitary Ramblings*, an account of his findings on public health matters in Bethnal Green. He stated his belief that the outbreaks of cholera and typhoid were due to the lack of proper water supply and sanitation. He described the squalor in which many people had to live, but praised their basic dignity and their struggle to keep clean rooms and back yards. He also gave evidence to the Analytical Sanitary Commission on his findings in Bethnal Green. He became Honorary

Secretary of the Tower Hamlets Sanitary Association in 1849.

Hector Gavin was editor of the journal *Public Health* and became a Medical Inspector for the General Board of Health.

He was sent to the Crimea as a member of a Royal Sanitary Commission to deal with the arrangements for Army and hospital hygiene and acted as adviser to Florence Nightingale.

He died at Balaclava in the Crimean War in tragic circumstances; while handing his pistol to his brother William Gavin, a veterinary surgeon, the weapon accidentally went off and he was killed.

Book
Sanitary Ramblings (Churchill, 1848)

GERBIER, Sir Balthazar
1591(?)-1667
Courtier and Adventurer

Born in Holland of French parents, Gerbier came to England in 1615 to serve under Sir George Villiers. For twelve years he was the representative of England at the court of Brussels.

In 1649 he opened an academy in Bethnal Green professing to teach, in addition to the more common branches of education; astronomy, architecture, perspective drawing, navigation, engraving, fortification, fireworks, military discipline, the art of speaking and civil conversation.

Once a week he would give a public lecture on one of the subjects advertised. A typical advertisement for December was 'The lecture next week is designed for ladies and honourable women of the nation on the art of speaking. Sir Balthazar Gerbier desires that any lady or virtuous matron attending his lecture will give notice, that they may be better accommodated according to their quality'.

The academy soon failed, and Gerbier went to America returning to England for the Restoration, 1660. Subsequently he became Master of Ceremonies to Charles II.

Biography
Williamson, H.R. *Four Stuart Portraits* (Evans Bros, 1949)

Article
Poer, M.J. 'Sir Bathazar Gerbier's Academy at Bethnal Green' in *East London Papers* Vol. 10 no.1 (Summer 1967)

DNB

GERSON, Phyllis Josephine
MBE, JP. 1903-1990
Social Work Administrator and Magistrate

Phyllis Gerson was born of German parents in North West London, going to school locally and then at Art College. Her first job was in a design office but she found it uninteresting, and was attracted by an advertisement for a helper in a girls group meeting in a Stepney school. In 1927 she began work with a group of ten girls, and commenced a sociology course at the London School of Economics.

She took over as Warden of the Stepney Jewish (B'nai B'rith) Club and Settlement in the old Beaumont Hall, Beaumont Square and introduced classes for cooking, art, and sport. During her 45 years at the Clubs and Settlement (1928-1973) the small organisation grew into a large welfare institution of clubs and social services. The rented room in the old Beaumont Hall where she began her work was succeeded in 1938 by the new Beaumont Hall, Beaumont Grove, E1, where Queen Mary performed the official opening. The Jewish Clubs and Settlement gained a place as a recognised training centre for youth workers and social science students from this country and abroad.

When the war came, Phyllis Gerson helped escort 300 children to South Africa. Returning to London she became an air raid warden, and delivered food and gave other help to those sheltering in Stepney Green Underground Station. At the end of the war she left the club to lead the first Jewish relief unit and followed the army through Egypt and Italy and then on to Albania. For this work she was awarded the MBE in 1949.

On her return to the Jewish Clubs and Settlement, the Beaumont Hall Nursery was merged with the Alice MODEL Nursery, and the new Alice Model Nursery and hostel for girls was opened by the Queen Mother in 1955.

Phyllis Gerson was appointed a Justice of the Peace for the Thames Division, where she later followed Basil HENRIQUES as Chairman of the Juvenile Bench.

The various voluntary activities that she undertook during her retirement included work as Vice-president of the Association for Jewish Youth, Governor of Stepney Green Comprehensive School, Honarary Secretary of the Alice Model Nursery, and working with the Jewish Welfare Board.

She is commemorated by Phyllis Gerson House, 2, Beaumont Grove, E1.

Ætatis suæ 42
A.º 1634

D. Balthazar Gerberius Eques Auratus primus post renouationem
Fœderis cum Hispaniarum Rege anno 1630. a Potentissimo
et Serenissimo Carolo Magnæ Britanniæ Franciæ et
Hyberniæ Rege, Bruxellas Prolegatus A.º 1631.

Anton van Dyck pinxit. Paul. Pontius sculpsit.

Sir Balthazar Gerbier

GERTLER, Mark 1891-1939
Painter

Born in Spitalfields, the son of Austrian Jewish parents, Mark Gertler spent his childhood in great poverty. He attended Deal Street School and began work with a manufacturer of stained glass. On the advice of Sir William Rothenstein, the Jewish Education Aid Society sent him to the Slade School of Art in 1908. He won a Slade scholarship in 1909 and continued his studies until 1912.

When he was 19 he painted the portrait of his mother, which together with four other paintings, are now in the Tate Gallery. In 1923 he painted a portrait of Sir George Darwin, now in the National Portrait Gallery, and another picture *The Merry-go-round* is in the Ben Uri Art Gallery in Soho. Gertler became a member of a group of artists and writers known as the 'Bloomsbury Set'.

All his life he suffered from consumption and spent much of his time in a sanatorium. He committed suicide in 1939.

He is commemorated by a Greater London Council Blue Plaque at 12 Elder Street, E1.

Biography
Woodeson, J. *Mark Gertler* (Sidgwick & Jackson, 1972)

DNB

GIBSON, Nicholas died 1540
Merchant

Nicholas Gibson was born in Ratcliff. He founded the Ratcliff Charity, and built a free school and almshouses for the poor and aged persons, both of which are mentioned in John Stow's *The Chronicles of England* (1580). Gibson became Prime Warden of the Grocers' Company and Sheriff of the City of London in 1538. He was buried in St. Dunstan's Churchyard.

The Coopers' Company took over the original school in 1549 and in 1891 a charities commission brought about the amalgamation of Coborn School (founded by the will of Prisca COBORN) and Coopers' School. Coborn School moved to 86 Bow Road, Bow and Coopers' School moved to Tredegar Square, Bow. In 1973 both schools moved to Upminster and became co-educational.

Biography
Foster, W. *Nicholas Gibson and his Free School at Ratcliff* (Cambridge Univ. P.,1936)
Foster, W. *The Ratcliffe Charity, 1536-1936* (Allenson, 1936)

GILBERT, Sir Humphrey 1539(?)-1583
Navigator

Humphrey Gilbert lived in Limehouse. In 1578 he received a royal patent 'to discover and occupy heathen lands', but his first expedition was frustrated by dissension, tempest and a brush with the Spaniards. The failure of this enterprise cost both Gilbert and his wife their entire estate.

He eventually sailed from Plymouth in June 1583 and landing in Newfoundland, he took possession of it for Queen Elizabeth I. Off Cape Breton he lost the largest of his three vessels, but steered for home with *Squirrel* and *The Golden Hind*.

The *Squirrel* went down with all hands on board on 9th September 1583. Gilbert is commemorated by a Greater London Council Blue Plaque in King Edward VII Memorial Park, Shadwell, E1.

Biography
Gosling, W.H. *The Life of Sir Humphrey Gilbert* (Constable, 1911)
Book
Quinn, D.B. *The Voyages and Colonising Enterprises of Sir Humphrey Gilbert* (Hakluyt Society, 1940)

DNB

GILBERT, Tony 1914-1992
Worker for Human Rights

Tony Gilbert was one of the key organisers in the struggle against racism in Britain for many years.

He was one of seven children born to Samuel and Esther Gilbert, Jewish immigrants who settled in Stepney before the first World War. The family later moved to Bethnal Green where Tony first encountered racist hostility. He took up boxing to be able to defend himself.

Greatly influenced by his mother, he became politically active at 14 and joined the Communist Party.

In 1936 he volunteered to fight in Spain with the International Brigade, he was taken prisoner and with his comrades, was only saved from the firing squad by the arrival of an American journalist.

After repatriation and convalescence he returned to work as a furrier and then as a building worker. He was called up in 1940 and served with the army in Burma, where he was wounded, and in India, where he worked with the movement for independence.

78

When he was demobilised he immersed himself in trade union activity. He worked in engineering, as a miner and on the railways. He was sacked from the railways after being involved in a strike and then returned to his old trade as a furrier, but spent a lot of time working for the Movement for Colonial Freedom founded by Fenner Brockway.

Later he was appointed General Secretary of Liberation, the new name for MCF and he organised conferences, demonstrations, and lobbies in many countries. Wherever there was discrimination, exploitation or abuse of human rights he sought to organise protest.

He wrote many pamphlets and articles and his book *Only One Died* (1975), gives an account of the National Front anti-demonstration outside Conway Hall, Red Lion Square, WC1, on 15th June 1974 at which a student, Kevin Gately was killed in a clash with the police. Tony Gilbert gave evidence to the Public Inquiry chaired by Lord Justice Scarman.

His friends knew Tony Gilbert to be a gentle and compassionate man.

GODLEY, Sidney Frank VC
1869-1957
Soldier

Sidney Godley was born at East Grinstead, Sussex and educated at Sidcup School. In 1909 he joined the 4th Battalion, Royal Fusiliers and 5 years later formed part of the British Expeditionary Force in Belgium in the early days of the first World War.

He was awarded the Victoria Cross for coolness and gallantry at Nimy, Mons on 23rd August 1914 for covering a withdrawal and holding up the enemy singled-handed despite being wounded, and allowing the Royal Fusiliers to retire. Two Belgian civilians helped him to hospital and it was there that the Germans captured him when they entered the town. He was a prisoner of war until the Armistice. The award was gazetted 25th November 1914.

On returning home after the war Sidney Godley received the VC from King George V. He took up his job as caretaker at Cranbrook School, Cranbrook Street, Bethnal Green and continued in this post until his retirement.

Sidney Godley was the first private soldier to be awarded the Victoria Cross in the first World War.

In 1938 he was presented with a special gold medal struck at Mons and together with other survivors of the battle, Sidney Godley was present in the spring of 1939 when a plaque was unveiled on the bridge at Mons commemorating his action.

A block of flats in Digby Street, E2 is named after him and in 1992 a plaque recording the official citation that accompanied the VC medal was unveiled by Councillor Blandford, Mayor of Tower Hamlets and Lieutenant Colonel Pettifer, Royal Regiment of Fusiliers.
Books
The Register of the Victoria Cross (This England Books, 1981)
O'M. Creagh and Humphries, E.M. (eds,) *The VC and DSO* (Standard Art Book, 1924)

GOMPERS, Samuel 1850-1924
American Trade Union Leader

Born in Tenter Street, Spitalfields, of Dutch parents, Samuel Gompers attended the Jews' Free School, Bell Lane, Spitalfields. On leaving school he was apprenticed to a cigar maker at the wage of one shilling a week. With Union help he emigrated to America with his family in 1863. Working again as a cigar maker, he became President of the Cigar Makers' Union 1876-1881 and President of the American Federation of Labour 1886-1924.
Autobiography
Seventy Years of Life and Labour (New York, A.M. Kelley, 1967)

GOSLING, Harry 1861-1930
Labour Leader

Born in Lambeth, Harry Gosling left school at 13 and began a seven year apprenticeship with the Watermens' Company. He was first elected to the London County Council in 1898 and then again in 1904, being one of the first Labour members alongside Will CROOKS.

He was Member of Parliament for Whitechapel and St. George's from 1923-1931, serving as Minister of Transport and Paymaster General in the governments of Ramsay MacDonald.

He was President of the Transport Workers' Federation, a forerunner of the Transport and General Workers' Union of which he also became President. Harry Gosling became Chairman of the Trades

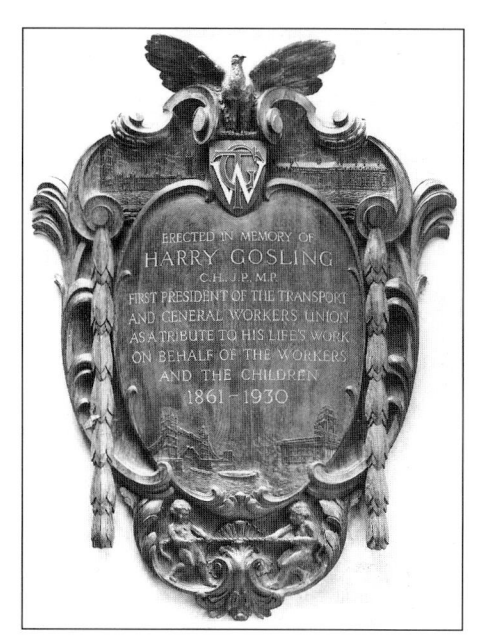

Memorial to Harry Gosling in Transport House, Westminster

Union Congress in 1916. He was also a member of the Port of London Authority.

He is commemorated by a Primary School in Henriques Street, Gosling House in Sutton Street, E1, and Gosling Gardens, Bigland Street, E1.
Autobiography
Up and Down Stream (Methuen, 1927)

DNB

GRANT, Clara Ellen 1867-1949
Teacher and Founder of Fern Street Settlement

Clara Grant was born in Wiltshire and was brought up in Frome, Somerset. She was educated at Salisbury Diocesan Training College and, coming to London, began work as a teacher in Wapping. She founded The Fern Street Settlement in 1907.

She initiated the popular 'farthing bundle' ceremony on Saturday mornings, when children small enough to pass through an arch would receive a parcel of toys, picture books etc., for a farthing.

The inscription on the wooden arch read;-

Enter all ye children small,
None may come who are too tall

She is buried in Tower Hamlets Cemetery.

She is commemorated by Clara Grant Primary School, Knapp Road, E3, and Clara Grant House, Mellish Street, E14.
Autobiographies
Farthing Bundles (Privately published, 1930)
From 'Me' to 'We' (Privately published, 1940)

GRANT, Julius 1901-1991
Forensic Scientist

Julius Grant was born into a poor East London family. He gained a part-time degree in chemistry at Queen Mary College, Mile End Road, E1. During the day he undertook research for the Marmite Food Extract Company. Following research at King's College, London, in 1931 he joined the John Dickinson Paper Company where his work on paper technology provided a foundation for his success in forensic science. After the excavation of Tutankhamun's tomb by Lord Carnarvon and Howard Carter in 1922, Julius Grant was asked to analyse a piece of cloth from the site.

During the war he invented edible paper for use by secret agents; developed special paper for prisoners of war which retained invisible writing and produced forgery-proof ration books. Post-war, he was involved in extending the use of re-cycled waste paper. He also experimented with new kinds of wrapping paper for butter, explosives and Mars bars.

Julius Grant appeared as an expert witness in the murder case of the Great Train Robbers. Tom Keating's forged Samuel Palmer paintings, The Mussolini Diaries and the Hitler Diaries were all exposed by him as being fraudulent. In the last episode of the television series *Selling Hitler* shown four days after his death, an actor playing the part of Julius Grant was seen denouncing the so-called Hitler Diaries as a forgery. As Julius Grant was an expert on paper technology he was able to prove that the paper on which the diaries were written was only manufactured after the war.

He wrote many scientific books, of which the most important is *Books and Documents; dating, permanence and preservation* (1937). He received many honours during his distinguished career and was President both of the Medico-Legal Society and the Forensic Science Society.

GREEN, George 1767-1849
Shipbuilder and Philanthropist

George Green was the son of a Chelsea brewer. At the age of 15 he became an apprentice at John PERRY's shipyard in Blackwall. As a youth, he walked daily to Blackwall from his home in Battersea, in time to start a twelve hour working day at 6.00 a.m. In 1796 he married Sarah Perry, the daughter of his employer, and in 1797 became a partner in the firm, which became known as Perry and Sons and Green.

In later partnerships with Robert Wigram and John Wells, he became one of the most successful shipbuilders of his day. The frigates built at Blackwall Yard between 1813 and the late 1830s were among the finest in their class.

A devout free churchman, George Green spent substantial money and energy to charitable educational projects. In 1815 he built and endowed Poplar and Blackwall Free School, on land given by the East India Company, to provide education for 300 girls and boys. A school still stands on the site in Woolmore Street, E14.

George Green also founded Chrisp Street School in 1828, Bow Lane, now Bazely Street School, and Trinity School, in 1843, now the site of Mayflower Primary School, Upper North Street, E14. Trinity School was moved to a new site on the corner of Kerby Street and East India Dock Road, Poplar, and re-named George Green's School in 1884, where it remained until moving to Manchester Road, Isle of Dogs, E14 in 1976. It was the first community school in London offering day and evening education to all.

A sailor's home, built in 1841, still stands at 133 East India Dock Road, E14. A row of almshouses built by George Green in 1849 remains in Upper North Street.

In 1841 he built a chapel in East India Dock Road, Poplar, first known as Green's Chapel and then Trinity Congregational Church, destroyed by enemy action in 1944. The Chapel was re-built and opened in 1951 as part of the post-war reconstruction of Poplar. The building passed from the Congregational Church to the Methodist Church in 1977.

George Green's tomb is in the churchyard of Trinity Church, East India Dock Road.

Biography
Moir, E.A. *George Green of Blackwall* (George Green's School,1934)

Books
Green, H. and Wigram, R. *Chronicles of Blackwall Yard* Pt. 1. (Whitehead, Morris and Lowe, 1881)
Wilks, H.C. *George Green's School 1828-1978* (Edward Arnold, 1979)
Taylor, Rosemary *Blackwall, The Brunswick and Whitebait Dinners* (The Author, 1992)

Rev. John Richard Green

GREEN, Rev. John Richard 1837-1883
Historian

Born at Oxford and educated at Magdalen School and Jesus College, Oxford, John Green became Vicar of St. Philip's Church, Newark Street, Stepney in November 1865.

He developed tuberculosis and was forced to retire as a parish priest and became Librarian at Lambeth Palace in 1868.

Green wrote *A Short History of the English People* (1874), the first social history of England. It was an instant success and was followed by a larger edition in 1877.

He also lived at 65 Approach Road, Bethnal Green.

A London County Council Blue Plaque was erected at the Newark Street Vicarage in 1910.

Biography
Snaith, S. (ed) *John Richard Green* (Unpublished Typescript, 1952)

DNB

GREEN, Richard 1803-1863
Shipbuilder

Born at Blackwall, the son of George GREEN, Richard Green became a partner in his father's firm at the Blackwall Yard, 1829. Many of the famous Blackwall frigates were built by him. A philanthropist, he supported the Training Ship *Worcester*, the *Dreadnought* Hospital Ship and Bow Lane school.

He is commemorated by a bronze statue by E.W. Wyon outside the old Poplar Baths, East India Dock Road, E14.

DNB

GREENHILL, Rev. William
1591-1671
Dissenting Minister

A native of Oxfordshire, William Greenhill graduated at Magdalen College, Oxford. He became a Chaplain to the Parliamentary Army and Minister of Stepney Meeting House in 1644.

After the execution of Charles I in 1649 and Oliver Cromwell rose to power, William Greenhill was appointed by the latter to be the tutor and guardian of the royal children, as well as Vicar of St. Dunstan's, Stepney.

During his time at Stepney Parish, William Greenhill appointed ministers to the newly built Chapels at Poplar and Shadwell; Matthew MEAD, appointed to Shadwell, later succeeded William Greenhill at Stepney Meeting House.

At the Restoration, 1660, he was made to leave St. Dunstan's and returned to the Meeting House until 1671.

Book
Hill, G.W. and Frere, W.H. *Memorials of Stepney Parish* (Privately published, 1890-91)
Article
Tower Hamlets Independent 9th May 1868

GRENFELL, Sybil Vera
MVO, CBE 1902-1990
Social Worker

Vera Grenfell was the daughter of Colonel Arthur Morton Grenfell, and granddaughter of Albert, 4th Earl Grey.

With financial assistance from Lady RAVENSDALE, she acquired 'Paddy's Goose', a Wesleyan Mission Hall for use as the headquarters of The Highway Clubs in East London where children of unemployed families could have tea, sandwiches and warm rooms. Both girls and boys were trained for a variety of simple jobs. Vera Grenfell helped to organise the Club summer camps and foreign holidays. During the second World War, she worked a 16 hour day. She provided breakfasts for the night's bomb casualties at Paddy's Goose Club and assisted many girl club members to escape to safety.

A contrasting break for these activities came from 1943-45, when she went to Canada as Lady-in-Waiting to Princess Alice, Countess of Athlone while the Earl of Athlone was Governor-General there. Her maternal grandfather, Albert, 4th Earl Grey, had been Canada's Governor-General from 1904-1911.

During her time there, she organised the sending of gifts of clothing to the Highway Clubs' members who were homeless. From 1945 Vera Grenfell began work for the National Association of Youth Clubs. She was Chairman, from 1949-60, of the Mixed Clubs and Girls Clubs. In 1958 she also became the last Chairman of the Highway Clubs in East London, taking over from Lady Irene RAVENSDALE. The clubs merged with the East London Family Service Unit in 1968.

She was awarded an MVO in 1945 and CBE in 1961.

Book
Burkes Peerage and Baronetage (1968)
Pamphlets
The Highway Clubs Annual Reports
Article
The Times 18th January 1990

GRENFELL, Sir Wilfred Thomason 1865-1940
Missionary Doctor

Wilfred Grenfell was born at Parkgate, near Chester, where his father was a headmaster. He was educated at Marlborough School and Oxford, where he gained a rugby blue.

He came to London in 1883 to begin medical studies at the London Hospital under Sir Frederick TREVES. Returning to the hospital after attending a maternity case in Shadwell, he came upon a large tent where D.L. Moody the American evangelist was conducting a campaign. Impressed by methods he used to enliven a bored audience, Wilfred Grenfell resolved to become a Christian and in his spare time helped in a boys' club in Ratcliff, worked with destitute people, as well as undertaking religious work in Bethnal Green. At this time he also obtained a Master Mariner's certificate.

Having qualified as a doctor, on the recommendation of Sir Frederick Treves he joined the National Mission to Deep Sea Fishermen in 1888, going to the North Sea as a missionary doctor. He became it's Superintendent at the headquarters in Gorleston, Norfolk, in the following year.

After visiting Labrador in 1892, he began his lifelong work there, founding hospitals, orphanages and other social services for fisherman. He also equipped hospital ships to serve the fishing fleets. Wilfred Grenfell was knighted in 1927. He is commemorated in the borough by Grenfell School, Myrdle Street, E1.
Biography
Kerr, J.L. *Wilfred Grenfell* (G.Harrap, 1959)

The signature of Sir Thomas Gresham

GRESHAM, Sir Thomas
1519(?)-1579
Merchant and Ambassador

Born in Bethnal Green, Gresham was the son of Sir Richard Gresham, Lord Mayor of London.

He became a leading member of the Mercers' Company and was employed as 'king's merchant' in Antwerp. In two years he paid off a heavy loan and restored the king's credit.

Gresham was knighted by Queen Elizabeth I in 1559 and appointed ambassador in Brussels.

Gresham devoted a great part of his wealth to the building of the Royal Exchange, similar to the one in Antwerp, and to the founding of Gresham College in the City of London.

He is said to have introduced the orange to England.
Biography
Laurent, H. *La Loi de Gresham au moyen age* (Bruxelles, L'Universite, 1933)
DNB

Father Groser in 1962

GROSER, St. John Beverley
1891-1966
Priest

Born in Australia, St. John Groser came to East London in 1922 as a Curate at St. Michael's Church, Poplar. In 1928 he was invited to be Priest at Christ Church, Watney Street, E1, at a time when the building was to be pulled down, but built up such a thriving congregation that the building was reprieved. He later became Rector of the St. George-in-the-East Church, E1.

When the Royal Foundation of St. Katherine returned to East London after the second World War, he was invited to be the second Master.

A socialist, he was a friend of G.D.H. and Margaret Cole, R.H. TAWNEY, George LANSBURY, and other local leaders.

St. John Groser was a fighter for the poor, the homeless, the under-privileged. Founder and Chairman of the Stepney Old People's Welfare Association, he was also Chairman of the Vallance Youth Club. He played the part of Thomas a Becket in the film of T.S. Eliot's play *Murder in the Cathedral*.

There is a plaque commemorating St. John Groser in front of the Royal Foundation of St. Katherine, Butcher Row, E14.
Autobiography
Politics and Persons (SCM, 1949)
Biography
Brill, K. (ed) *John Groser* (Mowbrays, 1971)

GURLE, (or GARLE, GERLE, QUARLE), Leonard circa 1621-1685
Gardener

Leonard Gurle had one of the earliest nursery gardens in London from the early 1640s, when he moved from Southwark to twelve acres between Brick Lane and Greatorex Street, north of Old Montague Street, Whitechapel. During the 1660s and 1670s his nursery was the largest in London and he was famous as a supplier of fruit trees, although he also sold ornamental trees, shrubs and seeds.

Records show that Leonard Gurle sold pear and other fruit trees, cypresses, jasmine and honeysuckle to Sir Roger Pratt for his garden at Ryston Hall near Downham, Norfolk.

By 1661, Leonard Gurle had raised the hardy nectarine Elruge and given it his own name backwards, with an extra 'e' for euphony.

Leonard Gurle succeeded John Rose as the King's Gardener in 1677. There he had an official residence, but he continued to run his Whitechapel nursery with another at London Fields.

The area in Whitechapel occupied by the nursery was called 'Gurle's Ground' for some time after his death.

In 1719 part of the nursery was still occupied by Martin Gurle, possibly the nurseryman's eldest son or grandson.

DNB Missing Persons (1993)

HANBURY, Cornelius 1796-1869
Pharmacist

Cornelius Hanbury was born at Ware, Hertfordshire. At 18 he joined his brother Daniel Hanbury at the Plough Court Pharmacy, where he was apprenticed for seven years to William ALLEN. He lived with William and Charlotte Allen at Stoke Newington and in 1822 married their daughter, Mary. She died after giving birth to a son, William Allen Hanbury.

Cornelius Hanbury was admitted to partnership in 1824 when the name of the firm was changed to Allen, Hanburys and Barry.

In 1826 he married Elizabeth (1793-1901), daughter of John Sanderson, a China tea merchant. Elizabeth became an acknowledged minister of the Society of Friends. She retained her clarity of mind until the end of her long life. She became the oldest subject of Queen Victoria and one of the oldest living people in the country. She took a keen interest in the work of her daughter, Charlotte (1830-1900) in prison reform and educational work. Their son, Cornelius II, (1827-1916) became a surgeon and apothecary. He began classes in chemistry at Birkbeck College, University of London and became a Fellow of the Royal Institute of Chemistry.

Books
Chapman-Huston, D. and Cripps, E.C. *Through a City Archway* (J.Murray, 1954)
Cripps, E.C. *Plough Court 1715-1927* (Allen and Hanburys, 1927)

DNB

HANBURY, Sampson 1769-1835
Brewer

Sampson Hanbury became a partner with Benjamin TRUMAN in the Eagle Brewery, Brick Lane, Spitalfields in 1789, taking charge of the business.

A country gentleman and keen sportsman, he was a shrewd business manager and his knowledge of book-keeping exceeded that of any of his employees.

He is commemorated by a tablet in St. Mary's Church, Thundridge, Herts.

Locally, Hanbury House and Hanbury Street, E1. are named after the family.

Book
Locke, A.A. *The Hanbury Family* (A.L.Humphreys, 1916)

HARRIS, Betsey 1809-1831
Resident

Inscription on tomb in St. Dunstan's Church 1831:-

> Sacred to the memory of Betsey Harris who died suddenly while contemplating the beauties of the moon 24th April, 1831, in her 23rd year.

HARRIS, Sir Percy 1876-1952
Politician

Born in London, educated at Harrow and Cambridge, Harris began work with the firm his father had founded in New Zealand. He returned to England in 1903, and became a Liberal politician.

In 1907 Harris was elected to the London County Council as member for South West Bethnal Green, beginning an association with the borough that lasted all his life. He became Chief Whip of his party and Deputy Chairman of the Council in l915-1916.

He entered Parliament in 1916 as Member for Market Harborough and in 1922 was elected MP for South West Bethnal Green. He held his seat for six successive general elections and for many years his was the only Liberal seat within 100 miles of London. He was defeated in 1945. In 1949 he won back his old seat on the London County Council and was the only Liberal member returned, with the other parties having equal numbers.

He was created baronet in 1932.

He is commemorated with Percy Harris House, 30 Barnet Grove, E2.

Autobiography

Forty Years In and Out of Parliament (Andrew Melrose, 1947)

DNB

HARRISON, Dr. John 1718-1753

Surgeon

Harrison was the leading spirit in a group of seven people who met on the 29th September 1740 at the *Feathers Tavern* in Cheapside in the City to found a new charity.

The group established an infirmary in Prescot Street, Whitechapel in May 1741, which was the forerunner of the London Hospital, opened in 1753.

John Harrison was resident surgeon at the infirmary and the London Hospital from 1741 until his death.

He is commemorated by a tablet in St. Paul's Church, Deptford.

Book

Clark-Kennedy, A.E. *The London* (Pitman-Medical, 1962)

HAWKSMOOR, Nicholas
1661-1736

Architect

Nicholas Hawksmoor was born in Nottinghamshire and educated at Durham Grammar School. He began work as a clerk to Justice Mellish of Doncaster. He later became the pupil, then the valued assistant and perhaps finally the partner of Sir Christopher Wren. In the first years of the eighteenth century, he worked for, and with, Sir John Vanburgh. He designed many buildings and churches and there are three splendid examples of his work in the borough; St George-in-the-East (1714-29), Christ Church, Spitalfields (1714-29) and St. Anne, Limehouse (1714-30).

Hawksmoor also designed the towers for the West Front of Westminster Abbey

He is also commemorated by Hawksmoor House, Maroon Street, E14 and Hawksmoor Mews, Cable Street, E1.

Biography

Downes, K. *Hawksmoor* (Thames and Hudson, 1969)

DNB

HEADLAM, Rev. Stewart Duckworth 1847-1924

Priest

Stewart Headlam was curate of St. Matthew's Church, Bethnal Green between 1873 and 1878, where he founded a radical Anglo-Catholic group, the Guild of St. Matthew.

As a young man Stewart Headlam was influenced by Christian Socialism, and always supported the deprived against the priviledged. He stood as a Radical candidate in the London School Board elections of 1888, when he called for free schools and free dinners for school children to be financed out of taxation. Such ideas were considered at the time controversial and even dangerous. Stewart Headlam was elected and served on the London School Board for Hackney district, which at that time included a large part of Bethnal Green, and served on the Board from 1907 until his death.

He was keenly interested in the theatre, and formed a church and stage guild. He encouraged young people to visit the ballet and stage productions, and this led the Bishop of London to accuse him of causing 'moral pollution'.

Stewart Headlam was associated with Oscar Wilde's last days in London. During Wilde's second trial for homosexuality (1895), Headlam became convinced that the outcome had been pre-judged. Although he did not know Oscar Wilde personally, he offered to stand bail for him, and escorted him to and from court each day. On the day of Wilde's release from jail in May 1897, Headlam collected him in a cab at 6 a.m. to avoid the press, and took him to his own home, before Wilde set out for exile in France

Biography

Bettany, F.G. *Stewart Headlam* (J.Murray, 1926)

Book

Orens, J.R. *The Mass, the Masses and the Music Hall* (Jubilee Group of East London, 1976)

HECKFORD, Nathaniel 1842-1871
Founder of East London Children's Hospital

Born in Calcutta into a shipping family, Nathaniel Heckford came to London to train at the London Hospital. On qualifying he won the gold medals for medicine and surgery in the same year. During this time he lived at 65 Philpot Street, Stepney.

During the cholera outbreak of 1866, in which some 4,000 East London people died, he was in charge of the Wapping District Cholera Emergency Hospital. It was there that he met his wife, Sarah, who had volunteered to be a nurse.

Together they founded the East London Children's Hospital, first in an old warehouse in Butcher Row, Ratcliff. One day Charles DICKENS visited the hospital and wrote an account of the work in *McMillan's Magazine*, giving it much praise. The publicity raised considerable funds and enabled the Heckfords to build a hospital in Glamis Road, Shadwell. Dr Elizabeth Garrett ANDERSON became the medical officer.

The hospital closed in 1963 when it was amalgamated with Queen Elizabeth's Hospital for Children in Hackney Road, E2.

After Nathaniel Heckford died, Sarah Heckford emigrated to South Africa and began buying and selling goods with the Boers.

Nathaniel Heckford is commemorated by Nathaniel Heckford School, Cable Street, E1, Heckford Street, E1, and Heckford House, Grundy Street, E14.

Book
Allen, V. *Lady Trader* (Collins, 1979)

HENDERSON, Robert 1884-1958
Headmaster

Robert Henderson was born in Poplar. His father was secretary of Millwall Football Club. He attended St. Luke's and Thomas Street Schools before going on to Mile End Pupil Teachers' Centre, Essex Street, Mile End, and to King's College, London.

He taught at Upper North Street School, Poplar and after a period in South London, returned to St. Matthias School, Grundy Street, Poplar as Headmaster. He was Head for 24 years, completing fifty years in teaching by the time he retired.

Henderson was President of the London Teachers Association and a prominent member of the National Union of Teachers.

HENDERSON, Rev. William John 1843-1929
Baptist Preacher

William Henderson was born in Poplar. He began work at Woolwich Arsenal and in his spare time often preached in the open air in that area. He became a travelling evangelist, visiting open fairs and race meetings. He entered Rawdon College, Leeds and on his ordination became minister at a church in Birmingham in 1868, and in Coventry in 1872. He remained in Coventry for 21 years, building up a large congregation – on Sunday mornings he would have a thousand men attending his Bible class.

In 1893 he was appointed President of the Baptist College in Bristol and was responsible for the new buildings erected 1914-15. In 1907 he became Chairman of the Baptist Union. He took an active part in the foundation of Bristol University.

Portrait of Sir Basil Henriques

HENRIQUES, Sir Basil Lucas Quixano 1890-1961
Community Worker and Magistrate

Basil Henriques was born in London and educated at Harrow School and Oxford. He came to Stepney and lived at Toynbee Hall. In

March 1914 he opened the Oxford and St. George's Club in Cannon Street Road, E1. The Club moved to the Bernhard Baron Settlement in Berner Street, now Henriques Street, in 1930.

He remained Warden there until his retirement in 1947. For many years he was Chairman of the East London Juvenile Court and was an acknowledged authority on delinquency. His portrait hangs in the Thames Magistrates Court, Bow Road, E3.

He was President of the London Federation of Boys' Clubs and a member of the House Committee of the London Hospital 1920-1940.

Autobiography
The Indiscretions of a Warden (Methuen, 1937)
Biography
Loewe, L.L. Basil Henriques (Routledge and Kegan Paul, 1976)

DNB

HENRIQUES, Lady Rose
1890-1973
Community Worker and Artist

Rose Loewe began training as a pianist but after meeting Basil Henriques she gave up this career and joined him in running the Oxford and St. George's Club in Stepney. They were married in 1916.

She started with a first aid class for boys, and went on to found the Oxford and St. George's Girls' Club. Concerned with every kind of social work, she was particularly keen to encourage young people to become interested in the arts.

She was air raid warden in the second World War; at the end of hostilities she went to Germany to organise relief for victims of the concentration camps.

Rose Henriques founded Workrooms for the Elderly and was interested in many schemes for young people in community service.

She painted many pictures of local scenes and held two exhibitions at the Whitechapel Art Gallery.

In 1966 she was invited by the BBC to give five talks on 'Fifty years in Stepney'.

HESSEL, Phoebe 1713(?)-1821
Female Soldier

Phoebe Hessel was born in Stepney, of respectable parents named Smith, and at the age of 15 she fell in love with Samuel Golding. When he was posted to the West Indies, she enlisted as a soldier in the 5th Regiment of Foot and followed him. She fought in different parts of Europe and in one battle was wounded by a bayonet. She was consequently forced to confess her sex to the General's wife and was discharged.

Phoebe married Golding and lived happily with him for 20 years. She became known as the 'Stepney Amazon' because of her war adventures. After Golding's death she married William Hessel and moved to Brighton where she became a 'local character'.

At the grand old age of 107 Phoebe Hessel took part in the coronation ceremonies of George IV and joined lustily in the singing of the national anthem.

Her tombstone in St. Nicholas' Churchyard, Church Street, Brighton describes her colourful career.

She is commemorated locally by Hessel Street, E1, and Amazon Street, E1. Golding Street, E1, was named after her husband.

DNB

HILLS, Arnold Frank 1857-1927
Shipbuilder and Philanthropist

Arnold Hills was born in London, the son of Frank Clarke Hills, a wealthy manufacturing chemist who acquired a majority holding in the Thames Iron Works and Shipbuilding Company, in Orchard Yard, Blackwall, formerly run by C.J. MARE. Arnold Hills was educated at Harrow School and Oxford. He distinguished himself by winning the University championships for the mile and the three miles, and also played football for Oxford against Cambridge.

He became a Director of the Thames Iron Works in 1880, and Chairman from 1905. The firm employed over 6,00 workers, building many of the early dreadnoughts in the 1900's, and the famous first iron battleship HMS *Warrior* (1859). Instead of re-organising the plant downstream on the Thames which might have been more profitable, Arnold Hills resolved to keep the firm on its 30 acre site in West Ham and five acre site in Blackwall, for the benefit of the local economy. The Thames Iron Works was the last and greatest of the Thames shipbuilding yards; it built the *Thunderer*, the last ship to be built on the Thames, in 1911. He fought hard but unsuccessfully to save the shipyard from competition from yards in the north of the country. Apart from ships, he diversified into electrical engineering, motor vehicles, and constructed new dock gates for the East India Dock, Hammersmith Bridge, and the roof of Alexandra Palace.

When he first joined the company he made his home in East India Dock Road, Poplar, a short walk away from the yard, and lived there for 5 years to be closer to his workers. After his daytime business work he spent his evenings on schemes for the improvement and recreation of his workers. In 1897 he built a recreation ground in West Ham, and helped to form the Thames Iron Works Football Club in 1895. He was a founder of the West Ham United Football Club in 1900.

In addition to his business involvement, Arnold Hills promoted his beliefs in temperance, vegetarianism and Christianity. He founded and was President of the Thames Iron Works Temperance League from 1884, which encouraged his workers to take the Pledge of total abstinence. Entertainments were arranged as a counter-attraction to the public house.

He also established, and generously funded The London Vegetarian Society, and its official journal, *The Vegetarian* from 1888 and used them to publicise his three causes. He inaugurated a scheme of providing penny vegetarian dinners for poor children attending elementary schools from 1901.

From 1891-1902 he was President of the Poplar Hospital, and Chairman for the last 15 years of his life.

Books
Banbury, P. *Shipbuilders of the Thames and Medway* (David and Charles, 1971)
Korr, C. *West Ham United* (Duckworth, 1986)
Obituaries
Vegetarian News April 1927
East London Advertiser 12th April 1927
East End News 11th April 1927
Articles
East London Observer 15th April 1927
Thames Iron Works Gazette 31st March 1905

DNB

HILSDON, George Richard
1885-1941
Footballer

George Hilsdon was born in Bromley-by-Bow, and, showing early promise as a footballer, he joined West Ham United. After he had been spotted at training by Chelsea's first manager, John Robertson, George Hilsdon was given a free transfer to Chelsea in 1906.

Playing in the first match of the 1906-07 season on the 1st September, he scored five goals in Chelsea's defeat of Glossop 9-2. That was a goal scoring record for a player making his first appearance in the Football League. This record still stands. In that season he scored 27 goals and was the spearhead in Chelsea's successful drive for promotion to the First Division.

He scored six goals in the F.A.Cup Tie for Chelsea against Worksop Town, 11th January 1908. For some time it was the highest number of goals scored by any player in an F.A Cup match, and was equalled, but not bettered by George Best.

George Hilsdon was chosen to play for England, was injured early in his first game, but went on to play several games for his country.

He returned to play for West Ham in 1912.
Book
Golesworthy, M. (ed) *Encyclopaedia of Association Football* (R.Hale, 12th rev.edn.,1976)

HILTON, Marie 1821-1896
Pioneer of the Creche

Marie Hilton was born in London. She was left an orphan at an early age and was brought up by her maternal grandmother in Richmond, Surrey.

When she was old enough, she obtained a post as governess to the children of a wealthy family living in Brighton. Whilst living there she joined the Society of Friends.

When her husband gained employment in London, the family moved to Bromley-by-Bow, witnessing the severe outbreak of cholera in 1866.

Concerned with the work of the Quaker's centres for social work, known as the Bedford Institute Association, she joined the Ratcliff Friends Meeting in Brook Street, Ratcliff. There she helped organise a sewing class and a soup kitchen.

During a visit to Brussels, Marie Hilton saw an infant nursery which gave her the idea to start similar work. She obtained premises in Stepney Causeway and began a creche in 1871. It was open from 8 a.m. to 8 p.m. to all local families at a cost of one penny a day. On arrival the children were bathed, given breakfast and their clothes were fumigated. The idea was new and caused much discussion but before long Marie and her helpers were looking after 100 children a day, enabling their mothers to go to work.

There was much interest in the scheme

and many visitors came, some from the London School Board, including Blanchard Jerrold who wrote an account of his visit in the *School Board Chronicle*.

Creche facilities were revived, in 1914 by Sylvia PANKHURST at the Mothers Arms, 438 Old Ford Road, Bow and again in the 1920s by Doris and Muriel LESTER at the Childrens House, Powis Road, E3.

Biography
Hilton, J.D. *Marie Hilton* (Isbister, 1897)

HIRD, James Wynne   1887-1959
Salesman and Promoter of Football to Russia

James Hird was born in Bow. His brother invited him to spend his holiday in Odessa, Russia in 1903. He returned home determined to go back there as soon as he was able.

In 1910 he got a job as a salesman for a firm making agricultural implements which took him over a large part of Russia. Travelling about, he was soon well known as 'Meester Jeem'.

He payed football with a group of English boys who had occasional matches with teams from British ships calling at the port. He suggested to his friends that they should teach Russian boys to play. At first there was little interest, but some schools took it up and in 1911, Hird formed the first football club in Russia for working boys – the Odessa Football Circle (OKF). The game spread to most of the big cities, largely through his enthusiasm in his travels.

Hird was in Russia during the Revolution and returned home to Poplar in 1921 where he opened a grocery shop.

HOBBS, Horace Edwin   1896-1935
Dog Lover

Horace Hobbs was born in Poplar at the Beehive Stores, East India Dock Road.

He became advertising manager and later director of Spratts, of Morris Road, Bromley-by-Bow, manufacturers of dog biscuits.

Hobbs was an authority on the welfare of dogs and organised several 'dog weeks'. From these came the Tail Waggers Club which enrolled 650,000 dogs from 58 countries. One of the Club's objectives was to finance the re-building of the canine department at the Royal Veterinary College and to found a professorship of canine medicine and surgery. The Club raised £20,000 for this purpose.

Horace Hobbs was also Treasurer of the Guide Dogs for the Blind Association.

HODGSON, Joseph Ray   1829-1908
Lifesaver

Joseph Hodgson was born in Sunderland. He received the name 'Stormy Petrel' for his courageous deeds and constant watch on the seas during storms off the North East Coast.

He distinguished himself by saving 150 lives from shipwrecks and drownings and was awarded medals from the Royal Humane Society, the National Life Boat Institution, the Board of Trade and the Emperor Louis Napoleon of France.

He travelled all over the world and had a varied career. When he settled in East London, he became a modeller for a firm of boat builders, and subsequently designed a life saving raft which gained the first prize at Tynmouth Exhibition.

The last years of his life were spent at 18 Suffolk Street, Poplar.

HODSON, Bishop Mark Allin
1907-1985
Rector of Poplar

Mark Hodson was born in Enfield and was educated at University College, London and Wells Theological College. He was a Curate at St. Dunstan's Church, Stepney, 1931-35, and Missioner at St. Nicholas Church, Perivale, 1935-40.

He was appointed Rector of Poplar in the summer of 1940, and in a few weeks the parish was devastated by the German air-raid attack on the Docks on 7th September.

Two initiatives began immediately *Poplar Pool* a magazine and newsletter to serve all the parishes, and the South Poplar Youth Club. Because of wartime restrictions the name 'Poplar' could not be included in the title so the club became known as the 'SPY' Club. It influenced many young people and quickly became the heart of much of the work of the parish. After several moves it occupied the old Railway Mission in Poplar High Street. At Christmas and Easter, dramatic presentations became a hallmark of the life of All Saints. In April 1949 *Picture Post* featured the Passion Play as a 'people's play', the cast drawn from Poplar people. Over two thousand people saw the play that year.

In 1945, the last German rocket fell about 40 yards from the Church whilst the staff were gathered there for their regular daily progress. The church began to fall in, the clergy were saved by the galleries as they crouched in the pews.

As Chairman of the Standing Committee of the Society for the Propagation of the Gospel, Mark Hodson was invited to tour countries in the Far East, visiting Borneo, Malaysia and Japan. He was given a great welcome on his return.

In 1956, Mark Hodson was appointed Suffragan Bishop of Taunton and in 1961 he became Bishop of Hereford. On his retirement in 1973 he became an Assistant Bishop of London.

Pamphlet
James, E. *Fire over Poplar* (Privately published, 1987)

HOLLAND, Sydney George, Lord Knutsford 1855-1931
Chairman of the London Hospital

Born in London and educated at Wellington School, Sydney Holland trained and practised as a barrister. He developed an interest in social reform and taught life saving in boys' clubs during his spare time.

Through an inheritance he became a shareholder in the East and West India Dock Companies and as they were in financial difficulties he proposed an amalgamation with their rival, the London and St. Katherine Dock Companies.

Sydney Holland's interest in the dock workers led him to visit Poplar Hospital, where many dockers were taken when they were injured. He was seriously disturbed by the poor facilities and was appointed to a committee of inquiry into management of the Hospital. After the report was published Sydney Holland was elected Chairman of Poplar Hospital and set about reform. Within four years the hospital had been rebuilt and enlarged, and its financial resources secured.

In 1895 he was asked to stand for election to the Committee of the London Hospital and was encouraged by Eva LÜCKES the Matron. He was elected and produced a report on the reforms needed to bring the Hospital up-to-date. In 1896 Sydney Holland was appointed Chairman, and by raising large sums of money was able to rebuild and extend the Hospital. He remained as Chairman until his death in 1931. Sydney Holland was a forceful administrator and brilliant fundraiser who was proud to be known as the 'Prince of Beggars'.

Sydney Holland became Lord Knutsford in 1914, inheriting the title from his father. He is commemorated by a tablet near the entrance to the London Hospital and his portrait by Oswald Birley hangs in the Committee Room.

Autobiography
In Black and White (E.Arnold, 1926)

Biography
Gore, J. *Sydney Holland* (J.Murray, 1936)

Books
Clark-Kennedy, A.E. *The London* (Pitman-Medical, 1962)
Collins, S.M. *The London Hospital; a brief history* (Royal London Hospital Archives and Museum,1995)
Daunton, C. (ed) *The London Hospital Illustrated; 250 years* (Batsford, 1990)

HOLMAN, Francis 1729-1784
Marine Painter

Francis Holman was baptised at St. Laurence Church, Ramsgate, son of Francis and Ann Holman. His father was a ship's master, trading between Mediterranean or North Sea ports and London. The Holmans were one of several Thanet seafaring families who traded from London, and built the strong eighteenth century connection between Wapping and Ramsgate.

Francis Holman's early career is unknown, but his paintings indicate he went to sea himself. In 1758 he described himself as a 'herald-painter', and by 1767 he is recorded as living in Wapping at Bell Dock; in 1770 at Broad Street; in 1774 at Johnson Street, Old Gravel Lane, and in 1778 at Fawden Fields, Old Gravel Lane, St. George's-in-the-East. He was a widower by 1781, when he married Jane Maxted of Ozengell, Thanet; he was recorded then, and at his death, as still resident in St. George's.

He was recognised as one of the most important British marine painters of the eighteenth century, having exhibited at the Free Society of Artists 1767-73, and at the Royal Academy 1774-84. His subjects included East Indiamen (a type of frigate), sea battles, Thameside shipbuilding yards and scenes along the Kent coast.

Exhibiting in 1782, he recorded that he had been on board a frigate during the action between Admiral Parker and the Dutch at the Doggerbank the previous year.

He was buried at St. Laurence's Church, Ramsgate; the parish register records the cause of death as 'lethargy'.

There are a number of his paintings in the National Maritime Museum, Greenwich.

HOOLE, Rev. Samuel 1770-1839
Priest

Samuel Hoole was born in a hackney coach which was conveying his mother to Drury Lane Theatre to see a performance of *Timanthes*, a play written by his father, John Hoole.

Samuel Hoole was educated at Merchant Taylor's School and Oxford and became the first Rector of Poplar (1823-1839) on the separation of the parish from St. Dunstan's, Stepney. He was also Chaplain to the East India Company.

As a result of his father's close friendship, Hoole was left a book in Samuel Johnson's will. He chose a two volume copy of *Terence*. The books contain Samuel Hoole's signature and a note of how he acquired them and they are now back in the Samuel Johnson Birthplace Museum at Lichfield.

Book
Timbs, J. *Curiosities of London* (Virtue, 1885)

HOW, Bishop William Walsham
1823-1897
Hymn Writer

Born in Shrewsbury, William How was educated at Shrewsbury School and Oxford. He was ordained in 1846.

In 1879 he was appointed the first Suffragan Bishop of East London and in 1888 he became the first Bishop of Wakefield.

He wrote many books but he is chiefly remembered for his hymns, the most famous being:-

For all the saints who from their labours rest (1864)

DNB

HOWELL, George 1833-1910
Labour Leader

George Howell was born at Wrington, Somerset. He began work at 12 year of age first as a mortar boy and then as bricklayer. In 1847 he joined a Chartist society and became a great reader, beginning on the religious classics. As he found bricklaying too heavy for him, he was apprenticed to a shoemaker who encouraged discussions on politics and religion in his workshop. Howell was one of the first members of the Young Men's Christian Association in Bristol.

He travelled to London to see the Great Exhibition of 1851, and made up his mind to return to seek his fortune. On his arrival back in London he worked for a time as a bricklayer, involving himself in union affairs, particularly in the building workers' strike of 1869.

He was involved in the formation of the 'Reform League' established in 1865 to 'promote the conquest of political power by the working, class'. He was appointed full-time secretary and organised two demonstrations in 1866 and 1867 which forced Disraeli to accept the number who were entitled to vote, and resulted in the 2nd Reform Act (1867).

Howell was appointed secretary of the London Trades Council and in 1871 was secretary of the parliamentary committee of the newly formed Trades Union Congress. He was also secretary to the PLIMSOLL Committee which promoted the Merchant Shipping Bill 1876, improving the conditions of merchant seamen and regulating loads carried by ships by marking of the Plimsoll Line.

George Howell was elected Member of Parliament for North East Bethnal Green from 1885-1892.

George Howell

In 1906 his library was purchased by public subscription for £1,000 and presented to the Bishopsgate Institute, Bishopsgate. The Institute also has two portraits of him.

Book
The Conflicts of Capital and Labour (London, 1878)
Biography
Leventhal, F.M. *Respectable Radical* (Weidenfeld and Nicolson, 1971)

DLB, DNB

HUDDART, Joseph 1741-1616
Marine Surveyor and Rope Manufacturer

Born at Allonby in Cumberland, Joseph Huddart was educated at a school kept by a local clergyman. He acquired great skill and scientific knowledge in navigation and astronomy. At the early age of 22 he commanded a brig, he then designed and built his own brig *Patience* in 1768. He entered the East India Mercantile Marine as chief officer in 1771, serving on the ship *Royal Admiral*.

During his time in the eastern hemisphere he pursued his hydrographical and astronomical activities. He ascertained the longitude of Bombay with great precision and then completed a survey of the Indian peninsula from Bombay to Coringo, going on to survey the River Tigris. He undertook many surveys of Britain.

In 1791 he was appointed an Elder Brother of Trinity House, Trinity Square and elected a Fellow of the Royal Society. A director of the East India Dock Company, he had a great deal to do with the laying out of the docks.

The accident of a parting cable on one of his ships had turned his attention to the making of rope, and he invented a process for the equal distribution of the strains upon the yarn. He went into business as a rope manufacturer in Copenhagen Place, Limehouse, specialising in making ships' cables. In the 1830s his firm built the cables for the London and Blackwall Railway.

DNB

HUFFAM, Christopher 1771-1839
Ship's Chandler

Christopher Huffam lived at 5 Church Row, Limehouse (now Newell Street) and was a partner in a firm dealing in supplies for merchant ships and the Navy.

Charles DICKENS' father and Huffam were old friends as they had worked together in the Navy Pay Office. Christopher Huffam was godfather to Charles DICKENS, who was named Charles John Huffam Dickens. When he was a boy, DICKENS visited the Huffams regularly.

In recognition of his work over the war with France, Huffam was appointed Gentleman-in-Waiting to William IV.

His portrait was painted by Sir Thomas Lawrence.

HUGHES, Mary 1860-1941
Social Worker and Philanthropist

Mary Hughes was born in Mayfair. She was the daughter of Tom Hugh's, a County Court Judge, and a leader of the Christian Socialist movement, and author of *Tom Brown's Schooldays*. At the age of nine she decided that she must give her life to the poorest people.

In 1883 she became the housekeeper of her uncle, the Vicar of Longcot, in Berkshire, and joined him in caring for the community. Mary Hughes was one of the first women members of the Board of Guardians in the country when she was elected in Longcot in 1894.

Despite inheriting a legacy from her deceased uncle, she preferred to have a simple way of life. She came to Stepney in 1897 to help at St. Jude's Church, Commercial Street, Whitechapel, where her brother-in-law, Ernest Carter, was the Vicar. She then assisted Muriel and Doris LESTER in their work at Kingsley Hall, Powis Road, Bow and stayed in a small room at the top of the building from 1915 to 1917.

From 1917 to 1924 she lived in Blackwall Buildings, Fulbourne Street, Whitechapel.

During the first World War, her pacifist views became stronger and in 1918 she decided to become a Quaker.

Mary Hughes was elected to the Whitechapel Board of Guardians, 1910-1925, and Stepney Poor Law Union, 1925-1930, and in 1917 became a JP.

She was elected Labour member on Stepney Borough Council, 1919-34 and was especially concerned about unemployment.

In 1926 she bought a disused public house at 71 Vallance Road, Whitechapel and converted it into a place of rest and refreshment for homeless and needy, which she called the *Dewdrop Inn*.

The London County Council Blue Plaque erected on the house in 1961 is inscribed:-

Mary Hughes
Friend of all in need
Lived and worked here 1926-1941

The house was later used by the Stepney Family Service Unit.

She is also commemorated by Hughes Mansions, Vallance Road, E1, and the Mary Hughes Clinic, Underwood Street, E1.

Biographies
Hobhouse, R. *Mary Hughes* (Rockcliff, 1949)
Pyper, H *Mary Hughes* (Quaker Home Service, 1985)

JACKSON, Sir Cyril 1863-1924
Educationalist

Cyril Jackson was born in Bodiam, Sussex, the son of Lawrence Jackson, a member of the Stock Exchange. He was educated at Charterhouse and Oxford. Although called to the Bar at Inner Temple in 1893 he decided not to enter the legal profession. He was inspired at Oxford by the University Settlement movements and after graduating, became one of Toynbee Hall's earliest residents, 1885-95. Here, his work included a survey on boy labour which was an important contribution to the Poor Law Commission report of 1906 and assisted the work of the Lewis Committee whose work resulted in the Education Act of 1918.

In 1886 he became a manager of Limehouse Schools and Central Secretary of the Children's Country Holidays Fund from 1888 to 1896 which gave children from the metropolis a taste of life away from home. Greater involvement in school activities came with his service on the School Board of London from 1891-1896 at a time when it was fighting for the right to provide advanced education.

Four hundred people bade him farewell at a party in Toynbee Hall before he emigrated to Western Australia. He took control of the Dept. of Education at a time when the expansion of the population had over-stretched a school system built for a very small community. From 1896 to 1903 he re-organised education so completely that it was soon recognised throughout the Commonwealth as one of the best systems in Australia.

He returned to London and accepted the post of Chief Inspector of the Board of Education from 1903-1906.

Cyril Jackson brought into public voluntary service a highly specialised knowledge and applied it ceaselessly to a very wide range of organisations and Royal Commissions dealing with social problems. He had an insatiable appetite for committee work and administration.

Cyril Jackson was elected to represent Limehouse on the London County Council in 1907. He became its leader in 1912. Whilst Chairman of the London County Council Education Committee (1908-10, and 1922) the Council adopted a far reaching scheme for reducing the size of elementary school classes and established Central Schools.

For many years he took an active interest in the Northey Street School Club in Limehouse. The school was re-named Cyril Jackson School in 1930. It is now in Three Colt Street, E14.

He was knighted in 1917.

Obituaries
East End News 9th September 1924
East London Observer 13th September 1924
Article
East London Advertiser 9th March 1907
Who Was Who 1916-1928, DNB

JACKSON, Rev. Thomas
1850-1932
Methodist Preacher

Thomas Jackson was born at Belper, Derbyshire. Entirely self-educated, he was working at the age of six, straightening nails in his father's shop. He studied theology and entered the ministry of the Primitive Methodist Church. When he arrived in London in 1876 he began work in Bethnal Green.

He offered a home and help in education to many boys, particularly first offenders, and established a centre of religious and social work for all in need. In 1896 he purchased the Working Lads' Institute next to Whitechapel Station and when he set up the Whitechapel Mission in the derelict Brunswick Hall Congregational Church a few yards east of the London Hospital in 1906 he was able to give destitute men supper, lodging and breakfast. For women, he started the 'Women's Bright Hour' which attracted average attendances of 300. Women working in the 'sweated trades' for a pittance persuaded Thomas Jackson into a rigorous lobbying campaign on Members of Parliament. He founded the Garment Workers' Trade Union to unite the anti-sweating movement at 21 Leman Street, Whitechapel in 1908, and in 1910 his efforts were partially rewarded when the Trade Boards Act was passed. Wages Boards were established to fix rates of pay exceeding the old scales of remuneration.

Rev. Thomas Jackson

Brunswick Hall was replaced in 1971 by a new building for the Whitechapel Mission on the site, and included a commemoration to his work, the Thomas Jackson Memorial Hostel, Maples Place, E1.
Biography
Potter, W. *Thomas Jackson of Whitechapel* (C.Tinling, 1929)

JACOBS, William Wymark
1863-1943
Writer

William Jacobs was born at 5 Crombies Row, Mile End Old Town, later re-designated 319 Commercial Road, E1. He was the son of William Gage Jacobs, a wharfinger's clerk. William Jacobs was educated at a private school in the City and then at Birkbeck College. His father became Manager of South Devon Wharf by Wapping Old Stairs and moved to Wapping. In 1883 William Jacobs became a clerk in the Savings Bank Department of the Post Office in Queen Victoria Street, EC, and continued there until 1899.

His first collection of stories, *Many Cargoes*, was published in 1896 and about 150

William Wymark Jacobs *National Portrait Gallery*

stories followed before 1926. The stories are mainly comic sketches of characters and situations associated with Wapping and the riverside. Many of the stories were illustrated by his friend Will Owen. *Many Cargoes, Monkey's Paw* and *Ship's Company* are still widely read.

There is a portrait of him by C.M. Park in the National Portrait Gallery. He is commemorated by Jacob's House, Carr Street, E14.
Book
Greene, H. (ed) *Selected Short Stories* (Bodley Head, 1975)

DNB

JAMES, Mary Eleanor Elizabeth, MBE 1859-1943
Social Worker

Mary James was born in London. Her father was a Church of England clergyman. When she was 21 she inherited £50,000.

Mary James started social work in Buckinghamshire. She came to Bethnal Green and lived at 5 Paradise Row for 41 years. Keeping 'open house', people came at all times for help and shelter. She was sometimes known as the 'Angel of Paradise Row'.

Elected to the Board of Guardians, in 1912 she was the first woman to preside over a Metropolitan Poor Law body. She was a

Mary James

Progressive Party Borough Councillor from 1919 to 1922 and a Liberal Party Councillor from 1928 to 1931.

She was interested in many causes and spent her fortune in helping the needy, for which she was awarded the MBE. Although she possessed a large house in Buckinghamshire, she seldom went there, using it to provide holidays for Bethnal Green people.

Greatly interested in Bethnal Green Hospital, she always had her Christmas dinner there or in the local workhouse.

She is commemorated by Mary James House, St. Peter's Avenue, E2.

JAMRACH, Johann Christian Carl 1815-1891
Importer of Wild Beasts

Johann Jamrach was born in Hamburg. He had a shop in St. George Street (now The Highway) which was always full of parrots and other exotic birds. He kept his wild beasts in Betts Street and always had orders for more than he could supply. He had no need to advertise but from time to time he would announce in the press that such and such beasts were at Jamrach's. He was so well known that there was no need to add his address.

> If ever you're my way
> Quite close to Ratcliff Highway
> Just look at my large stock-in-trade
> I've everything on sale-o
> From a winkle to a whale-o.
> *Old Song*

Book
Rubinstein, S. *Historians of London* (Peter Owen, 1968)

JEFFREYS, Baron George
1648-1699
'The Hanging Judge'

George Jeffreys was born near Wrexham. He was called to the bar in 1668, appointed Recorder of London 1683 and in the same year he was made Chief Justice of The King's Bench.

As a Royalist he earned the favour of James II and was involved in many political trials including those of Titus Oates and Richard Baxter. He had to try the followers of the Duke of Monmouth after the rebellion of 1685 and hanged, transported, whipped and fined hundreds of them at the 'Bloody Assize'.

He was appointed Lord Chancellor in 1685. On the downfall of James II in 1688, he tried to escape from London disguised as a sailor, but he was recognised in Wapping and was sent to the Tower of London, where he died.

Biography
Hyde, H.M.   *Judge Jeffreys* (Butterworth, 1948)
Parry, Sir E.A. *The Bloody Assize* (Ernest Benn, 1929)

DNB

JEROME, Jerome Klapka
1859-1927
Writer

Jerome K. Jerome was born at Walsall, Staffordshire. His father varied his occupations by being architect, coalowner, ironmonger and independent minister. The family came to Poplar and lived in Sussex Street after his father had lost his money in the flooding of a coal mine.

above The shop front of Jamrach, the wild animal dealer, in St. George Street, about 1896. *below* Inside the shop.

Judge Jeffreys in the disguise of a sailor seized at Wapping

Jerome first worked at Euston station, then on the stage and later as a teacher. He finally took up writing and the books that brought him fame were, *Idle Thoughts of an Idle Fellow* (1889) and *Three Men in a Boat* (1889). From 1893-1898 he founded and edited a magazine called *Today*.

He took up writing humorous fiction but one of his novels, *Paul Kelver* (1902) was of a more serious nature. He also wrote plays, of which the best known is *The Passing of the Third Floor Back*.

He is commemorated by Jerome House, Carr Street, E14, and Jerome Street, E1.

Autobiography
My Life and Times (Hodder and Stoughton, 1926)

JONES, Richard Cynfyn   1873-1964
Anglican Clergyman

Richard Jones was born in Ponterwyd, Cardiganshire. In 1897 he married Alice Gruss in St. James-the-Less Church, Bethnal Green, and the following year he graduated from St. Michael Theological College, Aberdare.

He served in various churches in South East England from 1900-1921, including the East End Mission in Stepney from 1902-1903. From 1921-1952 he was Vicar of St. Paul's Church, Gosset Street, Bethnal Green.

When he arrived at St. Paul's Parish there were only six members in the congregation on Sunday's. In the 1930s it was described as the poorest parish in London. After awhile the Sunday evening congregation grew to more than a thousand people, but the collections were only 16s. 6d (85p), mostly in halfpennies and farthings.

He spent all his money in providing amenities for his parishioners, and even mortgaged his own property to pay for a fortnight's holiday for a 1,000 children every year at Bicknacre, Essex.

In 1931 he was elected as a Progressive Party Member to Bethnal Green Council but lost the seat in l934.

Articles
The Star 31st March 1936
Bethnal Green News 15th July 1933
Crockford's Clerical Directory 1963-64

JOSEPH, Ernest Martin   1877-1960
Architect

Ernest Joseph was born in London, the son of an architect, and he was educated at St. Paul's School and Cheltenham College. Regular visitors to his home were H.G. Wells and Israel ZANGWILL.

On leaving school he joined his father's firm and became a voluntary manager at Brady Boy's Club in Whitechapel; he also became an officer in the Jewish Lads' Brigade. He was a keen photographer and ran a photography group in the club for many years. During the first World War he was in the Royal Army Service Corps and built numerous canteens for the armed forces. After the war he continued this work, becoming first, director of works and then consultant.

Joseph re-opened the Brady Boys' Club in 1919 and re-designed the building in 1936. In 1935 he designed the Brady Girls' Club in Hanbury Street, E1.

He was the founder of the Old Boys' Club and the moving spirit in purchasing Skeet Hill House - a country house in Kent for the use of club members.

He designed many buildings in London, his best known being Shell Mex House on the Victoria Embankment, Westminster.

Biography
Anon. *E.M.J.* (Privately Published, 1962)

KENTON, Benjamin   1719-1800
Vintner and Philanthropist

Benjamin Kenton was born in Fieldgate Street, Whitechapel where his mother kept a greengrocers shop. At the age of fifteen he was apprenticed to the keeper of the *Angel and Crown Inn*, Whitechapel, and he later became waiter and drawer at the *Crown and Magpie* in Aldgate. When the owner died Kenton took over. He made his fortune by discovering how to bottle ale that could pass through the changes of climate on the journey to India around the Cape, without the cork flying out of the bottle.

He amassed great wealth and retired to live in Gower Street, Holborn.

He was elected a Member of the Vintners' Company in 1734 and master in 1776; there is a portrait of him in the Court room.

He gave £5,000 to St. Bartholomew's Hospital and many other charities.

He is buried within the sanctuary of St. Dunstan's Church, where there is a monument by Westmacott.

Book
Locks, W.A. (ed) *East London Antiquities* (East London Advertiser, 1902)

DNB

refusing to levy Poplar's share of the London County Council, Police and Metropolitan Asylum contributions on the grounds that local rate payers were already impoverished with high levels of unemployment. He explained the councillors' position in his pamphlet – *Guilty and Proud of It; Poplar's Answer*.

He is commemorated by Charles Key Lodge, Southern Grove, E3, a home for physically disabled people.

Charles Key (left) receiving the casket containing the Freedom of the Borough scroll from Councillor Guy, Mayor of Poplar on the 9th November 1953

KEY, Charles William 1883-1964
Schoolmaster and Politician

Charles Key's father died when he was six and his mother took in a lodger, Ernest Linder who paid for Charles to go for training at the Mile End Pupil Teachers' School, Essex Street, Mile End.

Returning from the army in 1919 he settled in Poplar and began his career as a member of Poplar Borough Council which continued until 1940. He was the only person to have been Mayor of Poplar three times. In 1953 he was given the freedom of the borough.

Charles Key was headmaster of Dingle Lane School, Pennyfields, E14 for some years, resigning this position to enter politics full-time, with the Labour Party.

He was elected Member of Parliament for Bow and Bromley in 1940, succeeding George LANSBURY, and retained the seat for 24 years. He became Parliamentary Secretary to the Ministry of Health 1945-1946 and Ministry of Works 1947-1950.

In the second World War he was Regional Commissioner for Civil Defence.

Charles Key was sent to Brixton prison with other Poplar Councillors in 1921 for

LANE, James Charles (Jimmy)
1884-1956
Wrestler and Weightlifter

Born in St. Leonard's Road, Bromley-by-Bow, James Lane attended St. Leonard's Road School and on leaving, became a 'printer's devil', an errand boy in a printing office.

Seeing one of the printers lift the heavy litho stones he followed his example. He became interested in weightlifting and joined first the Poplar Club and then the Apollo Club, Bethnal Green. In 1902 and 1903 he was middleweight champion weightlifter and wrestler of Great Britain.

One of the most difficult bouts of his career was a contest with the Russian wrestler, Barney Shlitzer. When they were pitted against each other the contest lasted five hours five minutes without a break and without a fall, creating a world record. There were no rounds in those days; it was just one continuous effort to beat the other man. The following Saturday they started again but after two and a half hours they gave it up. Jimmy Lane later turned professional.

Jimmy Lane was also interested in rowing and was a stroke for the Viking Rowing Club.

He became licensee of the *Bombay Grab*, Bow Road, E3, 1942-1956.

LANE, William 1745(?)-1814
Publisher

William Lane was probably born in Whitechapel, the son of John Lane, poulterer, and his wife Mary.

He became a liveryman of the Poulterers Company in 1767 and in the same year was admitted to the Honourable Artillery Company in which he was to achieve some eminence.

He began his bookselling activities about 1770 from his father's shop, but had moved to 13 Aldgate High Street, City by the end of

1773. It was at this time that his first publications came out, among them the *Ladies Museum*, 1773-1814, and he then began to explore the possibilities of starting circulating libraries.

He retained his interest in the Honourable Artillery Company, but also joined the Stationer's Company, becoming a liveryman at the time of his move to 33 Leadenhall Street in the City.

About 1784 he set up a press there and founded an ambitious system of circulating libraries; he offered a stock of books, a catalogue and instructions to anyone wishing to set up a library.

William Lane was among the early backers of the first evening daily paper *The Star and Evening Advertiser*.

By 1790 he had adopted the title Minerva Press and under this imprint produced light romantic novels which mainly constituted the staple fare of his circulating libraries. The books were primarily intended for female readership and included a number of translations from the French and books by women novelists.

DNB, Missing Persons (1993)

LANSBURY, Elizabeth Jane
1860-1933
Suffragette

Born in Stepney, Elizabeth Brine attended St. Mary School, Whitechapel, where she first knew George LANSBURY. Her father was the owner of a saw mills and veneer works, where George LANSBURY eventually worked.

Elizabeth and George were married in 1880, when she was 19, and at first they had a very hard life. They had 12 children, four sons and eight daughters. It was a very happy partnership and they celebrated their Golden Wedding in 1930.

She was a supporter of the women's suffrage.

She is commemorated by Elizabeth Lansbury Nursery School, Cordelia Street, E14, and Brine House, Ford Road, E3.

LANSBURY, George   1859-1940
Politician

Born near Lowestoft, George Lansbury's association with East London began when his parents moved to Bethnal Green and then Whitechapel in 1868. He attended St. Mary School Whitechapel, his formal education ending at 14; for a time he worked unloading coal trucks.

In 1880 he married Elizabeth BRINE, daughter of the owner of a saw mills and veneer works, St. Stephen's Road, Bow. He sailed with his family to Australia in 1884, but the venture was a failure and he returned to England the next year. He was offered a partnership in the business of his father-in-law, and he made a home at 39 Bow Road, where he lived for the rest of his life.

Influenced by Christian socialists he entered local politics, first as a radical but in 1890 he was converted to socialism.

In 1892 he was elected to the Poplar Board of Guardians and was a moving spirit with Joseph FELS in setting up the Hollesley Bay colony for unemployed men.

George Lansbury had a remarkable knowledge of conditions and labour in inner London and was appointed to the Royal Commission on Poor Laws. At the end of its sittings he was one of our four signatories of what became a famous minority report.

Elected to Poplar Borough Council in 1903 he became Mayor in 1922 and 1936. He was sent to Brixton Prison with other Poplar Councillors in 1921 for refusing to levy Poplar's share of the London County Council, Police and Metropolitan Asylum contributions on the grounds that local rate payers were already impoverished with high levels of unemployment. He held meetings inside the prison with other councillors and spoke to crowds each day through the bars of his cell. The term 'Poplarism' became a word of national significance and was given an entry in the *Oxford English Dictionary*.

George Lansbury was elected Member of Parliament for Bow and Bromley in 1910, resigning in 1912 to stand again as a supporter of women's suffrage. He was defeated, and not re-elected until 1922. He founded the *Daily Herald* and edited it until 1922, when it became the official paper of the Labour Party. In 1929 he was appointed First Commissioner of Works in Ramsay MacDonald's Government and he opened up London's Royal Parks for games.

A great worker for peace, he undertook a series of journeys in 1937 to see heads of states, including Adolf Hitler, to attempt to persuade them to disarm.

From 1931 to 1935 he was Leader of the Labour Party and Leader of the Opposition in Parliament. He resigned over the re-armament issue and was succeeded by C.R. ATTLEE.

George Lansbury in 1921

He was a great friend to all working people in Poplar and gave of himself freely on their behalf. When he died on 7th May 1940 large crowds attended his funeral. His home at 39 Bow Road was demolished in an air raid shortly afterwards.

He is commemorated by the Lansbury Estate in Poplar, built in 1951 as part of the Festival of Britain, an exhibition of British trades and arts held to celebrate the centenary of the Great Exhibition of 1851. Lansbury Gardens and Lansbury Lodge, Grundy Street, E14, a home for the elderly, were also named after him.

Biography
Postgate, R. *The Life of George Lansbury* (Longmans, Green, 1951)

DLB, DNB

LAWRENCE, Arabella Susan
1871-1947
Politician

Susan Lawrence was born into a London legal family. After obtaining an honours degree in mathematics at Cambridge she began her political career as a Conservative member of the London School Board in 1900.

In 1910 she was elected Conservative member for West Marylebone on the London County Council. However, her practical experience there and new lines of thought led her to resign her seat, and in 1912 she joined the Independent Labour Party and came to live in Poplar, just off the East India Dock Road. She

Susan Lawrence in November 1923 *Newham Library Service*

was elected Member for South Poplar on the London County Council from 1913-1928. An Alderman of Poplar Borough Council 1919-1924, she went to Holloway Prison with other women councillors over the rates dispute.

Susan Lawrence was the first woman Member of the London County Council, and the first woman to be elected to Parliament for a London borough, representing East Ham North in 1923-1924 and 1926-1931. She was the first Labour woman to address the House of Commons and the first woman Chairman of the Labour Party, succeeding Herbert Morrison in 1930.

She was appointed Parliamentary Secretary to Arthur Greenwood, Minister of Health, 1929-1931.

She is commemorated in the borough by Susan Lawrence Primary School, Cordelia Street, E14, and Susan Lawrence House, Zealand Road, E3.

DLB, DNB

Rev. Lax, the Mayor, at the Old English Fair which he opened in Poplar Recreation Ground in August 1919

LAX, Rev. William Henry
1868-1937
Methodist Preacher

William Lax was born in Lancashire. After his training for the ministry he was appointed to Poplar Methodist Church in 1902 and was Minister for 35 years. At the time, this was a record period of service for a Methodist Minister at one church. He went on to become the Superintendent of the Poplar and Bow Methodist Mission.

He was an Alderman of Poplar Borough Council for 17 years and Mayor of Poplar in 1918. He claimed to be the originator of the 'street peace teas' and the 'street party' held in the first place to commemorate the Armistice of 1918. Almost every street had its own celebration.

William Lax realised that churchmen were generally reluctant to use the film medium with its predominantly unsuitable films, but he believed it could be improved. Poplar Mission's own cinema service for example was well attended. In 1934 J. Arthur Rank the industrialist and film producer whom Lax appreciated for his 'acute and sensitive perception of moral issues' made his first film, *The Mastership of Christ* featuring the work of William Lax.

Autobiography
Lax; His Book (Epworth Press, 1937)

Sir John Leake

LEAKE, Sir John 1656-1720
Admiral

John Leake was born at Rotherhithe. He served first in the merchant navy, then joined the Royal Navy, obtaining rapid promotion.

Elected M.P. for Rochester 1708-1714, he later became a Lord of the Admiralty and then Chairman of the Board of Admiralty.

He lived in Grove Place, now Adelina Grove, Mile End, and was buried in St. Dunstan's Church, Stepney.

Biography
Martin-Leake, S. *The Life of Sir John Leake* (Navy Records Society, 1920)

LEAN, Sir David 1908-1991
Film Director

David Lean was born in Croydon. He was forbidden to go to the cinema by his parents who were Quakers who regarded film-going as a sin. From school, he would go to see what films he could, and at the age of twenty he joined Gaumont British studios as an unpaid teaboy.

His rise there was rapid, within a few years he had become Chief Editor of Gaumont News.

In 1934 David Lean graduated to editing feature films, and by the end of the decade he was known as the best and reputedly highest paid editor of the British film industry. He regarded editing as the most interesting job, and even to the end of his career he insisted on cutting his own films.

His first assignment in 1942 was Noel Coward's *In Which We Serve*. The film was highly successful and led to the formation of Cineguild, a production company which included Noel Coward and himself as Directors.

The first three films were Noel Coward's *This Happy Breed*, *Blithe Spirit* and *Brief Encounter*. His other well known films included *The Bridge on the River Kwai* which won seven Oscars, *Dr. Zhivago*, *Passage to India*, and many more.

He was married five times.

In 1983 he bought four derelict warehouses at Sun Wharf, Narrow Street, E1, and spent £6 million converting it into a large four floor home which included a private cinema. He settled there in his last four years.

Book
Heaton, D. and Higgins, J. (eds) *Lives Remembered* (Blewberry Press, 1991)

Article
East London Advertiser 7th April 1994

LEDINGHAM, Professor John (Jack) 1916-1993
Professor of Medicine

Jack Ledingham was born in Edmonton. Although graduating in physics at University College, London, Jack Ledingham decided his main interest was in medicine and he qualified as a doctor in 1942.

Service in the Royal Army Medical Corps took him to France, Lebanon, Palestine and India. He joined his old medical college at the London Hospital, Whitechapel as a junior lecturer in 1948.

The prime interest at the time was to unravel the various causes of high blood pressure. In this field Jack Ledingham was to acquire an international reputation, concentrating on the connection between kidney disease and raised blood pressures and the part played by the heart in this condition.

His research work was permeated by a profound attention to detail and an objectivity and integrity, providing a lesson to all who worked with him.

He was awarded, in 1964, a personal Chair of Experimental Medicine, and he succeeded to the Chair of Medicine at the London Hospital Medical College in 1971.

Jack Ledingham was always interested in the patient as a whole person, combining a caring approach with a meticulous attention to detail. This was combined with a transparent kindness to his patients, his students and his junior staff.

He was much in demand as a teacher and examiner at home and abroad.

Obituary
The Independent 21st September 1993

Muriel Lester with Councillor Gillender, Mayor of Poplar at her 80th birthday party on the 9th December 1963

LEIJONHJELM, Baroness Emma
1847-1937
Seamen's Friend

Emma Leijonhjelm was born in Gothenburg. She married a Swedish Baron, the captain of a sailing ship, and sailed round the world several times. She later settled in Poplar and when her husband died, decided to devote herself to social work among seamen.

She lived at 7 West India Dock Road for nearly 50 years, where she held services for seamen and became known to seamen throughout the world as a 'kind mother' who would always help if they were in trouble. There was a constant stream of callers at her little house. She was quite fearless; there was no public house, street or court where she feared to go if needed.

LESTER, Muriel 1886-1965 &
LESTER, Veronica Doris 1883-1968
Founders of Kingsley Hall

Muriel and Doris Lester were born in Leytonstone of Baptist parents; their father was a wealthy shipowner, who offered them an income of £400 a year each, which they refused.

In 1903, both sisters became interested in the Bow branch of the Factory Girl's Evening Homes. They came to live at 60 Bruce Road, E3, and started a club for girls and a nursery school named 'Children's House'. In 1915 they also founded Kingsley Hall Settlement, named after their late brother. The settlement moved from its premises in Botolph Road, Bow to a purpose-built building in Powis Road, Bow, E3, in 1928

Their friendship with Mahatma GANDHI led to his residence at Kingsley Hall while visiting London in 1931 for the Round Table Conference on India. A London County Council Blue Plaque was erected in 1954 to mark this visit by Mahatma Gandhi.

Muriel Lester became a worker for the Peace Movement, the Fellowship of Reconciliation and was given the Freedom of the Borough of Poplar in 1964.

Autobiographies
Lester, M. *It Occurred To Me* (Harper, 1937)
Lester, D. *Just Children* (Privately Published, 1961)

LEVIN, Benjamin 1903-1977
Music Hall and Radio Entertainer

Benjamin Levin was born at 16 Brick Lane, Whitechapel, where his Russian-born father Rubin Levin, a master butcher, lived and had a shop.

He attended the Jews' Free School, Bell Lane, Spitalfields and later began working as a butcher's boy.

Mile End Empire theatre, Mile End Road, Stepney was the venue for his debut stage performance. By the 1930's he was a famous entertainer, calling himself 'Issy Bonn'. His first radio broadcast was in 1935 and he calculated that he had made over 100 broadcasts and sung over 500 different songs.

Over a million and a half records were sold in his career. His most popular songs were *My Yiddische Momma* and *When the Lights Go On Again*.

Ted (Kid) Lewis photographed in about 1915
East London Advertiser

LEWIS, Ted (Kid) 1894-1970
Boxer

Ted (Kid) Lewis was born Gershon Mendeloff at 56 Umberston Street, St. George's-in-the-East, the son of a cabinet maker. He began as a sparring boxer for a pittance, when he was 15, at the Wonderland in Mile End Road, and the Premierland, Back Church Lane, Whitechapel, and fought under the name Ted (Kid) Lewis. Altogether he recorded 249 fights with only 24 defeats.

His first title was British featherweight, which he won when he was 18. He then went on to become European champion. Later he won British welterweight and middle weight titles.

He was the first British boxer to win a world title in America, by beating Jack Britton in August 1915. He lost to Britton in April 1916, regained the title from him in June 1917 and lost again to him in March 1919.

Biography

Lewis, M. *Ted Kid Lewis; his Life and Times* (Robson, 1990)

Morrison, I. *Boxing Who's Who* (Guinness Publishing, 2nd edn.,1993)

LIEBERMAN, Aaron 1849-1880
A Founder of Socialist Zionism

Aaron Lieberman was born in Grodno, Russia. His early education was strictly religiously orthodox, and he became a fine orator and linguist. As a young man he joined a revolutionary circle and was recruited to write for a radical socialist journal. In 1875 his revolutionary group was broken up by the Czar's police, and Aaron Lieberman made his way to London.

Shocked by the living and working conditions of the Jewish immigrants in Whitechapel, with other radicals, Aaron Lieberman set up a Hebrew Socialist Union. His first meeting was held at 40 Gun Street, Old Artillery Ground, Spitalfields on 13th May 1876, and he was the secretary and leading speaker.

His subsequent career was as a writer for socialist journals in Europe; he was imprisoned in Vienna in 1878 for ten months; returned to Whitechapel in 1879 and lived at 21 Elder Street, Spitalfields, where he attempted to set up a Jewish Working Mens' Benefit and Educational Society.

Dissillusioned, he emigrated to America in 1880 and committed suicide there in that year.

Book

Fishman, W.J. *East End Radicals* (Duckworth, 1975)

LINTON, William James 1812-1898
Engraver, Poet and Political Reformer

Born at Ireland Row, Mile End Road, Mile End Old Town, William Linton was educated at a school in Stratford. In 1828, he was apprenticed to George Bonner, a wood engraver. In association with a fellow engraver, John Orrin

Smith, Linton introduced considerable improvements in English wood engraving.

William Linton developed radical views of religion and politics, and in 1839 he established *The National*, a weekly newspaper for the reprint of extracts of political publications inaccessible to the working man. However, the paper did not last long.

Linton worked on engravings for the *Illustrated London News* established in 1842. By 1855 he had firmly established himself as the best wood engraver of his day and was much in demand for book illustrations.

He went to America in 1866 and devoted much time to the regeneration of American wood engraving, producing a number of books on the subject. His best known book *The Masters of Wood-Engraving* was published in 1889. His drama *Claribel* was published in 1865 and he also produced a volume of verse from his private press.

Linton wrote a life of the American poet John Greenleaf Whittier and an autobiography in 1895. He was described as a man 'amiable and helpful, full of kind actions and generous enthusiasms'.

A collection of his pamphlets and other material is in the British Library.

Biography
Smith, F.B. *Radical Artisan* (Manchester University Press, 1973)

LITTLE, Dr. William John
1810-1894
Physician and Surgeon

William Little was born at the *Red Lion*, Aldgate, where his father was the landlord. At the age of two he contracted poliomyelitis, leaving him with a club foot. He went to school at Dover and Calais and when he was 15 he was appprenticed to a surgeon-apothecary in Whitechapel. He then became a student at the London Hospital, qualifying MRCS in 1832.

In 1832 he went to Europe, visiting Leyden, Leipzig, Dresden and Berlin, where he met the surgeon Stremeyer who operated on his foot. The result was successful and Little was allowed to perform similar operations in Hanover and Berlin.

In l837 as the result of his studies in Berlin he was awarded the degree of M.D. and he returned to the London Hospital, Whitechapel where he became Assistant Physician and later Physician.

He practised as a consultant in Finsbury Square and with friends collected funds to start the Orthopaedic Institution in Bloomsbury Square. Opened in 1840 it was the first such hospital established in England. In 1845 the hospital moved to Hanover Square and was re-named the Royal Orthopaedic Hospital.

In 1861 he published a paper providing the first investigation into the cause of spastic rigidity of the limbs of new-born children. This led to the universal use of the term 'Little's Disease' for the group of disabilities – spastic diplegia.

He retired from practice in 1884 suffering from deafness.

William Little was the father of Louis Stremeyer Little, Surgeon to the London Hospital, and E. Muirhead Little, also an orthopaedic surgeon.

A commemorative plaque was placed outside the *Red Lion* in 1961.

LONDON, Jack   1876-1916
Writer

Jack London was born in America and his father was probably a wandering astrologer called Professor Chaney. Jack London spent an adventurous youth in smuggling oysters, worked in the gold mines of the Klondyke, and went to sea with the whaling fleet.

His writing skills developed in observing and describing animals – *The Call of the Wild* (1903), being one of his best known books.

In 1902 he came to Whitechapel, obtaining lodgings in Flower and Dean Street, and wrote *The People of the Abyss* (1903), which gives an account of his two months experience in local doss houses and workhouses, and describes the living conditions of some East Londoners at the time.

Biography
Barltrop, R. *Jack London, the Man, the Writer, the Rebel* (Pluto, 1977)

LOSS, Joshua Zalig (Joe)
MVO, OBE   1909-1990
Band Leader

Joe Loss was born at 16 Grey Eagle Street, Spitalfields, the son of Israel Loss who was a cabinet maker. At the age of thirteen he won a scholarship to Trinity College of Music, and he began working by playing the violin during the showing of silent films.

At the age of twenty he was Britain's youngest band leader at the Astoria ballroom in Charing Cross Road, WC1 He became, by

Royal Appointment, Band Leader to HM Queen Elizabeth II, playing at the wedding balls for Princess Margaret, Princess Alexandra and Princess Anne. He also played for the Queen's fiftieth birthday party.

His famous signature tune *In the Mood*, borrowed from Glenn Miller, sold over a million copies, and he became EMI's longest serving artist. Among performers he helped to launch were Vera Lynn, Eamonn Andrews, Spike Milligan and Michael Bentine.

His band played all over the world, his purpose he said, "was to bring people together". He claimed to have married more people than the average vicar!

Joe Loss was a tireless worker for charity, particularly helpful to 'Age Concern'.

He was created MVO and OBE.

LOWDER, Rev. Charles Fuge
1820-1880
Priest

Charles Lowder was born in Bath, and educated at King's College School, London and Oxford. After several curacies he came to St. George-in-the-East Church to set up a preaching Mission which was based in Calvert Street, and Wellclose Square, E1.

He became widely known and respected for his work among poor people. The High Church views and practices of Charles Lowder and the clergy team at St. George-in-the-East provoked riotous behaviour in 1859, and there were disturbances at a number of services. The church was closed down for a time by order of the Bishop but re-opened a month or two later when order was kept by police.

Charles Lowder was responsible for raising the money to build St. Peter's Church, London Docks, consecrated 1866, and his work for local people during the severe cholera epidemic of that time earned him great respect.

He died on holiday in Austria and was buried in the churchyard at Chislehurst, Kent.

He is commemorated locally by Lowder House, Wapping Lane, E1.

Book
Lowder, C. *Twenty-one Years at St. George's Mission* (Rivington, 1877)

Biographies
Trench, M. *Charles Lowder* (Kegan Paul, 1882)
Ellsworth, L.E. *Charles Lowder and the Ritualistic Movement* (Darton, Longman and Todd, 1982)
DNB

Eva C.E. Lückes *The Royal London Hospital Trust Archives*

LÜCKES, Eva Charlotte Ellis CBE 1855-1919
Matron of the London Hospital

Born in Gloucestershire, Eva Lückes was educated at Malvern School and Cheltenham Ladies College. She trained at Middlesex and Westminster Hospitals. For a few months in 1779 she was a night sister at the London Hospital, Whitechapel.

She was appointed Lady Superintendent at Pendlebury Childrens' Hospital in Manchester. In 1880 she became Matron at the London Hospital at the age of 25 and was there for nearly forty years. Immediately on her appointment she began to introduce reforms, improving cleanliness, the quality of food, and general nursing standards in the wards.

Eva Lückes improved the standards of nursing by training and examinations in the Nursing School established by her predecessor Miss Swift in 1879. In 1895 the Preliminary Training School was opened at Tredegar House, 97-99 Bow Road, E3, the first in the country.

She persuaded the hospital governors to build the first nurses' home, the Eva Lückes Home in 1906 in Oxford Street, later Stepney Way.

She was awarded CBE in 1917.

Books
Collins, S.M. *The Royal London Hospital; a brief history* (Royal London Hospital Archives and Museum, 1995)
Clarke-Kennedy, A.E. *The London* (Pitman-Medical, 1962)
Biography
McEwan, M. *Eva C. Lückes* (London Hospital League of Nurses, 1958)

LUCY, Joseph (Joe) 1930-1991
Boxer

Joseph Lucy was born at the London Hospital. He was the son of a dock labourer and his wife who lived at 24 Stayners Road, Stepney.

He was a member of the Repton Boxing Club, and achieved the unique distinction of winning the London Federation of Boys' Clubs Championships in four successive years.

Joseph Lucy represented the Army at welterweight, and when he was demobilised in 1950 he turned professional, under the guidance of Jim Wicks. He began well by only losing one of his first fifteen fights. In 1954 he beat Tommy McGovern for the Southern Area Championships, and nine months later beat him again for the British Lightweight title.

As British champion he went to Johannesberg in 1955, but lost a close contest of fifteen rounds to Johnny van Rensberg for the Empire title. In April, that year, he lost his British title to Frank Johnson but regained it from Johnson in 1956 and defended it successfully against Sammy McCarthy.

He had difficulty in making the lightweight limit of 9st. 9lbs., and lost the Championship to Dave Charnley in 1957.

On retiring from the ring, he became a publican at several well known public houses with gymnasiums attached.

DNB

McCallum, Colin Whitton
1852-1945
Comedian

Colin McCallum was born at 25 Sydney (now Sidney) Square, Mile End Old Town. He took his stage name, Charles Coborn, from Coborn Road, Bow near to where he lived as a child.

He immortalised two songs which were sung for the first time at the Paragon Music Hall, Mile End Road in 1886, *Two Lovely Black eyes* and *The Man Who Broke the Bank at Monte Carlo*.

McCallum was an active campaigner for improvement of music hall working conditions and was largely responsible for forming the Music Hall Artists Association and later the Music Hall Benevolent Fund.
Autobiography
Coborn, C. *The Man Who Broke the Bank* (Hutchinson, 1928)

MACCOBY, Rabbi Hayim Zunden 1858-1916
Maggid-Preacher

Hayim Maccoby was born in Russia and had a troubled boyhood and early manhood, through persecution. He escaped from Russia and came to London in 1890, living in Charlotte de Rothschild Dwellings, Thrawl Street, Spitalfields.

Rabbi Maccoby was a champion of orthodoxy and pioneer of Zionism whose preaching attracted large crowds. Many individuals called at his home for advice and inspiration.
Biography
Jung, J. *Champions of Orthodoxy* (J.Jung, 1974)

McDOUGALL, Sir John 1844-1917
Miller

John McDougall was born in Manchester. In 1845 his father, Alexander McDougall began in business as a manufacturing chemist, selling sheep dip, scouring soap and disinfectants. Alexander's five sons, Alexander, Isaac Shimwell, James Thomas, John and Arthur were eventually recruited into the business, and in 1864 they took up the search for, and production of raising agents other than yeast. They revolutionised home baking with McDougall's self-raising flour.

In 1869 John and James McDougall came to London to expand the milling business. In partnership with the other three brothers from the chemical side of the business, they leased land in Millwall in 1871 and built a fertilizer factory. From about 1879 the factory was partially used for the production of McDougall's Self Raising Flour when the great increases in grain imports began arriving at Millwall Dock. In 1887 or 1895 the first Wheatsheaf Mill was built there and John McDougall became responsible for its management.

He was a Member of the Port of London Authority which controlled Millwall Dock and the other London Docks, and was elected to the first London County Council in 1889, representing the Progressive Party. He was the Council's Chairman in 1902-1903, when he was knighted, and remained a Member of the Council until 1913. His main interests there, were in the Main Drainage Committee and the Asylums Committee, where he did much to improve administration and conditions for mental patients.

During the air raids of September 1940 which set fire to the docks, the Wheatsheaf Mill was the only building in the area to remain unscathed.

Ranks Hovis McDougalls Ltd, as the company later became known, closed the mill in 1982 and the buildings were demolished in 1984-1985.

He is commemorated by Sir John McDougall Gardens, E14.

Pamphlet
A Matter of History (McDougall's Ltd.,1964)
Obituaries
East London Advertiser 19th May 1917
East London Observer 19th May 1917
Survey of London Vol. 43 Poplar, Blackwall and the Isle of Dogs (Athlone, 1994)

McMILLAN, Margaret CH, CBE
1860-1931
Educationalist

Margaret McMillan was born in New York. At the age of five, both her father and a sister died, and her mother, who was from the Scottish Highlands, brought Margaret and her sister Rachel to live in Inverness. Margaret was educated at Inverness High School and Academy, later studying music at Frankfurt and languages at Geneva and Lausanne. Moving to Bradford, she joined the Independent Labour Party, becoming widely known as the 'Labour Prophetess of the North'.

She became interested in education, and served on the Bradford School Board; she encouraged the development of physical education, and in 1899 she arranged the first recorded medical inspection of children in an English elementary school.

Margaret McMillan came to London in 1902, and together with her sister Rachel opened a children's clinic at Devons Road School, Bow, in 1908. As the clinic served only one school, it was not cost-effective, and the work moved in 1910 to Deptford where there was the opportunity to provide for children from a group of schools. A pioneering open-air nursery school was opened, arousing worldwide interest, and in 1930 the Rachel McMillan Training College was founded for the training of nursery school teachers. The College is now part of the Deptford Campus of the University of Greenwich.

Her biographer Albert MANSBRIDGE, who first met Margaret McMillan in 1903 when he sought her help in developing the newly-founded Workers' Educational Association, wrote that: 'In operative power and influence in promoting legislation, Margaret McMillan affected the education of elementary school children more than any other person'.

She was appointed CBE in 1917, and made a Companion of Honour in 1930.

Biography
Lowndes, G.A.N. *Margaret McMillan* (Museum Press, 1960)

DNB

MACPHERSON, Annie P.
1824-1904
Founder of the Home of Industry and Bethnal Green Medical Mission

Annie Macpherson was the eldest of seven children and educated in Glasgow. Her father, a Quaker, was a teacher who studied the work of the educational reformers Pestalozzi and Froebel. Attending classes with her father she became interested in the techniques and was later trained as a teacher in Froebel's methods in Gray's Inn Road, City.

In 1858 Annie Macpherson and her widowed mother moved to Cambridgeshire to be near one of her married sisters. Whilst attending an evangelical meeting in Shoreditch in 1861 she had a profound spiritual experience and started to preach and teach among the rural population in Cambridgeshire.

The following year she moved to London and through her involvement in the revival movement learned of the misery and squalor that existed in the East End. On discovering that children, as young as three years old, were engaged in the home industry of making matchboxes she wrote *The Little Matchbox Makers* to publicise their plight. As a result of this publicity, money was sent for the young matchboxworkers and Annie Macpherson was able to arrange evening classes.

By 1866 sufficient money had been collected for her to acquire a former warehouse and cholera hospital at 60 Commercial Street, Spitalfields. For the first three years the Home of Industry's main work was with children. They were trained in simple tasks and taught reading and writing. The Home's expenditure for the first year was met entirely by readers of *The Christian* newspaper.

In 1869 Annie Macpherson put out a circular, headed 'Emigration is the only remedy for chronic pauperism in the East End'. She pioneered a policy of emigration to Canada and over a period of 55 years sent nearly 9,000 East London children to begin a new life.

In 1869 Miss Macpherson developed the Bird Fair Mission on Sunday mornings in the market streets around Petticoat Lane. She was Vice-president of the Bible Flower Mission, founded in 1876, which distributed flowers with texts to patients in the London hospitals. The warehouse in Commercial Street, Spitalfields was given up in 1887 and the Home of Industry moved to 29 Bethnal Green Road. In 1901 Miss Macpherson's nephew, Dr. Merry, began treating people at the Home and this medical work became an integral part of the Home providing poor people with free medical care. The change in emphasis of the work made new premises essential and in November 1925 the Home of Industry acquired the present site at 305 Cambridge Heath Road, E2. The following year the name was changed to The Bethnal Green Medical Mission with the addition in brackets of the words The Annie Macpherson Home of Industry Inc.

Books

Wagner, G. *Children of the Empire* (Weidenfeld and Nicolson, 1982)

Walker, H. *East London; Sketches of Christian Work and Workers* (The Religious Tract Society, 1896)

Pamphlet

Bethnal Green Medical Mission, *A Clean Thing Out of an Unclean; A Short History of Bethnal Green Medical Mission, 1866-1966* (Bethnal Green Medical Mission, c.1966)

MALLON, James Joseph 1875-1961
Warden of Toynbee Hall

James Mallon was born in Manchester. After going to University he joined the staff of Ancoats Settlement, Manchester.

He came to work at Toynbee Hall, a university settlement in 1906 and was appointed Warden in 1919, serving for 35 years. He was passionately interested in problems of poverty, employment, wages, education and all forms of social betterment. Under him Toynbee Hall became a centre of social experiment and action, an educational institution and a place for community life and arts.

In his early days he was secretary of the National League to establish a minimum wage. This led to the passing of the Trade Boards Act, 1909, which set minimum wages in several industries. He organised the building of the education block, opened in 1938, and Toynbee Hall became known as the 'poor man's university'.

In 1935 he formed the Council of Citizens of East London to combat anti-semitism, and he had much to do with the passing of the Public Order Act which prohibited the wearing of uniforms by political organisations.

He became a Governor of the BBC, served on the committees of the Whitechapel Art Gallery, the People's Palace and the London Museum, and on many other public bodies.

There is a bust of him by Sir Jacob Epstein in Toynbee Hall.

He is commemorated by Mallon Gardens, Commercial Street, E1, and Mallon House, Carr Street, E14.

MANN, Sir Edward 1854-1943
Brewer

Edward Mann was born in Norfolk. He was the grandson of James Mann who founded the Albion Brewery, Whitechapel Road, in 1808.

In 1900 he was elected the first Mayor of Stepney and then elected for a second term. He was created baronet in 1905 and became Chairman of Mann, Crossman and Paulin in 1916. He was Master of the Worshipful Company of Brewers and Chairman of the London Hospital.

His son, F.T. Mann and his grandson, F.G. Mann, both played cricket for Middlesex and England.

He is commemorated by Edward Mann Close, Pitsea Street, E1.

Book

Janes, H. *Albion Brewery 1808-1958* (Harley Publishing Co., 1958)

Burke's Baronetage

MANN, Tom 1856-1941
Trade Union Leader

Tom Mann was born near Coventry. His mother died when he was two years old. He had only three years of schooling; and by the age of nine years he worked on a colliery farm. When Tom was ten he became a pit worker, dragging boxes of coal to keep the air courses clear. He had to crawl on all fours, harnessed to the box by a belt and chain.

Tom Mann was later apprenticed to a toolmaker in Birmingham and after a five month's strike in 1872 his working hours were reduced from 14 to 9 hours a day.

The shorter hours of work enabled him to attend general and technical courses in the evenings; he also joined a Bible class and became a Sunday School teacher. He moved to London and then went to New York for a few months. It was at this time that he developed a friendship with Frederick Engels, Eleanor Marx and John Burns while he was working for the Social Democratic Federation.

On his return to London in 1889 he was enlisted by Ben TILLETT to help in the London Dock Strike. He became, until 1893, first President of the Docker's Union. He was a great orator, and with Ben Tillett, formed a famous partnership, both becoming greatly sought after as speakers at meetings.

In 1891 he was one of seven Labour members appointed to the Royal Commission on Labour. He was the first secretary of the London Reform Union, campaigning for a simplification of the administration of London. He became first secretary of the Independent Labour Party in 1894 but gave this up to work for the International Federation of Ship, Dock and River Workers which he had founded and of which he was the first President.

Autobiography
Memoirs (McGibbon and Kee, 1967)
Biography
Torr, D. *Tom Mann* (Lawrence and Wishart, 1944)
DLB, DNB

MANNING, Rev. Henry Edward
1808-1892
Cardinal

Henry Manning was born at Totteridge, Herts. He was educated at Harrow School and Oxford and ordained into the Church of England.

He became a Roman Catholic in 1851 and in 1865 was appointed Archbishop of Westminster, the diocese including the borough of Tower Hamlets.

Cardinal Manning was the prime mover in the settlement of the Dock Strike of 1889, a member of the Royal Commissions on Housing (1885) and Education (1886).

He was buried in Westminster Cathedral, where there is a bronze effigy of him. He is commemorated locally by Manning House, Halley Street, E14.

Biographies
McClelland, V.A. *Cardinal Manning* (Oxford University Press,1962)
Reynolds, E.E. *Three Cardinals* (Burns, Oates, 1958)
DNB

MANSBRIDGE, Albert 1876-1952
Founder of the Workers' Educational Association

Albert Mansbridge was born in Gloucester, from where his family moved to London and he attended Battersea Grammar School. Leaving school at 14 he became a copyist in the Department of Inland Revenue and after several other jobs came to work for the Co-operative Wholesale Society. In 1901 he became cashier of the Co-operative Permanent Building Society. During these years he had continued his studies at King's College, London, becoming an evening class teacher in industrial history and economics.

His mother, who was one of the earliest members of the Women's Co-operation Guild at St. Jude's Church, Whitechapel, introduced him to Toynbee Hall, Whitechapel, a university settlement, where he became an occasional student.

From his experience of evening classes both as a student and teacher, Mansbridge concluded that the time was ripe for a big step forward in adult education. The University Extension Movement founded in 1873 had made some appeal to the working class, but was largely a middle class movement. What Mansbridge had in mind was an organisation in which the demand for further education would come from the workers themselves.

In 1903 he formed the Association to Promote the Higher Education of Working Men, the title later being changed to the Workers' Educational Association (WEA). Later that year an important conference was held at Toynbee Hall with BARNETT, BEVERIDGE and TAWNEY all giving active support. The Toynbee Hall library was to serve as a central library for students all over the country.

The first branch of the WEA was formed at Reading in 1904. Albert Mansbridge was appointed full-time Secretary in 1905 and for the next ten years was occupied in starting branches all over the country. By 1914 there were 145 classes in England and Wales with over 3,000 students. In 1913 he was invited to Australia by the University of Melbourne, where he organised the foundation of the WEA in every state.

Through ill health he was forced to retire as Secretary in 1914.

In 1916 through financial help from educational trusts and friends a trust was formed to enable him to found the National Central Library (which was later taken over by the British Library) for WEA students.

Albert Mansbridge received many honorary degrees from universities and was made a Companion of Honour in 1931.

There is a portrait of him by his son, John Mansbridge in the National Portrait Gallery.

Books
An Adventure in Working Class Education (Longmans, 1920)
Price, T.W. *The Story of the Workers' Educational Association from 1903-1924* (Labour Publishing Co., 1924)

DNB

MARCH, Samuel 1861-1935
Labour Leader

Samuel March was born at Romford, Essex where his father was an agricultural labourer. Sam March worked as a part-time farm labourer from the age of nine. Between the ages of 12 and 14 he worked as a bakery assistant for 6d. a week. He came to Poplar in 1878, becoming first a milk roundsman and then a carman.

He became secretary of the London Carmens' Union and when that was amalgamated with the Transport and General Workers' Union he became national secretary of the transport section.

He was elected a Poplar Councillor in 1903, continuing until 1927 and being Mayor in 1920. He went to prison with other councillors in 1921 for refusing to levy Poplar's share of the London County Council Police and Metropolitan Asylum contributions on the grounds that local rate payers were already impoverished with high levels of unemployment. He also served on the London County Council as member for South Poplar from 1919 to 1925. He was the first Labour JP in East London and was elected Member of Parliament for South Poplar from 1922-1931.

He is commemorated by Sam March House, Blair Street, E14.

DLB

MARE, Charles John 1815-1898
Shipbuilder

Charles Mare was born in Derbyshire. His first career was in the legal profession but he did not find it congenial. With some capital from the sale of of a house he had inherited, he began a shipbuilding business.

In 1837 he formed a partnership with Joseph DITCHBURN, taking over Dudman's Dock, Deptford. Soon after they had moved in,

Councillor Sam March, Mayor, speaking in Poplar Recreation Ground to raise funds to carry on the fight for equalization of rates in August 1921

the yard was gutted by fire and they then moved to Orchard Shipyard, Blackwall.

Joseph Ditchburn retired from the partnership in 1846 and the firm was then re-named C.J. Mare and Company. In 1856 the firm was re-organised. His father-in-law Peter Rolt took over control and re-named it Thames Ironworks and Shipbuilding Company. This company, and Millwall Ironworks were both distinguished by being the only companies to manufacture iron on their sites at this time. For the next ten years Charles Mare ran the Millwall Ironworks and Ship building Company, and after the third bankruptcy in his career, he ended his shipbuilding activities, 1866.

As an enlightened employer, he provided workers with a spacious dining hall and permitted workmen who did not reside in the area to use the stove. His employees were given a reading room, and a rowing club, cricket club and band were established.

Between 1840 and 1911, Mare's shipbuilding companies built 143 warships and 287 merchant ships. They also built parts of Westminster Bridge, Saltash Bridge near Plymouth, Blackfriars Railway Bridge, London and Hammersmith Suspension Bridge and seven sections of Robert STEVENSON'S Britannia Bridge, which crosses the Menai Strait.

Charles Mare was influential, and assisted in the founding of Poplar Hospital, East India Dock Road in 1855, a much needed facility as the London Hospital was some distance away in Whitechapel. It especially provided care for accidental injuries occurring in the docks and shipyards. He was a Governor of the Hospital and Dr. Matthew BROWNFIELD became the first surgeon there.

In July 1852 he was elected Concervative Member of Parliament for Plymouth but was unseated in May 1853 when his election was declared void after a petition. He was a great friend of Benjamin Disraeli, later Prime Minister.

He had a passion for horse-racing on which he spent a great deal of money.

He died at 82 Whitehorse Street, Mile End, and a public subscription had to be raised to bury him.
Obituary
Daily Mail 18th February 1898
Book
Banbury, P. *Shipbuilders of the Thames and Medway* (David and Charles, 1971)

MARTELL, Philip 1906-1993
Conductor and Director of Film Music

Born in Whitechapel, Philip Martell trained at the Guildhall School of Music, becoming an orchestral player and a fine player of chamber music. Later he was to become a distinguished theatre conductor.

He began his work in film music as an arranger, but with the end of the silent film era, he formed his own orchestra.

He returned to the film industry after the second World War, starting work for Hammer Films in 1955. He was appointed Music Director of the company in 1963 and remained in that position for thirty years.

Philip Martell raised and maintained the standard of film music, choosing young and unknown composers together with more experienced writers to compose special music.

He made a huge contribution to British film music and to the composers who worked and learned from him.
Obituary
The Independent 23rd August 1993

MARX-AVELING, Eleanor
1855-1898
Socialist

Eleanor Marx was the daughter of the Russian revolutionary, Karl Marx, and she was the only member of his family to be British. Eleanor Marx-Aveling, as she became known, played an important part in the introduction of Marxian Socialism and internationalism in Britain. She was Hon. Secretary to the Dock Strike Committee in 1889, working from their headquarters at *Wade's Arms*, Jeremiah Street, Poplar.

She founded the first women's branch of the National Union of Gasworkers and at their conference in 1890 she was the only nominee to be unaminously elected, a position she held until she retired in 1895.

She was deeply attached to Jewish workers in Whitechapel and addressed many meetings; she also spoke on behalf of Russian persecuted Jews.

Eleanor Marx was in the forefront of every effort to improve the condition of working people, children and the aged.
Biographies
Kapp, Y. *Eleanor Marx* Vol. 2. (Lawrence and Wishart, 1976)
Tsuzuki, C. *The Life of Eleanor Marx, 1855-1898* (Oxford University Press, 1967)

MAY, Francis 1803-1885
Match Manufacturer

Francis May was born at Alton, Hampshire, the fourth son of a wealthy merchant and member of an old Quaker family. The family moved to Ampthill, Bedfordshire when Francis May was young.

After leaving school he served a three year apprenticeship with a grocer in Epping and then set up in business on his own account as a tea dealer and grocer, at 20 Bishopsgate Without, in the City.

The original association between Francis May and William BRYANT is not recorded but it is possible that May acted as agent for the products of Bryant's firm Bryant and James, formed 1833.

At one stage Bryant and May were members of the Society of Friends' Peckham Meeting, May living in Peckham until 1853, when he moved to Reigate.

For some time Bryant remained in Plymouth looking after his business there while May managed the firm in London.

In 1844 the business became Bryant and May with premises at Philpot Lane, in the City and Tooley Street, Southwark. The firm imported matches from Sweden and then, moving in 1861 to Fairfield Road, Bow, began to manufacture them.

Francis May left the business in 1875.

William Bryant and Francis May are commemorated by a Purbeck Stone bird bath in the Quaker Burial Ground, Hanover Street, Peckham.

Sources
Bryant and May Company pamphlets.

MAYHEW, Henry 1812-1887
Journalist

Henry Mayhew was the son of a solicitor who brought up his children very strictly. He was sent to Westminster School and disgraced his family by running away from what he regarded as an unjust flogging. He was then sent to India as a midshipman.

Interested in writing and journalism, he became acquainted with Thackeray, DICKENS and Douglas Jerrold, whose daughter he married. Through Jerrold he was involved in the founding of the satirical magazine *Punch*, becoming joint editor in 1841, and being credited with some of the most famous jokes. In 1849 he was appointed Metropolitan correspondent of the *Morning Chronicle*.

Mayhew embarked upon a national survey of working people and the poor, which pioneered the method of recording the history of ordinary people through their own words. Many of his articles were written about people in East London.

His book *London Labour and London Poor* was produced in weekly parts selling around 13,000 copies each week and was published in 1861 in nine volumes.

A London County Council Blue Plaque was erected at 55 Albany Street, W1, in 1955.

Biography
Humphreys, A.   *Travels into Poor Man's Country* (Calibran, 1977)

MEAD, Rev. Matthew 1630(?)-1699
Minister of Stepney Meeting House

Matthew Mead was born at Leighton Buzzard and educated at Cambridge. In 1658 he was appointed by Oliver Cromwell to be Morning Lecturer at St. Dunstan's Church, Stepney. He was then appointed to the living of St. Paul's Church, Shadwell, but ejected under the Act of Uniformity 1662. Matthew Mead's supporters built Stepney Meeting House, completed 1674 (re-built 1863).

Matthew Mead lived at Worcester House, opposite St. Dunstan's Rectory. In 1683 he was accused of complicity in the Rye House Plot – a plan to murder Charles II and James, Duke of York. He fled to Holland but subsequently returned and died in Worcester House. He was buried in St. Dunstan's Churchyard.

DNB

MEAD, Dr. Richard 1673-1754
Physician

The son of Matthew MEAD, Richard was born at Worcester House, Stepney Green, educated by his father at home and then sent to private school. He continued at the University of Utrecht and then qualified as a Doctor of Physick at Padua University. He returned to England and began his practice in Stepney at Worcester House.

In 1702 he published a paper entitled *The Mechanical Account of Poisons*. Appointed a physician at St. Thomas's Hospital in 1703, he became a Fellow of the Royal Society in 1704.

Asked to give advice about the spread of the plague he wrote *A Discourse Concerning Pestilential Contagion*, of which seven editions were printed in 1720. He was one of the first supporters of inoculation for smallpox.

On Mead's resignation from St. Thomas's Hospital in 1715 he was appointed a Governor and later Vice-President. He continued in private practice, being appointed Physician-in-Ordinary to George II.

He had begun to collect paintings and antiquities, having a library of about 10,000 books. He was the leading physician of his time, treating many famous patients. He lived in Great Ormond Street, Holborn on a site now occupied by the Hospital for Sick Children.

There is a monument to Richard Mead in Westminster Abbey and Temple Church where he was buried. He is commemorated by a bust in the Royal College of Physicians and by a portrait in the National Portrait Gallery.

MENDOZA, Daniel 1764-1836
Prize Fighter

Daniel Mendoza was born in Aldgate and lived for a time in Paradise Row, Bethnal Green. He started work in the service of a Jewish family and took to fighting at an early age as he was often drawn into defence of his employer when insulted.

He won his first fight for money in the Mile End Road. Daniel Mendoza is said to have established a scientific style in boxing and set up an academy by the Royal Exchange in the City, where boys could train and receive advice.

In 1790 he successfully defended his title as champion of England in a fight which lasted 72 rounds. He was champion of England at least three times.

Attacks on Jewish people, prevalent at the time, are said to have declined with the rise of Mendoza and his successors.

His death was reported in the *Gentleman's Magazine* in 1836, giving his address as Horseshoe Alley, Petticoat Lane.

A plaque at 3 Paradise Row, Bethnal Green states that he 'proudly billed himself "Mendoza the Jew" and lived here when writing *The Art of Boxing*'.

Autobiography
Magriel, P. (ed) *The Memoirs of the Life of Daniel Mendoza* (Batsford, 1951)

DNB

MERCERON, Joseph 1763-1839
Magistrate

Joseph Merceron was born in Bethnal Green. He became a clerk in a lottery office and subsequently he managed to obtain positions of influence and power which he used to his own advantage. As Chairman of the Watch Board and Treasurer of the Poor Rate Fund, he altered the rate books, reducing rates for his tenants and friends, and increasing them for his enemies.

Despite his position as a magistrate he encouraged every kind of disorder and vice. He owned many public houses or had the landlords in his power. He was able to get appointed the most ignorant characters to fill parochial offices or audit his books. He was finally found out and prosecuted for theft and corrupt practices as a magistrate and was sentenced to 10 months imprisonment and a heavy fine, but was re-elected to office on his return from prison.

Merceron was buried in St. Matthew's Church, Bethnal Green, where he was churchwarden.

He is commemorated locally by Merceron Houses, Globe Road, E2, and Merceron Street, E1.

Book
Gurney, W.B. *Merceron's Trial for Fraud and Corruption* (Printed for W.Wright, 1819)

MERRICK, Joseph Carey (John)
1862-1890
'The Elephant Man'

Joseph Merrick was born in Leicester and spent his childhood in a workhouse and in hospital following a hip operation. He suffered from neurofibromatosis or Von Recklinghausen's Syndrome. He had an enormous misshapen head, a humped-back, and his body was covered with a growth likened to a brown cauliflower. Today, about 20,000 people in the United Kingdom carry the defective gene which causes the disease for which no cure has yet been discovered.

He was exhibited as 'The Elephant Man' in 1884 in an old shop opposite the London Hospital and it was there that Sir Frederick TREVES, surgeon and lecturer in anatomy at the Hospital, first saw him. Treves examined him in detail at the hospital and wrote an account for the *British Medical Journal* in 1886 and 1890.

Joseph Merrick was taken around Europe by Mr Ferrari, an Italian, but he was abandoned in Brussels having only his ticket to London. Arriving at Liverpool Street Station he had nowhere to go. The police were perplexed, but discovered Sir Frederick Treves's card in his pocket.

Treves was sent for and admitted Joseph Merrick to the London Hospital in 1886, where he lived for four years in isolated rooms. Mr Carr Gomm, Chairman of the Hospital, wrote a letter to *The Times*, which produced enough money to keep Joseph Merrick without charge on the hospital funds.

The account by Sir Frederick Treves shows 'John' Merrick to have been a remarkably intelligent man, and he became a great reader. In spite of his experiences he was without a grievance or an unkind word for anyone. The Princess of Wales, later Queen Alexandra, visited him as did a number of society ladies.

Joseph Merrick died from the effects of a dislocation of his neck, his head having fallen back in his sleep.

Books
Treves, F. *The Elephant Man and Other Reminiscences* (Cassell, 1923)
Howell, M. and Ford, P. *The True History of The Elephant Man* (Allison and Busby, 1983)

MIKARDO, Ian 1908-1993
Politician

Ian Mikardo's parents arrived in this country during the Jewish exodus from the Russian empire about 1900, his mother from the Ukraine and his father from Kutno, near Warsaw.

When his father, Morris, disembarked in London, his total possessions were the clothes he stood up in, a little bag containing a change of underclothes, his accessories for prayer, and one rouble.

Settling in Stepney, the family left to set up home in Portsmouth in 1907. Ian Mikardo was born a year later. When he went to school at the age of three he only had a few words of English, which put him at a disadvantage with his classmates. He was to say later that he understood the problems of the Bangladeshi families who formed part of his parliamentary constituency.

His mother's ambition was that he should become a rabbi, and he went to a college in Portsmouth for the training of young men as Jewish divines, but after a while he transferred to Portsmouth Grammar School, and on leaving had a number of jobs. His great delight at that time was to watch Portsmouth playing football and he retained an encyclopaedic knowledge of those games.

He met his wife Mary Rosette in 1930; she was his partner for over sixty years. He joined the Labour Party in the same year. By 1935 he had returned to Stepney where both his daughters were born.

In the 1930's he had various jobs in factories and with marketing and distributing agencies and during the second World War he became interested in advising about improvements to industrial planning and control of production, especially in aircraft factories.

In 1945 Ian Mikardo was elected Member of Parliament for Reading, but lost the seat in 1959 and also his place on Labour's National Executive. He regained the executive place in 1960 retaining it until 1978.

He was elected Member of Parliament for Poplar from 1964-74, for Bethnal Green and Bow 1974-83 and for Bow and Poplar 1983-87. 'Mik' as he was always known, was Chairman of the Labour Party 1970-71, Chairman of the Parliamentary Labour Party 1974, and Chairman of the Select Committee on Nationalised Industries.

Ian Mikardo was an expert at bridge and chess, he also wrote a pamphlet on betting called *A Mug's Game*.

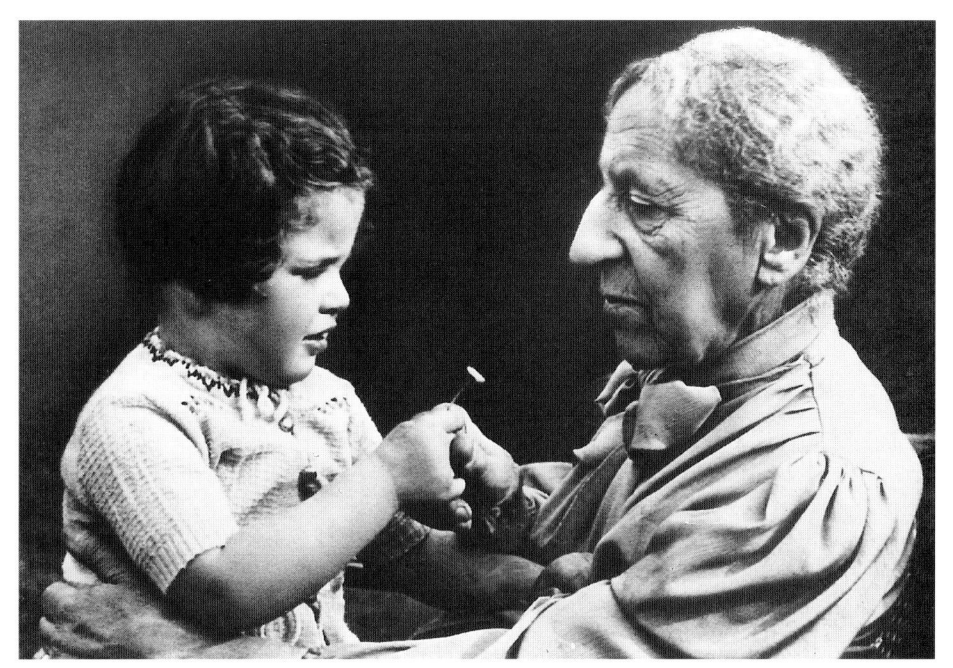

Alice Model

He was a friend and mentor to many in the Labour Party and Movement. His concern for his constituents and their many problems occupied much of his time. He made a great impact as a backbench Member of Parliament.
Autobiography
Back-bencher (Weidenfeld and Nicholson, 1988)
Obituary
The Independent 7th May 1993

MODEL, Alice 1856-1943
Community Worker

Born Alice Sichel into a middle class family, she met and married her husband in Hampstead in 1880.

She began her social work by starting an organisation which sent trained nurses to homes when needed, called Sick Room Helps, based in Underwood Street, now Underwood Road, Stepney. This also acted as a maternity home.

Alice Model was a pioneer in the founding of nursing homes and health visiting. The maternity home in Underwood Street became the Jewish Maternity Hospital and later the Bearstead Memorial Hospital, which moved to north London, admitting both Jews and Christians.

In 1896 she started a Jewish day nursery for the infants of working parents. The nursery also offered training for girls wishing to become nursery nurses. She is commemorated by the Alice Model Nursery in the Stepney Jewish Club and Settlement, Beaumont Grove, E1.

MONTAGU, Sir Samuel, Lord Swaythling 1832-1911
Merchant Banker

Samuel Montagu was born in Liverpool where his father was a watchmaker and silversmith.

Coming to London, he was a co-founder of the Jewish Board of Guardians, now Jewish Welfare Board, and among his many activities he established a Working Men's Club in Hutchinson Street, Aldgate. It later grew to a membership of 1,000, moving to Alie Street, E1. He was a Trustee of the People's Palace, Mile End. He gave 26 acres of land in Tottenham to the London County Council to build houses to ease the overcrowding in Whitechapel.

In 1887 he founded the Federation of (Minor) Synagogues which became centres of religious activity and learning. He was a Member of the Jewish Board of Deputies and

Sir Samuel Montagu

was elected Liberal Member of Parliament for Whitechapel 1885-1900. In 1892, Samuel Montagu purchased at auction for 30 guineas a 17th century oil painting of London and presented it to the Whitechapel Library Commissioners to mark the official opening of the Library. The painting was removed to Stepney Central Library and was sold to the Museum of London in 1991 for £170,000.

An authority on immigration, he was a member of the House of Commons Select Committee on Alien Immigration in 1888.

It was mainly due to his efforts that the Royal Exchange was roofed over in 1880 to protect the merchants at their business.

He was created Lord Swaythling in 1907.

Biography

Montagu, L. *Samuel Montagu* (Truslove and Hanson, 1911)

DNB

MONTEFIORE, Robert M. Sebag
1882-1915
Barrister

Robert Montefiore was educated at Clifton College and Oxford, studied law and became a member of the Inner Temple.

Arthur Morrison

In 1907 he was elected to the London County Council as Member for South West Bethnal Green. He became Vice-Chairman of the Education Committee. As Chairman of one of the sub-committees he was involved in the purchase of the site and the building of Vallance Road School.

His life was cut short after being wounded in the first World War. In 1916 Vallance Road School was re-named Robert Montefiore School.

Robert Montefiore Secondary School, Vallance Road, E1, was closed in 1984, and became Osmani School in 1986. Robert Montefiore Primary School, Buxton Street, was re-named Thomas Buxton School in 1982.

MORRISON, Arthur 1863-1945
Writer

Arthur Morrison was born in John Street, Poplar. In 1886 he was appointed Clerk to the Beaumont Trustees, who established the People's Palace, now part of Queen Mary and Westfield College, in the following year.

Morrison became a journalist and a freelance writer, and his first book of detective stories was published in 1894. His best known

Elected Mayor of Stepney in 1931, she was the first woman Mayor of Stepney and the first Jewish woman Mayor in the country.

In 1958 Miriam Moses was the subject of the television programme *This is your life.*

She was awarded OBE in 1945.

Article

Jewish Chronicle 2nd July 1965 and 9th July 1965

MUDD, Captain Henry   died 1692

Sailor

Henry Mudd lived for many years in Ratcliff and was a member of the Stepney Vestry.

An elder brother of Trinity House, a religious order which had considerable jurisdiction over the River Thames and advised on the construction and purchase of ships and rigging, he gave the ground on which Trinity Hospital (now Almshouses) Mile End Road, E1, is built.

He was buried in St. Dunstan's Church and the inscription on his tomb reads:-

> This tomb was re-built by the Corporation of Trinity House in the year 1776 as a grateful testimony of his benefactions to that Charity, for the decay'd seamen, their widows and families. *Restored 1876.*

Miriam Moses, photographed in 1965 *Jewish Chronicle*

Book

book is *A Child of the Jago* published in 1896 which describes the life of a boy living in the Old Nichol Street area of Bethnal Green. Wapping is featured in *The Hole in the Wall* which he wrote in 1902.

Ashbee, C.R. *The Trinity Hospital in Mile End* (Guild and School of Handicraft, 1896)

MUSSELL, Ebenezer   died 1764

Antiquary

MOSES, Miriam   OBE   1886-1965

Community Worker

Miriam Moses was born in Stepney. She became interested in the activities of her father, Mark Moses who was a magistrate, borough councillor, synagogue worker and master tailor. On his death in 1921, Miriam Moses succeeded him as borough councillor and magistrate.

For many years she was a member of the Whitechapel Board of Guardians and served on the East London Juvenile Court at Toynbee Hall.

In 1927 she founded the Brady Girls' Club and was club leader and then Warden of the Settlement until her retirement in 1958.

Miriam Moses was Chairman of the Stepney Youth Committee for many years and involved herself in many organisations and activities for children, young people and women.

Ebenezer Mussell was a magistrate who lived at Aldgate House (built 1643), on a site now occupied by the Church of the Assumption, Victoria Park Square, Bethnal Green.

In 1760 the city gate at Aldgate was demolished to widen the thoroughfare and Mussell bought some of the remains and had them built into the front of his house, re-naming it Aldgate House.

Ebenezer Mussell was an original member of the Vestry of St. Matthew's Church, Bethnal Green for which he laid the foundation stone in 1745. The church was designed by George DANCE the Elder.

Mussell was a collector of Greek and Roman coins and the catalogue of his collection is in the library of the Society of Antiquaries. He also had a vast library which was sold in 1782.

Tower Hamlets Local History Library has a Chinese soapstone figure which is thought to have belonged to him.

He is commemorated by Ebenezer Mussell House, Patriot Square, E2.

MUSTO, Sir Arnold Albert
1883-1977
Civil Engineer

Arnold Musto was born in Mile End and educated at Coopers' Company School and Birkbeck College. He began work as an engineering pupil and in 1905 he worked on the construction of the Rotherhithe road tunnel.

In 1907 he became assistant engineer for the Bombay Government. He was responsible for the world's largest irrigation scheme after his initial survey of the River Indus in 1907. An essential part of this project was his design and construction of the Lloyd Barrage across the gorge at Sukkur. It was completed in 1932, by which time he was the Superintending Engineer. The barrage is one mile long with sixty-six spans, each sixty feet wide. It provides water to the province of Sind, an almost rainless area about the size of England.

There are 5,400 miles of main and branch canals bringing irrigation to cover eight million acres of cultivation, abolishing drought and famine. Parts of the barrage were built at Robert BAILLIE's yard in Blackwall.

Arnold Musto was knighted in 1932.

NEALE, Thomas   died 1699(?)
Master of the Mint

Thomas Neale was appointed Master of the Mint, when it was still situated within the walls of the Tower of London, during the reign of Charles II, continuing in office under James II and William III. He was responsible for devising a re-coinage scheme after writing *A Proposal for Amending the Silver Coins of England* (1696), a copy of which can be seen in the British Library.

In 1684 he was appointed Groom Porter to Charles II and held the same post under William III. The duties were to see that the King's lodgings were adequately furnished, to provide cards and dice for the gaming tables and to decide disputes. He also had authority to licence and suppress gaming clubs.

He was also Master of the Transfer Office and as such organised a lottery – loan for £1 million on the security of a new duty on salt.

Engaged in building and mining schemes, in 1694 he began the building of the London streets known as Seven Dials, Westminster.

He lived in Shadwell and was mainly responsible for its development after two great fires in 1673 and 1682 had destroyed much of it. He built a waterworks in 1684 providing piped water for surrounding districts; he also built a chapel at which Matthew MEAD was the first minister.

There is a public house in Watney Market, E1, named after him.

Book

Rose, M. *East End of London* (Cresset Press, 1951)

NEWLAND, George Alexander
1891-1975
Borough Librarian

George Newland was born in Stepney and commenced his 51 year library service as a boy assistant in St. George's Library in 1905. During the first World War he was in the Army in the Middle East and during the second World War he was in the ARP, experiencing the whole of the blitz, doodlebug and rocket attacks on East London.

During a long period as Stepney Borough Reference Librarian, when the population peaked to over 300,000, the libraries were crammed with young people studiously trying to improve their chances of getting out of that impoverished area.

Being appointed Stepney Borough Librarian (1946-56) he had the task of trying to build up the system again after War-time disruption. He centralised book selection and cataloguing, began Local History and Gramaphone collections and developed a programme of lectures and films for adults and children.

NEWTON, Sir Isaac   1642-1727
Mathematician and Physicist

Isaac Newton was born at Woolsthorpe in Lincolnshire and was educated at the local grammar school, going to Trinity College, Cambridge in 1661. Following his degree he began his studies on gravitation, on the nature of light and on the construction of telescopes with John DOLLOND.

His association with the Borough lay in his appointment in 1696 as Warden of the Royal Mint. In 1699 he succeeded Thomas NEALE as Master (an office now held by the Chancellor of the Exchequer) continuing in office until his death.

During 1717-1718 he was responsible for the issue of new coins, replacing the debased and chipped silver coinage. The new coins had

a milled edge and were more practical and satisfactory. Milled money had first been introduced in 1665.
He was buried in Westminster Abbey, where there is a monument to him.
On a tablet in the room at Woolsthorpe where he was born there is inscribed the famous epitaph by Alexander Pope:-

Nature and Nature's laws lay hid in night: God said "Let Newton be" and all was light

Biography
Andrade, E.N. *Isaac Newton* (Max Parrish, 1950)
DNB

NEWTON, Rev. John 1725-1807
Priest and Hymn Writer

John Newton was the son of John Newton, a sea captain, and his wife Elizabeth. The baptism register of Old Gravel Lane Chapel in St. George's-in-the-East has an unusual note with his baptism entry for the 26th July 1725:-

This is the celebrated John Newton whose early history is so full of awful depravity – but who was at length arrested by the Almighty – say "thus far shalt thou go but no further". He was afterwards Rector of St. Mary Woolnoth Church in the City for many years – and died at a good old age riper for glory – He was interred in the vault under the Church of Saint Mary Woolnoth.

He lived in Wapping during his childhood. His mother died when he was seven and he spent much of his time at sea with his father.
When John Newton was older, he was engaged in the slave trade, voyaging from Liverpool to Africa and America. One night at sea in the midst of a furious storm he had a remarkable Christian conversion experience, and under the influence of Mary Catlett, who later became his wife, he gave up the sea.
Meeting John WESLEY and George Whitefield, he was encouraged to prepare for ordination. He found some difficulty in finding a parish, but eventually went to Olney, Buckinghamshire, where he met the poet William Cowper, and together they wrote the Olney hymnbook.
In 1780 John Newton became Rector of St. Mary Woolnoth, where he remained until his death.
There is a monument to him in the Church.
Biography
Martin, B. *John Newton* (Heinemann, 1950)
DNB

NEWTON, William 1822-1876
Politician and Newspaper Publisher

William Newton was born in Congleton, Cheshire and settled in London from 1840. After being sacked for trade union activity whilst a foreman in Henry O. and Albert Robinson's engineering firm in Millwall, he ran *The Phoenix Tavern* in Phoenix Place, Ratcliffe (1848-51), a frequent meeting place for trade unionists. He then spent a short time as a secretary of an insurance company before deciding to take up journalism.
He edited the *East London Observer* from its foundation by him in 1857 until his death in 1876. This was the first local newspaper for Tower Hamlets and carried his editorials and extensive reports of his own speeches. By the late 1860s the newspaper became closely identified with the Liberal Party.
He was elected a vestryman of Mile End Old Town and later added to his responsibilities by serving on the vestry as the representative from 1862-76 on the Metropolitan Board of Works, which was instrumental in carrying out the improvements under the Metropolitan Street Acts, 1872. Improvements in Tower Hamlets included the widening of Wapping Basin, the London Docks and the entrance to St. Katherine's Dock. Commercial Road, Whitechapel was extended in 1870 and a new street, Great Eastern Street, Shoreditch, was completed in 1876.
William Newton was a founder and first President of the Amalgamated Society of Engineers in 1851. In the 1852 general election he was the first Independent Working Class candidate to stand for Parliament in Tower Hamlets and fought both Liberal and Tory for the Tower Hamlets seat. Few workers, however, had the vote at that time and he was bottom of the poll. Even so he received over 1000 votes.
He died at his home at 41 Stepney Green, Mile End.
Pamphlet
Amalgamated Engineering Union *William Newton 1822-76* (AEU, London North District, 1951)
Book
Metropolitan Board of Works Report 1888
Article
East London Observer 27th March 1915
DLB

THOMAS OKEY

OKEY, Thomas 1853-1935
Basket Maker and Professor of Italian

Thomas Okey was born in Quaker Street, Spitalfields and later lived in Middlesex Street, Bethnal Green. He attended St. James-the-Less School. Canon BARNETT met him repairing baskets in Whitechapel and encouraged him to attend classes at Toynbee Hall, a university settlement. He later attended the Working Men's College in Camden Town.

He was always interested in languages and gained greater knowledge with his Sunday visits to the French Protestant Church at St. Martin's Le-Grand, the German Church in Whitechapel and the Italian Chiesa Evangelica. He became a teacher of Italian at Toynbee Hall but continued with the basket-making, becoming recognised as an authority on the craft.

In 1918 he was appointed examiner in Italian to the Civil Service Board and in 1919 was appointed Professor of Italian at Cambridge University, being elected a Fellow of Caius College.

He wrote many books and translated the Italian classics into English.

His career could be summed up: Early life-vocation-basket-making, hobby-learning-languages. Later life-vocation-teaching-languages, hobby-basket-making.
Autobiography
A Basketful of Memories (J.M.Dent, 1930)

ORTON, Arthur 1834-1898
Imposter

After the death of Sir Alfred Tichborne, a member of an ancient Roman Catholic family, Thomas Castro, otherwise Arthur Orton of Wapping, came forward to impersonate an elder brother, Roger Tichborne, who had been lost at sea, and to claim the family fortune.

A famous case in law history, in 1871-1872 it created much interest for its length and expense. Orton's case collapsed on the 103rd day of its hearing and after 22 days of cross examination by Sir John Coleridge.

Orton was committed for perjury, for which he received a sentence of fourteen years hard labour. He confessed the imposture in 1895.
Books
Atlay, J.B. *The Tichborne Case* (W.Hodge, 1916)
Maugham, F.H. *The Tichborne Case* (Hodder and Stoughton, 1936)
Gilbert, M. *The Claimant* (Constable, 1957)
Woodruff, D. *The Tichborne Claimant* (Hollis and Carter, 1957)

DNB

PACE, Rev. Richard 1482(?)-1536
Priest and Diplomat

Richard Pace was born near Winchester and educated at Oxford and in Italy, where he met the scholar Desiderius ERASMUS, who became his friend. He was appointed Vicar of St. Dunstan's, Stepney 1519-1527 and he succeeded John COLET as Dean of St. Paul's.

Richard Pace became Secretary of State to Henry VIII and was sent as ambassador to the Emperor Maximillian of the Holy Roman Empire; he also conducted diplomatic missions to Rome and Venice on behalf of Cardinal Wolsey.

DNB

PANKHURST, Estelle Sylvia
1882-1960
Suffragette Crusader

Sylvia Pankhurst was born in Manchester, and educated at Manchester High School for Girls. On leaving school she intended to

Sylvia Pankhurst, circa 1915, in the mother and infant clinic in Old Ford Road

become a painter and studied in Manchester, Venice and at the Royal College of Art in London (The National Portrait Gallery has portraits by her of the Labour MP Keir Hardie and herself).

With her mother Emmeline and her sister Christabel, Sylvia became one of the leading campaigners in the fight to establish votes for women which began in Manchester in 1905. She was one of the founders of the campaigning organisation, the Women's Social and Political Union.

In 1912, through association with George LANSBURY, she had taken up the cause of women's suffrage, Sylvia came to work in East London and established a local branch of the WSPU at 198 Bow Road, Bow.

Moved by the situation of working class women, she organised them to speak out about their working conditions and poverty. This involvement led to a break with her mother and sister over the policies of the WSPU, and the foundation of the East London Federation of Suffragettes in 1913.

In 1913 Sylvia Pankhurst led a deputation of women from East London to see Sir Edward Grey and Lloyd George. The demonstrations and activities which followed led to her imprisonment. She went on hunger strike in prison, was released and then re-arrested under the Prisoners' Temporary Discharge for Ill-Health Act, which became known as the 'Cat and Mouse' Act (1913), so named because the effect was like that of a cat catching its prey, then letting it go again, then catching it again.

Sylvia Pankhurst lived in and around Bow from 1912-1924, and founded a day nursery and toy factory at 45 Norman Road (now Grove), Bow. a mother and baby clinic, called the Mother's Arms in Old Ford Road and a cut price restaurant.

She was arrested in 1921 under the Defence of the Realm Act for giving support to Russian revolutionaries. A great worker for the poor and the old, she became a champion for Ethiopia when that country was invaded by Mussolini in 1936.

She is commemorated in the Borough by Sylvia Pankhurst House, Warley Street, E2, and with a plaque at 45 Norman Grove, E3.

Biography
Pankhurst, R. *Sylvia Pankhurst* (Paddington Press, 1579)

Books
Pankhurst, S. *The Suffragette Movement* (Longmans, 1931)
Taylor, R. *In Letters of Gold* (Stepney Books, 1993)

PARKER, Edward, Lord Morley
1555-1618
Public Servant

After spending some time abroad as a nonconformist, Edward Parker seems to have agreed to conform to the Church of England rituals.

He resigned the office of Lord Marshall in Ireland and received in exchange the sole right to print and publish a book called *God and the King*, a manual of instruction for children in the oath of allegiance.

Edward Parker was a Commissioner for the trials of Queen Mary Stuart in 1586 and of Philip, Earl of Arundel in 1589 and married the heiress of the third Lord Monteagle. He was auditor for Limehouse in 1584 and a vestryman of Ratcliffe in 1586.

In 1605 there was a conspiracy of some Catholic sympathisers which resulted in explosives being planted in the Houses of Parliament to kill the King. Edward Parker, at the time living in a house off Stepney Green, received a letter addressed to his son Lord Monteagle advising him not to attend Parliament on 5th November. Lord Monteagle passed the letter to Robert Cecil, Lord Privy Seal, whose investigations led to the arrest of the conspirators, the most famous of whom was Guy Fawkes. When Fawkes confessed after being tortured in the Tower of London, he was hung, drawn and quartered. Edward Parker's son, Lord Monteagle, received a reward of £100 a year.

Book
Williamson, H.R. *The Gunpowder Plot* (Faber and Faber, 1951)

DNB

PARMITER, Thomas died 1682
Silk Merchant

A Bethnal Green resident, Thomas Parmiter became wealthy through his business. In his will dated 28th February 1682 he bequeathed money for the establishment of a school for ten poor children and six almshouses for poor and deserving old people. They were to be maintained by rents from Parmiter's two farms in Suffolk.

The school and almshouses were eventually built in St. John Street, off Brick Lane, Bethnal Green, later demolished to make way for the Eastern Counties Railway to Bishopsgate. From the beginning, in 1722, the school and almshouses were supported from other charitable funds. They were rebuilt in Gloucester Street, now Parmiter Street, E2, but were demolished in an air raid in 1945.

The present school building in Approach Road, E2, was built in 1887 and is now used by Raine's Upper School.

Parmiter's School has now moved to Garston, Hertfordshire.

PASSMAN, Florrie 1888-1986
Youth Worker

Florrie Passman was born in Leeds. Her family moved to East London and she was educated at Aldersgate Street Grammar School, in the City. Her father died when she was ten and she learned to take on responsibility at an early age.

She joined the Butler Street Club, Spitalfields in 1903, and was Leader of the club from 1913 to March 1953.

In 1940 Florrie Passman decided that it was time to change from a girl's club to a mixed club, and Butler Street became the first mixed club in the Association for Jewish Youth.

During the war, the club remained open and when the air-raid sirens went, the members would transfer to the shelter between the nearby Fruit Exchange and continue their activities.

When the club lease expired and had to close in 1953, Phyllis GERSON invited her to help at the Stepney Jewish Club.
Article
Hackney Gazette 19th June 1966

PATER, Walter Horatio 1839-1894
Writer

Walter Pater came from a family of doctors and was born in 1 Honduras Terrace, Commercial Road, Mile End Old Town. Educated at King's School, Canterbury and Oxford, he became associated with the pre-Raphaelites, particularly the poet, Algernon Swinburne.

In 1864 he became a Fellow of Brasenose College, Oxford and combined tutorial duties with writing. His first book was *Studies in the History of the History of the Renaissance* (1873) and his later books were about English and Greek writers.

Book
Levey, M. *The Case of Walter Pater* (Thames and Hudson, 1978) DNB

PENN, William 1644-1718
Founder of Philadelphia

William Penn, son of Admiral Sir William Penn, was born on Tower Hill. As a student of Christ Church, Oxford, he came under the influence of some of the earliest Quakers, and was sent down from 1661 for holding nonconformist views.

During the late 1660's, William Penn attended Quaker meetings held in a private house in Wheler Street, Spitalfields along with George Fox and George Whitehead, the early founders of the movement. In 1668 William Penn was imprisoned in the Tower for seven months after publishing a pamphlet critical of the established church doctrines. He was imprisoned twice more for his religious views.

In 1681 he received a grant of territory in America from the Crown in lieu of his father's claim upon it. The land was called Pennsylvania after his father. William Penn sailed for Delaware in 1682 and in November held his famous interview with the Lenni Lenape Indians. He concluded a peace treaty with them which the philosopher, Voltaire described as the only agreement of the kind which was neither sworn to, or broken. This treaty gave the Quakers sufficient assurances to peacefully plan and build the city of Philadelphia.

He returned to England to help with the release of many dissenters in prison. William Penn's father was a friend and almost like a guardian to James II in his youth, and in 1686, King James, who, as a Catholic wished to promote religious tolerance, made a proclamation of pardon, probably at William Penn's insistence, for all who were in prison for consciences sake. Twelve hundred Quakers, amongst others, were released.

He wrote over forty books and pamphlets on Quakerism, religion and the history and description of Pennsylvania and Philadelphia.

Biographies
Dunn, M.M. *William Penn* (Princeton University Press, 1967)
Pearce, C.O. *William Penn* (Dobson, 1959)
DNB

PENNETHORNE, Sir James
1801-1871
Architect

James Pennethorne was born into a family connected with John Nash, architect to the Prince Regent. He trained under Augustus Pugin, who worked with Charles Barry in building the Houses of Parliament.

After two years travelling abroad he became personal assistant to John Nash. When John Nash retired from a government post he recommended James Pennethorne for the position.

Employed to prepare plans for improving central London, James Pennethorne designed New Oxford Street and Endell Street, WC2, as well as many public buildings. He also designed Battersea Park. James Pennethorne was appointed architect for Victoria Park and submitted his first report in 1841. The Park fences were erected by 1845 and the superintendent's house, designed by him, stood at the main gate until it was bombed during the second World War.

Book
Poulsen, C. *Victoria Park* (Stepney Books, 1976)
DNB

PEPPERELL, Elizabeth OBE
1914-1971
Champion of Working Women

Elizabeth Pepperell was born in Bow and lived with her family at 22 Whitethorn Street, E3. She attended Devons Road Infants School.

After leaving school she worked on the factory floor at Bryant and May's, attending evening classes in economics at Toynbee Hall and the London School of Economics.

In 1938 she won a Mary McArthur Scholarship, which enabled her to attend the London School of Economics full-time. Completing her studies she began work as a Welfare Officer in a carpet factory. When the firm closed she went as Chief Welfare Officer to the tobacco company, Carreras, and was there for eleven years.

In 1949 Elizabeth Pepperell was elected a Fellow of the Institute of Personnel Management, the youngest Fellow to be elected.

She joined the Industrial Welfare Society (re-named The Industrial Society in 1965) as Assistant Director and was responsible for much of their pioneering work. She was awarded the OBE in 1966.

R.L.Wessel, Chairman of the Industrial Society's Executive Committee said of her 'Probably no other woman in Britain has done more to improve the climate of industrial relations in this country. No individual ever did more or worked harder to improve the working status and career prospects of

women, and persuade employers to recognise their abilities and use them to the full'.
Biography
Reed, M. *Elizabeth Pepperell* (The Industrial Society, l973)

PEPYS, Samuel 1633-1703
Diarist and Secretary of the Admiralty

Samuel Pepys was born in Fleet Street, in the City, and educated at St. Paul's School and Cambridge. He was twice Master of Trinity House, then situated in Stepney. Between 1660-69 Samuel Pepys kept a private diary which was written in cypher because it gave vivid details of his personal life, alongside descriptions of public events such as the Great Plague of 1665 and the Great Fire of London, 1666. During the Fire, he deposited his diary for safe-keeping with Sir William RYDER at Bethnall House, Bethnal Green. The Diary was not decyphered until 1825 and the first complete and unexpurgated edition was not issued until 1970.

Samuel Pepys was Secretary to the Admiralty and responsible for enlarging the Navy under Charles II. He was Member of Parliament for Harwich in 1685, elected Fellow and then President of the Royal Society, 1684.

There is a monument to Pepys in St. Olave's Church, Hart Street, EC3, a portrait by John Hayls in the National Portrait Gallery and another by Sir Godfrey Kneller in the National Maritime Museum.

He is commemorated locally by Pepys House, Kirkwall Place, E2.
Biography
Bryant, Sir A. *Samuel Pepys* (Collins, 1947-48)
DNB

PERKIN, Sir Henry William
1838-1907
Chemist

Henry Perkin was born in Stepney, the son of a builder and decorator, of King David Lane, Shadwell. Henry Perkin was educated at the City of London School, where he became interested in chemistry.

Assistant to Professor August Hoffmann at the Royal College of Chemistry (founded 1845), in 1856 Henry Perkin made the discovery of the first aniline or coal-tar dye, mauve, which led to the foundation of the modern dye-stuff industry.

In 1857 Henry Perkin built a factory at Sudbury, near Wembley, for tile manufacture of synthetic dyes, but he sold his interest in 1894, returning to experimental chemistry. He was appointed Fellow of the Royal Society in 1866 and knighted in 1906.

His son and namesake (1860-1929) became Professor of Chemistry at Oxford University in 1912.
Book
Perkin Centenary Celebration Committee *Perkin Centenary, London* (Pergamon Press, 1958)
DNB

PERRY, John 1743-1810
Shipbuilder

John Perry was born into a family of engineers and shipbuilders. His grandfather, Philip Perry, ran a shipyard at Blackwall, and John Perry entered the family business, succeeding his father as owner in 1772.

In 1789 he began the construction of Brunswick Dock, which opened in 1790. This was the first dock to be built on the north side of the Thames. It was divided into two deep basins, each with an exit to the river. The dock was large enough to contain twenty-eight vessels of the East India Company, and sixty Greenland Sloops. At the time it was said to be the largest dockyard in the world.

George GREEN, who was an apprentice at Brunswick Dock, married John Perry's daughter Sarah in 1796, and was taken into partnership with his father-in-law.

Brunswick Dock became known as East India Export Dock in 1806.

He is commemorated by Perry's Close, E14.
Books
Green, H. and Wigram, R. *Chronicles of Blackwall Yard* Pt.l. (Whitehead, Morris and Lowe, 1881)
Lubbock, B. *The Blackwall Frigates* (James Brown, 1922)
Taylor, R. *Blackwall, The Brunswick and Whitebait Dinners* (R.Taylor, 1991)

PHILLIPS, Roland 1890-1916
Scout Commissioner

Roland Phillips, the son of Lord St. Davids, was born in Westminster, and educated at Westminster and Oxford. During his university vacations he spent time at Oxford House in Bethnal Green.

Having made up his mind to work in East London he purchased 29 Stepney Green, E1, as a home. In 1912 Sir Robert Baden Powell appointed him Assistant Scout Commissioner for East and North East London, and in

November 1913 he was appointed Scout Commissioner for Bethnal Green, Poplar and Stepney.

When war was declared in August 1914, he joined the Army, winning the Military Cross, but was killed at the battle of the Somme in 1916.

In 1920, his house was developed by his friends and named Roland House, becoming the headquarters for Scouts in East London. Used as an activity centre, it also provided accommodation for young men interested in scouting. A chapel in the basement was dedicated to St. Francis.

Roland House was closed in 1982 and the chapel moved to the East End Methodist Mission where it was formally opened on 23rd March 1985, continuing the link with Roland Phillips and his interest in young people in East London.

Book
Barber, D.H. *The House on the Green* (Roland House Scout Settlement, 1960)

PHILPOT, Sir John died 1384
Grocer

Sir John Philpot owned the Manor of Mile End. He was elected the Member of Parliament for the City of London 1369, 1371 and 1383. He was Alderman for the Cornhill ward in the City, Sheriff from 1372-1373 and became Lord Mayor of London from 1378-1379.

During the Peasant's Revolt of 1381 he became actively involved in suppressing the rebellion which been sparked off by Wat Tyler. At a mass gathering of the rebel forces at Mile End, the young Richard II granted concessions that appeased the bulk of the Essex and Hertfordshire peasants, but not all.

The King, together with many notable men, including John Philpot and William Walworth, Lord Mayor of London, met with the remaining rebels at Smithfield.

Unbeknown to the peasants, William Walworth had amassed a concealed armed force in the City, and secure in this knowledge, he struck down and badly wounded the belligerent Wat Tyler. In the confusion that followed, William Walworth summoned his forces.

Wat Tyler temporally escaped but Lord Mayor Walworth found the dying man and had him beheaded. Wat Tyler's death marked the collapse of the revolt, and the day culminated in Richard II knighting William Walworth and John Philpot. The King declared that he was much beholden to them for their part in restoring 'my heritage that was lost and the realm of England also'.

John Philpot also was responsible for helping to clear the River Thames of pirates.

He is commemorated by Philpot Street, E1.

Book
Beaven, A.B. *Aldermen of the City of London* (Guildhall Library, 1908-13)

DNB

PIATKOV, Peter (alias SCHTERN) active circa 1910-1911
Political Activist

Peter Piatkov, known as 'Peter the Painter', was the most notorious member of a gang of Russian communists, living in Stepney in 1910-1911.

Having escaped from Russia following the revolution of 1905, he travelled widely in Europe earning his living as a house painter. He came to London and lived at 59 Grove Street, off Commercial Road, Stepney and at 36 Lindley Street, Stepney.

The first crime of the gang was in January 1909– a wage snatch in which three policemen were killed. The affair became known as the 'Tottenham Outrage'.

In 1910 the gang tried to rob a jewellers in Houndsditch, and in making their escape, killed three policemen and injured two more. Armed police hunted the killers and for a time they were not detected, but an informer led the police to a house in Sidney Street, Stepney where two of the gang were hiding.

On 3rd January 1911, the famous siege of Sidney Street began and armed police and troops attacked the house. They were directed by Winston Churchill, who was Home Secretary.

Eventually the house caught fire and at the end, the charred bodies of two men were found. They were identified as Fritz Svaars and William Sokoloff, commonly known as Joseph.

Although 'Peter the Painter' caught the imagination of the press and public, there is no evidence to show that he was one of the gang who had murdered the policemen in Houndsditch. It is probable that he returned to Russia in 1911 to continue working for the revolutionary movement and died there.

Book
Rumbelow, D. *The Houndsditch Murders and the Seige of Sidney Street* (Macmillan, 1973)

PLATT, Sir Hugh 1552-1608
Horticulturalist and Pioneer Food Preserver

Hugh Platt was the third son of a rich brewer of Hertfordshire. After graduating from Cambridge, he studied law and became a member of Lincoln's Inn, but never practised.

Following his marriage he came to live at his new country house, Bishops Hall, Bethnal Green, moving later to Bethnall House. He became interested in the cultivation and the preservation of fruit and flowers and developed his own garden. He also grew tobacco, and the wine that he made was from grapes grown in Bethnal Green.

He discovered that by excluding air from freshly picked fruit, it could be kept for a considerable time. He thus became the pioneer of fruit bottling. He also experimented on meat and discovered that if this was partly boiled in brine it would keep for some time.

The preservation of food at sea was a great problem for Elizabethan explorers, and Sir Francis Drake, who was at the time fitting out the *Defiance* rode out from London to Hugh Platt's house at Bishops Hall to watch the final tests on meat. Sir Francis Drake was very impressed with the meat he sampled and took some when he next sailed. The tests with Sir Francis Drake were successful and Hugh Platt wrote that 'it benefitted the whole Navy of England'. Sir Francis Drake was also interested in Platt's experiments to keep water fresh by adding powdered brimstone and frequently changing the hogshead containers.

Beauty culture was one of his sidelines. For his second wife and three daughters, he wrote a pocket manual of household hints discreetly entitled *Delights for Ladies* (1602). In the 17th century the book became a best-seller. Apart from advice on cosmetics it gave instructions for erecting a 'Delicate Stove to Sweat In' where 'gentlewoman' sat or stood in the steam for two hours or more, her head 'helde above the tubbe'.

After a series of bad harvests, new ideas were needed and Hugh Platt soon became an authority on agriculture, advocating the rotation of crops and the use of artificial fertilisers.

He was knighted by James I in 1605 for his services as an inventor.

He is commemorated by Hugh Platt House, Patriot Square, E2.
Books
Sundrie New and Artificall Remedies Against Famine (1595)

The Garden of Eden, or, An Accurate Description of all Flowers and Fruits Now Growing in England etc (W. Leake, 1653)

DNB

PLIMSOLL, Samuel 1824-1898
Sailors' Friend

Samuel Plimsoll was one of 12 children of Thomas and Priscilla Plimsoll. In spite of a limited income, his parents had him well educated at schools in Penrith and Sheffield. He began work as a solicitor's clerk. After several ventures he came to London in 1855 and engaged in the coal trade. Between 1860 and 1880 he pursued a relentless crusade against the increasing losses of vessels and sailors at sea.

He became a familiar figure in Poplar, where he was a frequent speaker at riverside meetings. The National Amalgamated Sailors' and Firemens' Union found him a ready and hearty supporter when it was formed, and elected him as its first President, 1890.

During the period that he was the Liberal Member of Parliament for Derby, 1868-1880, he adopted the reforming ideas of a philanthropic shipowner, James Hall of Tynmouth and brought bills in 1871 and 1874 before Parliament to bring the attention of the country to the need to reform maritime laws.

Eventually the Merchant Shipping Act of 1876 was enacted which empowered the Board of Trade to detain vessels deemed unsafe by overloading. The Plimsoll Line, the compulsory load line marked on the hull of every ship, indicating the maximum load, was enforced in the 1890 legislation instigated by George HOWELL, MP.

Samuel Plimsoll is commemorated locally by Plimsoll Street, E14, and there is a monument to him on the Victoria Embankment, EC4.
Biography
Masters, D. *The Plimsoll Mark* (Cassell, 1955)
Obituary
Illustrated London News 11th June 1898
Articles
Maritime History Vol. 1. (April 1971) no. 1. pp73-90
Illustrated London News 7th August 1875

POTTER, Henry III 1848-1928
Chemist

Henry Potter was born in Farringdon Street, in the City, and educated at the City of London School. He went straight into the family business at the age of fourteen, becoming apprenticed to his father, Henry Potter II.

The business of Potter and Clarke was founded by Henry Potter I in 1812, in Farringdon Street, opposite the Fleet Prison. Henry Potter was seedsman, herbalist and dealer in leeches. There was a herb farm at Carshalton, Surrey, and as the business grew, additional premises were taken in Duke Street, Spitalfields, and later a head office was established in Artillery Lane. Charles Goddard-Clarke became a partner in 1873.

Henry Potter was a keen business man and took much interest in local affairs. He was Churchwarden of Christ Church, Spitalfields. Elected to Stepney Borough Council, he presided over its first meeting and was elected Mayor in 1902. He became an Alderman, Justice of the Peace and Commissioner for Income and Land Tax. As Mayor, he raised £5,000 for the London Hospital and also funds to equip three tuberculosis dispensaries.

In 1908 he went to live at Westcliff-on-Sea and was elected Councillor for the Chalkwell ward on Southend Council.

He was keen on bowls and became Chairman of the Essex Bowling Club.

Book

Baker, P.S. *The Acorn That Grew Into An Oak* (Potter and Clarke, 1948)

PRELLEUR, Pierre or Peter circa 1705-1741

Organist and Composer

Pierre or Peter Prelleur was a Huguenot, that is, one of those who were religiously persecuted for their Protestant faith in France. He was perhaps the 'Pierre Preleur', son of Jacque Preleur, weaver, 'over against Crispin Street', who was baptised on 16th December 1705 at the French Church, Threadneedle Street in the City. He lived in Rose Lane and, at the time of his death, in Corbet's Court, Spitalfields.

He began his career as a writing-master in Spitalfields, and in his spare time played the harpsicord at the 'Angel and Crown' tavern in Whitechapel. In 1728 he became organist at the City church of St. Alban, Wood Street. He wrote an *Introduction to Singing*, first published in 1731 as Part 1 of a much larger instructional work called *The Modern Musick Master*, which in addition to singing, also dealt with playing the recorder, flute, violin and harpsicord. In 1732 he co-edited *The Harmonious Companion, or The Psalm Singer's Magazine*.

In 1736 he was appointed as the first organist at Christ Church, Spitalfields, which then had the largest organ in England, at a salary of £30 per year. While there, he wrote fifteen hymn tunes, which were posthumously published in 1758 in the anthology *Divine Melody*.

From about 1728 he was also harpsicordist at Goodman's Fields Theatre until it was closed under the Licensing Act of 1737; he then transferred to the New Wells (or Goodman's Fields Well) Theatre in Leman Street. There, he wrote a good deal of music for stage performance, including the opera *Baucis and Philemon*, produced in 1740. This has been described as a 'very cheerful affair' and songs from it were performed at Christ Church in 1979 as part of the church's 250th anniversary celebrations.

Pierre or Peter Prelleur was buried in Christ Church, Spitalfields.

Book

Dawe, D. *Organists of the City of London 1666-1850* (The Author, 1983)

The New Grove Dictionary of Music and Musicians

PUDDEFOOT, Sydney Charles 1894-1972

Footballer

Sydney Puddefoot was born in Limehouse. He attended Park School, West Ham where he gained a reputation as an outstanding schoolboy footballer.

He came into prominence as a West Ham player towards the end of 1913 and was a regular at centre forward or inside forward until professional football was brought to a close because of the war.

He played with West Ham in the London Combination competitions during the war and was picked for the Victory Internationals in 1919.

He was transferred to Falkirk in 1922 for £5,000, then a record transfer fee. He moved to Blackburn Rovers in 1925 and was in that Club's F.A. Cup winning team in 1928. He was capped for England twice in 1926.

He returned to West Ham in 1932 and was later involved in coaching in Turkey.

RAINE, Henry 1679-1738
Brewer

Henry Raine was born in Wapping into a brewing family. In 1694 he was apprenticed to Anthony Bond, a brewer in the City of London, and by 1723 he was the proprietor of the *Star Brewhouse* at New Crane Wharf, Wapping. He married Sarah Petre, the daughter of a Mile End sea captain.

In 1716 Henry Raine founded his first school for 50 boys in Old Gravel Lane, Wapping, and records show that in 1718 the school was expanded to take in 50 girls. Raine's Hospital, a boarding school for 40 girls, was built and endowed in 1736. The girls received training for employment as domestic servants. A trust fund was set up to provide 'marriage portions' of £100 each for two former pupils every year. The marriage purses were drawn by lottery, and the money paid out on the marriage, which was to take place at St. George's-in-the-East Church. The trustees of Henry Raine's Will also gave the couple a wedding feast. This trust continued, with some interruptions, until 1892.

In 1875 the boys' school moved from Wapping to Cannon Street Road, St. George's-in-the-East. In 1913 both schools moved into premises in Arbour Square, Stepney and remained there until 1985, when the present site of the school in Approach Road, Bethnal Green was acquired.

The original 1719 building still stands in Raine Street, Wapping.

Book
Rose, C.M. *Raine's Foundation; an East London Charity School 1716-80* (Unpublished thesis, University of Bristol, 1985)

Pamphlet
Raine's Foundation *Raine's Prospect 1719-1969* (Raine's Foundation, 1969)

RALEIGH, Sir Walter 1552-1618
Explorer and Statesman

Walter Raleigh was born at Hayes Burton in South Devon and was educated at Oriel College, Oxford.

He is reputed to have lived in Blackwall, and a house said to have been occupied by him was demolished in 1890 to make way for the first Blackwall Tunnel approach.

Sir Walter Raleigh's house at Blackwall, demolished to make way for the Tunnel

He was knighted in 1584, and in 1595 he led an expedition to South America which he described in his book *Discovery of Guiana*. There were also expeditions to Cadiz in 1596 and 1597.

After James I's accession in 1603 he was condemned to death for conspiracy and imprisoned in the Tower of London, where he wrote his unfinished *History of the World*.

In 1616 he was reprieved and led a gold seeking expedition to the Orinoco, but this failed disastrously and on his return he was beheaded under his former sentence.

Walter Raleigh is popularly supposed to have introduced tobacco and potatoes to this country.

He is commemorated by a statue by W. McMillan (1959) in Whitehall, SW1.

Biography
Wallace, W.M. *Sir Walter Raleigh* (Oxford University Press, 1959)

DNB

RAMSAY, Edith MBE 1895-1983
Educationalist and Community Worker

Edith Ramsay was born in Highgate, where her father was the first minister of the Presbyterian Church. She won an open scholarship to North London Collegiate School and then went to London University, where she obtained B.A. degrees at Bedford College and the London School of Economics.

Edith first came to Stepney to teach at Old Castle Street Day Continuation School. From 1922-25 she was Childrens Care Organiser. During this time she stayed at local Women's hostels to understand the conditions under which many women and children had to live.

Appointed Head of Stepney Women's Evening Institute in 1931, she held the post until her retirement in 1960. The Institute was a warm and welcoming place for all. Literacy was a high priority, and over a period, the Institute served the Jewish population, refugee children from the concentration camps in the aftermath of war, and Hungarians who fled from their country during the uprising in 1956. From 1950 to 1960 she was active in the campaign to highlight the plight of prostitutes in the area.

During her time in Stepney, she continued her voluntary social work, with children, alcoholics and several organisations like the People's Palace, Toynbee Hall and the London Hospital. She was also concerned with the conditions of colonial seamen and served on a Colonial Office Advisory Committee.

When war came, she assisted in the evacuation of local children and spent her evenings working in the air-raid shelters. She was awarded MBE in 1947.

Edith Ramsay was elected to Stepney Borough Council as a Labour member, 1945-48, as an Independent member, 1959-62, and as a Liberal member, 1962-65, serving each time the residents of Cable Street (Tower Hamlets ward).

A devoted Christian, popular and greatly trusted, she was welcomed in churches of all denominations, synagogues and mosques.

Following her retirement, she continued her social work and there would often be a morning queue outside her home in Turner Street, waiting to get her advice and help.

Biography
Sokoloff, Bertha *Edith and Stepney; the life of Edith Ramsay* (Stepney Books, 1987)

Obituary
The Times 8th July 1983

RANDOLPH, Jane 1720-1776
Mother of President Thomas Jefferson

Jane Randolph was the eldest daughter of Colonel Isham Randolph and his wife Jane, of Dungeness. For a time they lived in Wapping and Jane Randolph was baptised at St. Paul's Church, Shadwell on 20th February 1720.

The family emigrated to America where Jane married Colonel Peter Jefferson, who became Justice of Goochland County Court, High Sheriff and County Lieutenant.

One of her nine children, Thomas, was third President of the United States of America from 1801-1809. He created the Republican Party and helped to draft the Declaration of Independence. He tried unsuccessfully to bring an end to slavery.

Through the Randolph family, President Jefferson derived a Royal descent from Edward I.

Book
Montgomery-Massingberd, H. (ed) *Burkes Presidential Families of the Unites States of America* (Burkes Peerage, 2nd edn.,1981)

RAVENSCROFT, John
died 1735-1745(?)
Musician

John Ravenscroft was one of the waits (professional musicians) of Tower Hamlets. He played the violin in the band of Goodmans

Fields Playhouse, opened in October 1729, received benefit performances in the 1729-30 and 1730-31 seasons, and seems to have been replaced by 1735.

He was much sought after to play at balls and dancing parties, being particularly good at the hornpipe. He wrote hornpipes and other dance tunes for the violin, and also composed some songs.

Being a very corpulent man, his performance was all the more remarkable.
The New Grove Dictionary of Music and Musicians

RAVENSDALE, Lady Mary Irene
1896-1966
Social Worker and Philanthropist

Irene Curzon was born at Carlton Gardens, London SW1, the daughter of 1st Baron Curzon of Kedleston, 1st Baron Ravensdale (Foreign Secretary from 1919-24) and Mary Victoria Leiter of Washington, USA. Irene Curzon succeeded to her fathers titles in 1925.

Her prospects of an entirely aristocratic life-style were changed after 1917 when she involved herself increasingly in raising money and organising entertainments at the Highway Clubs in East London. The clubs were all based in the vicinity of High Street, Shadwell, where severe conditions of poverty, unemployment, bad housing and crime existed. From modest beginnings the Highway Clubs soon became the centre where children, adolescents, parents and old people found friendship and creative activity. Many younger members of the aristocracy followed her and visited the clubs, but none were as consistent and faithful in their support as herself. In 1928, 224 High Street, Shadwell was purchased and established as the Ravensdale Girls Club in her honour. Her regular and generous donations to the clubs greatly assisted the activities to flourish.

During the second World War the clubs became centres for evacuation, for the homeless, for the provision of food in the shelters, and acted as playcentres and day nurseries for babies. Lady Ravensdale slept on a mattress on the floor by night in a room shared with club members, while the bombs fell.

Her efforts to replace the damaged club buildings came to a successful conclusion in 1958 with the opening of the new headquarters in Lowood Street.

In 1959, after 25 years as Chair of the Clubs, Lady Ravensdale was succeeded by Vera GRENFELL.

Other charitable works included the Vice-Presidency of the National Association of Girls Clubs and Mixed Cubs, Joint Presidency of the London Union of Youth Clubs, Presidency of the Musicians Benevolent Fund and Presidency of the World Congress of Faiths.

In 1958 she became a Life Peer, and took the title of Lady Ravensdale of Kedleston.

She was sister-in-law of the fascist leader Oswald Mosley but had no sympathy for his political activities.
Autobiography
In Many Rhythms (Weidenfeld and Nicolson, 1953)
Article
East London Advertiser 22nd May 1959
Who Was Who 1961-70

REED, Rev, Andrew 1787-1862
Philanthropist

Andrew Reed was the son of a watchmaker and was privately educated. In 1807 he became a student at Hackney Congregational College and in 1811 after his ordination he became Pastor of New Road Chapel, St. George's-in-the-East, where he had previously been a member.

Early in his ministry he rescued three orphan apprentices. Their master, a shoemaker in Rosemary Lane, now Royal Mint Street, had become bankrupt. Andrew Reed took over the master's debts and assumed responsibility for the boys.

In 1813 he began the London Orphan Asylum in premises in Cannon Street Road, St. George's-in-the-East. When the numbers increased, the asylum moved to Bethnal Green. He began the Infant Orphan Asylum in Hackney, moving to Dalston and finally to Wanstead where some 600 infants were cared for.

He also began the Reedham Orphan Asylum in 1841 and a Hospital for Incurables, 1855.

He wrote a number of hymns, including, *Spirit Divine, attend our prayers.*
Biography
Grist, D. *A Victorian Charity* (R.V.Hatt, 1974)
DNB

REEVE, Ada 1874-1966
Musical Comedy Actress

Ada Reeve was born Adelaide Mary Isaacs in Jubilee Street, Mile End. Her mother was a dancer and her father an actor who worked under the name of Charles Reeves.

She appeared in juvenile roles at the Pavilion, Whitechapel, and the Britannia, Hoxton. She went to America in 1893 to appear in music hall and returned a year later to appear in musical comedy at the Gaiety Theatre, where she had a long run of successes.

She made eight films and her television debut was in 1947 as Queen Victoria in Hugh Ross Williamson's play *Mr Gladstone*.
Autobiography
Take it for a Fact (Heinemann, 1954)
Book
Busby, R. *British Music Hall* (Elek, 1976)

RENNIE, John 1761-1821
Engineer

John Rennie was born in Scotland. He studied at Edinburgh University and in 1784 entered the employment of James Watt, the famous engineer and inventor

In 1791 John Rennie came to London and began business on his own account. He was Consultant and Engineer for West India and East India Docks, also for the London Dock. He designed the first Waterloo Bridge, Southwark Bridge and prepared designs for London Bridge, but died before they could be considered. London Bridge was subsequently built by his son, Sir John Rennie.

In 1798 John Rennie was elected Fellow of the Royal Society and he is commemorated by Rennie Cottages, Colebert Avenue, E1, and John Rennie Walk, E1.
Books
Pudney, J. *Crossing London's River* (J.M.Dent, 1972)
Pudney, J. *London's Docks* (Thames and Hudson, 1975)

DNB

RICARDO, David 1772-1823
Economist

David Ricardo grew up in Bromley Saint Leonard and later lived in Poplar. He was the son of a Dutch Jewish stockbroker and began work in his father's business and made a fortune when he was quite young. He married a Quaker and became a Christian.

Ricardo was interested in the scientific treatment of economic questions and in 1817 published his *The Principles of Political Economy and Taxation*. This book established him as an authority on his subject and he is generally regarded as the founder of the classical school of political economy. He was one of the founders of the Geological Society.

He purchased Gatcombe Park Estate, Gloucestershire in 1813 and became Member of Parliament for the Irish borough of Portarlington from 1819 until his death.

He is commemorated by Ricardo Street, E14.
Biography
Weatherall, D. *David Ricardo* (Hague, Martinus Nijhoff, 1976)

DNB

Dr. Harry Roberts

ROBERTS, Dr. Harry 1871-1946
General Practitioner

Harry Roberts was born in Somerset and qualified at St. Marys Hospital, London in 1895. After a short spell in Whitechapel, he acquired a surgery in Harford Street, Mile End Old Town, and remained there until his retirement.

He soon became known as 'the doctor' to half of Stepney and by 1912 had developed the practice into the largest and best run in East London. There were three other doctors, nurse midwives, a dentist and a masseur on his staff. It was a model of the panel system and a pioneer of the group practice. The staff were fully committed to their work and turned out day and night when needed.

Harry Roberts was an early member of the Fabian Society and a friend of Bernard Shaw and H.G. Wells. He founded the Stepney Labour League and was a member of the Mile End Board of Guardians, playing a large part in the many campaigns for better social conditions. Later in his career his political activity was mainly confined to journalism.

His surgery was bombed during the second World War and although a temporary surgery was obtained, the strain of the war years affected his health and he retired.

He is commemorated in the Borough by Harry Roberts Nursery School, Harford Street, E1.
Biography
Stamp, W. *Doctor Himself* (Hamish Hamilton, 1949)

ROCKER, Rudolf 1873-1958
Political Activist

Rudolf Rocker was born in Germany and came to Whitechapel in 1895. He lived at 33 Dunstan House, Stepney Green, Mile End, until 1914. He was a powerful leader of the Jewish immigrant poor, particularly tailors and could be described as a libertarian philosopher, teacher and trade unionist.

In 1906 Rudolf Rocker was the leader of a group which took over an old Salvation Army depot in Jubilee Street, Mile End Old Town, and transformed it into a club, education centre, library and reading room. The club was an early centre of adult education and was available to all workers whatever their creed. Lenin was a visitor to it in 1907.

Rudolf Rocker was the principal leader of the Jewish tailor's strike of 1912 which dealt a severe blow to the sweatshop system, and he was an active supporter of the docker's strike of the same year.

During the first World War he was interned at Alexandra Palace in North London. After his release he emigrated to the United States.
Autobiography
The London Years (Robert Anscombe, 1956)
Book
Fishman, W.J. *East End Jewish Radicals* (Duckworth, 1975)

ROGERS, Frederick 1846-1915
Social Reformer and Journalist

Frederick Rogers was born at 11 Gowers Walk, Whitechapel and lived for over 40 years at 9 Green Street, later called 62 Nicholas Street, Mile End.

When the University Extension Movement began in 1879 Frederick Rogers was the movement's secretary. He was also involved with the London School Board (formed in 1870), as a School Manager and took part in the activities of the working men's club in East London.

Frederick Rogers believed in an educated democracy giving equal opportunities for full self-development and that class jealousy and hatred were to be opposed. This led to his early involvement in the settlement movement. In the autumn of 1883 he spoke at a series of lectures organised by students at Oxford, his subject being artisan life in East London. The talk without doubt helped in the foundation of Toynbee Hall, the first settlement, in 1884. Frederick Rogers became active in its life and remained so for thirty years. In 1886 he was elected one of the first non-resident associates of Toynbee Hall, serving on its education committee from 1890-98. He was vice-President from 1886-1915 of the Elizabethan Literary Society which met at Toynbee Hall. It enabled him to meet many of the leading literary figures of the day.

He was also a journalist, contributing regularly to the *Weekly Dispatch* in the 1880s under the pseudonym of 'Artisan'.

He was elected Organising Secretary of the National Committee of Organised Labour in 1899, the year it was established, because of his ability in writing, speaking, and organising and his middle of the road Labour background. One of his activities was the promotion of the idea of state pensions.

Being convinced of the proposals put forward by Charles BOOTH regarding Old Age Pensions he was appointed in 1899 to a Select Committee. It was largely due to his efforts that the 9 year campaign finally succeeded, and the Liberal Government introduced the Pensions Act, 1908.

He became an active trade unionist for 40 years and a skilled vellum bookbinder specialising in the binding of account books. From 1892-98 he was President of the Vellum Binder's Trade Society and represented them at the founding conference of the Labour Representation Committee, the forerunner of the Labour Party in 1900.
Autobiography
Labour, Life and Literature (Smith, Elder, 1913)
Article
East London Record no.15 (1992) pp.10-14

ROSENBERG, Isaac 1890-1918
Poet and Painter

Isaac Rosenberg was born in Bristol, one of five children of parents who had emigrated from Lithuania. They moved to London in 1897, and lodged at 47 Cable Street, St. George's-in-the-East. Isaac Rosenberg attended St. Paul's School, Wellclose Square, Whitechapel, and when the family moved to Jubilee Street, Stepney in 1900 he attended nearby Baker Street Board School. He showed early talent at drawing and painting, and his headmaster arranged for him to attend classes at the Stepney Green Art School. From the age of fourteen he was writing poetry. He was encouraged in his ambitions by the Librarian at Whitechapel, Morely Dainow, who lent him books and guided his reading.

In 1905 he was apprenticed to a Fleet Street engraver and platemaker and attended evening painting courses at Birkbeck College. In 1911 he was able to go to the Slade School of Fine Art as a full-time student, as a result of the generosity of friends who recognised his talent.

His first collection of verse, *Night and Day* was published at his own expense.

Isaac Rosenberg joined the Army in October 1915, and served in France. He was killed in action 1st April 1918.

His *Poems from the Trenches* are now recognised as some of the most outstanding written during the first World War. Paintings by Isaac Rosenberg hang in the National Portrait Gallery and the Tate Gallery.

He is commemorated with an English Heritage Blue Plaque at Whitechapel Library, Whitechapel High Street, E1.

Biographies
Cohen, J. *Journey to the Trenches* (Robson Books, 1975)
Liddiard, J. *Isaac Rosenberg* (Gollancz, 1975)
Wilson, J.M. *Isaac Rosenberg, Poet and Painter* (Cecil Woolf, 1975)

Book
Parsons, I. (ed) *The Complete Works of Isaac Rosenberg* (Chatto & Windus, 1979)

RUSSELL, John Scott 1808-1882
Engineer and Shipbuilder

John Russell was born in Glasgow. As a boy he displayed considerable aptitude and interest in mechanical inventions. He went to Glasgow University, where he graduated MA at the age of 17 and then became a teacher of mathematics.

In 1832 he was appointed Professor of Natural Sciences at Edinburgh University. He began research into the nature of waves, with a view to improving the design of ships, and recommending that the greatest section of a vessel should be behind the middle. In 1837 he received the gold medal of the Royal Society of Edinburgh for his paper on the results of his studies; *On the Laws of Resistance of Floating Bodies*. His system of shipbuilding was adopted for the new fleet of the West India Royal Mail Company.

He came to London in 1844 and for a time was secretary to the Royal Society of Arts, being involved in the discussions for the Great Exhibition of 1851.

He was one of the earliest advocates of ironclad Warships and was the joint designer with Isaac Watts, admiralty constructor, of the first sea-going iron frigate, the *Warrior*, built at Blackwall.

With Isambard Kingdom BRUNEL he built the Atlantic cable-laying ship *Great Eastern*, launched from Napier's Yard at Millwall in 1858. Its length of 680 feet made it a wonder of the world. John Scott Russell designed the paddle engines and boilers.

Biography
Emmerson, G.S. *John Scott Russell* (J.Murray, 1977)

DNB

RUSSELL, William 1777-1813
Organist and Composer

William Russell was the son of an organ builder and started taking lessons from eminent organists at the age of eight.

In 1798-1801 he became organist at St. Anne's Church, Limehouse. He was probably the earliest composer to write a pedal part in solo organ music. In 1800 he was appointed pianist and composer at Sadler's Wells Theatre and moved to Covent Garden Opera House in 1805.

Between 1800 and 1803 he wrote six pantomimes for Sadler's Wells. During his life he wrote oratorios, edited psalms, hymns and anthems and composed overtures and incidental music for theatrical entertainment. For Sadler's Wells, he composed an overture to *Highland Camp* in 1800. In 1805 he was engaged as a pianist at Covent Garden Opera House. He was organist at the Foundling Hospital from 1801 to 1813.

He composed two books of organ voluntaries and was much in demand as an organ inspector.

He was a great friend of Samuel Wesley, organist of Gloucester Cathedral, who praised his work highly.

Part of Russell's music library is now in the British Library.

DNB, Groves Dictionary of Music

RYDER, Sir William died 1669
Deputy Master of Trinity House

William Ryder purchased Bethnall House, Bethnal Green in June 1660. During the Great Fire of London, on 3rd September 1666, his great friend Samuel Pepys wrote in his diary:-

about four o'clock in the morning, my Lady Batten sent me a cart to carry away all my money, and plate and best things, to Sir W. Rider's at Bednall-greene. Which I did, riding myself in my nightgown in the cart; and Lord! to see how the streets and the highways are crowded with people running and riding, and getting of carts at any rate to fetch things away. I find Sir W. Rider tired of being called up all night, and receiving things from several friends. His home full of goods, and much of Sir W. Battens and Sir W. Pens

As member of the Stepney Vestry, William Ryder was given special permission to drive his coach across Mile End Common when attending St. Dunstan's Church.

He was knighted in 1660.

Book
Hill, G.W. and Frere, W.H. *Memorials of Stepney* (Privately Published, 1890-91)

SALMON, Robert 1567-1641
Merchant

Robert Salmon lived in Limehouse and married Joan, daughter of John VASSALL. In 1623 he was elected a vestryman at St. Dunstan's Church, Stepney. He became Master of Trinity House and Sheriff of the City of London 1640. He was also a member and director of the East India Company.

He is commemorated in the borough by Salmon Lane, E14.

SAMUDA, Joseph D'Aguilar
1813-1885
Engineer and Shipbuilder

Joseph Samuda was born in London. He studied to be an engineer and went into partnership with his brother Jacob in a yard at Blackwall. Between 1832 and 1842 they were principally concerned with building engines, but in 1843 they began shipbuilding.

The *Gipsy Queen* was one of their first ships and on the trial run off Blackwall, Jacob was killed in an explosion when an expansion joint in the engine gave way.

The firm continued building iron steamships for the Royal Navy as well as for passenger and mail services. Among those built for the Navy was the *Thunderbolt*, the first armour-plated iron vessel.

In 1860 Joseph Samuda was among the founders of the Institute of Naval Architects, becoming a Vice-President and first treasurer. He was also a member of the Institution of Civil Engineers. He was appointed to the Metropolitan Board of Works from 1860-1865.

He was elected Member of Parliament for Tavistock in 1865 and in 1868-1880 was Liberal Member for Tower Hamlets. He lost the next election through giving support to Disraeli's foreign policy.

He is commemorated by the Samuda Estate and Samuda Street, E14.

Book
Banbury, P. *Shipbuilders of the Thames and Medway* (David and Charles, 1971)

SAUNDERS, Thomas Henry
1813-1870
Papermaker

Born in Limehouse, Thomas Saunder's parents were John Saunders, a hoop bender and his wife, Mary. Little is known about his early life.

Thomas Saunders entered the paper making trade in the late 1830s and eventually owned six paper mills in Kent and Buckinghamshire. His mills had the reputation for supplying everything from newsprint (for *The Times*) in the 1860s to security paper, building up a huge export business to Europe. The quality of his paper is confirmed by the fact that he exhibited and won some dozen prize medals at international exhibitions. His business expanded entirely by acquisitions, one of his mills was probably the largest in the country. He rebuilt the Phoenix mill in Dartford as one of the major industrial buildings in South East England.

He went twice on deputations to see the Prime Minister (Viscount Palmerston), during the 1860's controversy about the abolition of paper duties and the continuing import duties on rags.

In 1862, Thomas Saunders with his mill manager, took out a patent on an improved way of drying machine-made paper, and of regulating the supply of pulp to the paper machine.

He was an active Baptist and a strong supporter of the Shaftesbury Society.

DNB Missing Persons (1993)

Alderman John Scurr and Councillor Mrs Julia Scurr

SCURR, John 1876-1932
Labour Leader

John Scurr was brought up in Poplar. He was adopted by his uncle, Captain John Scurr after his mother died when he was an infant. He was educated at George Green's School and then at King's College School. He started work in a Poplar office.

In the 1890s he worked with Will CROOKS, George LANSBURY and others to improve conditions for working people. He became a member of the Poplar Labour League, 1897 and then became its secretary. In 1910-11 he played a major part in the Dock Strike as District Chairman of the Dockers' Union. At the invitation of George LANSBURY, he worked for the *Daily Herald*. His wife, Julia SCURR was a member of the Board of Guardians and was prominent in the suffragette movement. Elected to Poplar

Borough Council in 1919, he was later made an Alderman, and was Mayor 1922-23. John Scurr was sent to Brixton Prison with other Poplar Councillors in 1921 for refusing to levy Poplar's share of the London County Council, Police and Metropolitan Asylum contributions on the grounds that local rate payers were already impoverished with high levels of unemployment. From 1925 to 1929 John Scurr was an Alderman of the London County Council.

After several attempts to get into Parliament he was elected for Mile End in 1923 and again in 1924 and 1929, increasing his majority of votes each time. He was defeated in the election of 1931.

As a Roman Catholic he was prominent in the discussions on the Education Bill before Parliament in 1930, particularly over the role of the voluntary schools. He is commemorated in the borough by John Scurr House, Branch Road, E14., and by John Scurr Primary School, Cephas Street, E1.

DLB

SCURR, Julia 1871-1927
Suffragette and Councillor

Born Julia O'Sullivan, her family came from County Cork, but she spent her early years in Limehouse and lived in East London all her life. Julia married John SCURR in 1900 and they made a formidable partnership.

Julia Scurr was first active in the Irish movement and then became particularly concerned with women's rights and the improvement of their conditions. One of her earliest activities was to organise a deputation of women to meet Prime Minister Balfour on unemployment.

A friend and colleague of Sylvia PANKHURST, she was active in the East London Federation of Suffragettes. In 1914 she led a deputation from the Federation to meet Herbert Asquith, Prime Minister, over low wages paid to women.

In 1907 she was elected to fill the vacancy on the Poplar Board of Guardians caused by the resignation of Will CROOKS and remained a Guardian until her death. A Poplar Councillor from 1919-1925, she was sent to Holloway Prison with other women Councillors in 1921 for refusing to levy Poplar's share of the London County Council, Police and Metropolitan Asylum contributions on the grounds that local rate payers were already impoverished with high levels of unemployment.

In 1925 Julia Scurr was elected a member of the London County Council for Mile End.
Book
Branson, N. *Poplarism, 1919-1925* (Lawrence and Wishart, 1979)

SHEA, Danny 1887-1960
Footballer

Daniel Shea was born in Wapping in 1887. After success in amateur football locally, he was taken on by West Ham United for whom he signed as a professional in 1908.

He had several successful seasons in the Southern League before being transferred to Blackburn Rovers for the then record fee of £2,000.

While at Blackburn he won a League championship medal in 1914 and was twice capped for England in the same year.

His career was interrupted by the first World War, but he appeared regularly as a guest player for West Ham and was selected for two Victory Internationals in 1919. He played for Fulham, Coventry, and Clapton Orient, retiring from League football in 1926. He later worked in the London Dock.

SHEPPARD, Rev. Hugh Richard Lawrie (Dick) 1880-1937
Priest

Dick Sheppard was born at Windsor, where his father was a Canon at St. George's Chapel. Educated at Marlborough School and Cambridge, he began working in Bethnal Green as manager of a boys' club at Oxford House, Derbyshire Street, in 1904. He was ordained in 1907, and took charge of Oxford House, 1909-10.

In 1914 he was appointed Vicar of St. Martin's-in-the-Fields Church, Trafalgar Square, Westminster and remained there until 1926.

He was appointed Dean of Canterbury in 1929 and a Canon of St. Paul's Cathedral in 1934.

He was one of the founders of the Peace Pledge Union in 1936.

There is a portrait of him and a memorial in St. Martin's-in-the-Fields Church and commemorated in the borough by Sheppard House, St. Peters Avenue, E2.
Autobiography
Dick Sheppard by his friends (Hodder and Stoughton, 1938)

Biographies
Roberts, R.E. *H.R.L. Sheppard* (J. Murray, 1942)
Scott, C. *Dick Sheppard* (Hodder & Stoughton, 1977)

DNB

Jack Sheppard

SHEPPARD, Jack 1702-1724
Highwayman

Jack Sheppard was born in Stepney. He consorted with criminals and in 1720 committed many robberies. He was caught in 1724 and imprisoned. Four times he managed to escape but was finally imprisoned at Newgate and executed at Tyburn in the presence of an estimated 200,000 spectators.

He caught the public imagination and was the subject of many plays and ballads, a tract by Daniel Defoe and a novel by Harrison Ainsworth.

His portrait was painted by Sir James Thornhill in the cell at Newgate and is in the Print Room of the British Museum.

He was buried at the old Churchyard of St. Martin's-in-the-Fields, Trafalgar Square, SW1, now the site of the National Gallery.

Biography
Hibbert, C. *The Road to Tyburn* (Longmans, Green, 1957)

DNB

SHINWELL, Emanuel (Lord 'Manny') 1884-1986
Labour Leader

Manny Shinwell was registered at birth as Emmanuel Shinewell, 17 Freeman Street, Spitalfields. He was the eldest of thirteen children of Samuel Shinewell, an immigrant Polish tailor and Rose who was of Dutch descent. He went to school in Old Castle Street, Whitechapel. When he was six, his parents moved to Glasgow, and the remainder of his childhood was spent there, in the Gorbals district.

He left school when he was eleven and worked for a time for his father, and later as a delivery boy for a tobacco firm. His ambition was to go to sea, but his parents were against it.

When he was twenty six, he was appointed an official of the National Union of Seamen. He was a splendid orator who spoke his mind.

In 1922 he was elected Member of Parliament for Linlithgow in MacDonald's Labour Government and was appointed Parliamentary Secretary to the Department of Mines. He held several cabinet offices and remained in the House of Commons until 1970 when he was given a life peerage.

On his one hundredth birthday he was invited to unveil a plaque presented by his fellow peers to hang in the House of Lords Library. He had so much post on that day, that by the time of the unveiling he had failed to find the congratulatory telegram from the Queen. "I have got to have that telegram", he said, "or nobody will believe that I am a hundred; and nor will I".

On 26th March 1985 he returned to Tower Hamlets to unveil a plaque on Brune House, Bell Lane, E1, which has replaced 17 Freeman Street where he was born on 18th October 1884.

Obituary
The Daily Telegraph 9th May 1986
Autobiography
Lead With the Left, My First Ninety Six Years (Cassell, 1981)

SILLEY, John Henry 1872-1941
Shipbuilder

John Silley was born at Chepstow. After an engineering apprenticeship, he went to sea and on his return he began business as a ship repairer in partnership with John Weir. The firm eventually became R. and H. Green and Silley Weir Ltd., which had extensive ship repairing facilities in Blackwall, E14. In 1934-35 he was President of the Institute of Marine Engineers.

John Silley was always concerned about the welfare of his workers and especially interested in those who had retired. He built Jubilee Crescent, Cubitt Town, E14, and other houses for retired workers of the shipping industry in Blackwall.

SMITH, George Joseph 1872-1915
Bride Murderer

George Smith was born in Roman Road, Bethnal Green. He achieved notoriety as the accused in what became known as 'The Brides in the Bath Case'. All three of Smith's wives died mysteriously in the bath on the first night of their honeymoon, and he collected the insurance money.

The trial took place at the Old Bailey, where he was defended by the famous barrister, Sir Edward Marshall Hall. George Smith was convicted of the murder of Constance Munday at Herne Bay on 13th July 1912. Evidence was also given in regard to the death of Alice Burnham at Blackpool in 12th December 1913 and Margaret Lofty at Highgate on 18th December 1914.

The jury took twenty minutes to find him guilty and the Judge then sentenced him to death. George Smith made no confession, he was hanged protesting his innocence.

SMITH, Sir Hubert Llewellyn
1864-1945
Civil Servant

Hubert Llewellyn Smith was born in Bristol. After leaving Oxford he lived at Toynbee Hall, a university settlement, from 1888-89. He then moved to a house in Beaumont Square, Mile End Old Town from which he organised the Craft School, first in Globe Road, and later at 37, Stepney Green. The Craft School was an evening school. It included a gymnasium, facilities for carpentry, metalwork, drawing, painting and drama. Boys and girls acted in a wide variety of weekly Shakespeare's plays.

Hubert Llewellyn Smith became Permanent Secretary to the Board of Trade. In 1919 he was appointed Chief Economic Adviser to the British Government and attended the peace talks at Versiailles which concluded the first World War.

His writings included *The Story of the Docker's Strike* (1889), and *The History of East London*, published in 1939.

He was Chairman of the National Association of Boys' Clubs 1935-1943.
Book
History of East London From the Earliest Times to the Eighteenth Century (Macmillan, 1939)

SMITH, Corporal Issy VC
1886-1940
Soldier

Issy Smith was born in Stepney and educated at Berner Street School. He served in the 1st. Battalion of the Manchester Regiment from 1906 to 1912. For some time before 1914 he worked with the Metropolitan Gas Company as a plumber and gas fitter.

In 1914 he emigrated and joined the Imperial Australian Force serving in New Guinea, Mesopotania and Palestine. He transferred to the 1st Battalion, Manchester Regiment again and was sent to France. He was awarded for his brave action of 26th April 1915 in the 2nd Battle of Ypres.

His citation records that:-

He went well forward on his own initiative to assist a severely wounded man, carrying him a distance of 250 yards into safety, while exposed the whole time to heavy machine gun and rifle fire. He later displayed great gallantry when casualties were very heavy to bring in more wounded men during the day, attending them with the greatest devotion to duty, regardless of personal risk.

Apart from the VC he was awarded the Russian Cross of St. George and the French Croix de Guerre. Leeds and Bradford Cities invited him to visit after his award and he was feted. Issy Smith also received a presentation at Berner Street School. He was also a guest at the wedding in Westminster Abbey in 1923 of the Duke of York and Lady Bowes-Lyon (later King George VI and Queen Elizabeth).

After the war he worked for S.T. Davies and Co., of Bethnal Green, a cycle accessory firm. He later toured with several musical comedies. He became a music hall manager, film actor and business man.

Issy Smith emigrated to Australia and was an unsuccessful candidate in the Federal Elections. He died in Melbourne, Australia.
Books
The Register of the Victoria Cross (This England Books, 1981)
Creagh, Sir O'M. and Humphries, E.M. (eds) *The V.C. and D.S.O.* (Standard Art Book, 1924)

SNELL, Hannah 1723-1792
Female Soldier

Hannah Snell was born in Worcester, the youngest of nine children of a hosier and his wife. All her brothers joined the armed forces and all her sisters, except one, married servicemen. Her parents died in 1740, and she went to live in Ship Street, Wapping with her sister, Susannah who was married to James Gray, a carpenter. There, she met a Dutch sailor, James Simms or Summs whom she married in 1743. When he deserted her, she decided to search for him, and, to ensure her personal safety she dressed as a man and adopted her brother-in-law's name on her journey. She reached Coventry and, realising the advantages of travelling more safely with companions, she enlisted as a soldier, and marched with her regiment to Carlisle. Here she came into conflict with her sergeant by revealing to a young lady that her sergeant had dishonourable intentions upon her virtue. Hannah was falsely accused of dereliction of duty and her punishment was to be stripped to the waist, tied to the castle gate and whiplashed 600 times. She tried to conceal her womanhood by pressing tightly onto the gate to flatten her breasts. Not surprisingly she soon deserted from the Army and joined the Marines, serving on the sloop *Swallow*, where she became steward and cook in the officers' mess. She saw action at Pondicherry, India, and was wounded several times. She joined another ship and returned home after discovering that her husband was dead.

She wrote a book *The Female Soldier; or, the Surprising Life and Adventures of Hannah Snell* (1750).

Her fame spread and she was engaged to sing at the Royalty Theatre, Wellclose Square and performed military ballads and drill routines at the New Wells Theatre, Goodman's Fields.

Hannah Snell received a pension from the Army which enabled her to take a public house in Wapping, which she called *The Female Warrior*.

In 1759 she married Richard Eyles in Newbury, Berkshire and in 1772 she married Richard Habgood at Wickham Chapel, near Newbury.

She was buried at her request in the graveyard at the Royal Hospital, Chelsea, London, SW1, the home for retired soldiers.

Book
Wilson, H. *Wonderful Characters* Vol. 1.(J.Robins,1821)

Articles
Family Tree Magazine December 1992, pp.4-5, and January 1993, pp.27-28

DNB

SOLOMONS, Jack 1902-1979
Boxing Promoter

Jack Solomons was born the son of a Russian Jew who had a fishmonger's business. He attended Old Castle Street School, Whitechapel. He boxed as 'Kid Mears' to earn money, but gave up boxing at the request of Fay, the girl who was to become his wife.

In 1932 he began promoting fights in an old church hall in Hackney where ringside seats cost one shilling. During his career Jack Solomons promoted 26 world title fights, featuring boxers such as Randolph Turpin, Henry Cooper, Sugar Ray Robinson and Muhammed Ali.

SOMES, Joseph 1787-1845
Ship Owner

Joseph Somes was born in the parish of St. George's-in-the-East. His father was a waterman and lighterman and Joseph Somes entered the family business.

As the business prospered he became a ship owner possessing ships of all types. When the East India Company sold their ships he bought some of the best of the vessels and hired them to the Government, mainly for the transport of convicts. He also owned whaling ships and vessels of his fleet were used in the Crimean War.

Joseph Somes claimed that every captain in his employ had originally entered his employ as an apprentice. The fleet was well known for providing good seafarers.

Joseph Somes was a promoter and member of the Committee of Management of Lloyd's Register of Shipping which was an authorised classification society which surveyed ships under construction and issued certificates of sea worthiness.

He died at his house in New Grove, Mile End Old Town, where St. Clement's Hospital, Bow Road, E3, now stands. He left property to the value of between one and two million pounds. After his death the firm was known as Somes Brothers and later as the Merchant Shipping Company.

He was buried in St. Dunstan's Church, Stepney, where there is a monument to him.

SPERT, Sir Thomas died 1541
Founder and First Master of Trinity House

Thomas Spert lived in Stepney and for a time was Comptroller of the Royal Navy. In approximately 1511 he founded Trinity House at Deptford Strand. He became its first Master and was knighted in November 1529. Trinity House is still responsible for all lighthouses, lightships and pilot services around the coast of Britain. Thomas Spert obtained from Henry VIII the charter of incorporation for the Deptford Mariner's Guild of the Holy Trinity, as Trinity House was known as, in 1514.

The Corporation of Trinity House's connections with Stepney began about 1610 with their meetings being held near Ratcliff Cross or White Horse Lane. The formal move to Ratcliff Cross appears to have taken place in 1618 where the majority of their meetings were held. In about 1650 Trinity House acquired the rental of the 'Great House', opposite St. Dunstan's Church, Stepney but prior to the Great Fire of London 1666, had already moved to new premises in Water Lane, near the Tower of London. It was burnt down during this conflagration. The Trinity Brethren took temporary accommodation in White Horse Lane in 1670. By 1683 the Trinity House lease at the 'Great House' had expired.

At the end of his life, Thomas Spert's main residence was 'Newburns' in West Ham.

He was buried in St. Dunstan's Church and there is a monument to him in the church.

He is also commemorated by Spert House, Carr Street, E14, and Spert Street, E14.

STEEVENS, George 1736-1800
Shakespearian Scholar

George Steevens was born in Poplar, the son of a Captain in the East India Company's fleet. He was educated at Eton and Cambridge, but left without completing his degree.

The main activity of Steevens' life was devoted to preparing accurate editions of Shakespearean texts. His first was printed in 1769, and in 1773 he collaborated with Dr. Samuel Johnson on a ten-volume annotated edition of the plays.

George Steevens is buried in St. Matthias Church, Poplar where there is a monument to him by the English sculptor John Flaxman.

DNB

George Steevens

STEPHENSON, Robert 1803-1859
Civil Engineer

Robert Stephenson was the son of George Stephenson, the railway pioneer, and was born near Newcastle-upon-Tyne. On leaving school he was apprenticed to Nicholas Wood and assisted his father in the survey for the Stockton to Darlington railway. He was also involved in the Rainhill trials in preparation for the Liverpool to Manchester railway, the first passenger railway in the world.

In 1836 Robert Stephenson moved his office to London. He built the Blackwall railway which ran from Fenchurch Street Station to Brunswick Wharf, Blackwall from 1841 to 1926. This was the second local railway in London, the first being London Bridge to Greenwich.

One of his many achievements was the Britannia Bridge over the Menai Strait, a channel between Anglesey and the Welsh mainland. The giant tubes were made in Blackwall at Robert BAILLIE's yard. Robert Stephenson also designed the great bridge over the St. Lawrence River at Montreal; here also the ironwork was made at Blackwall and shipped to Canada. The bridge is 6,588 feet long. In 1858 he went to Napier's Yard, Millwall to assist I.K. BRUNEL in launching his giant ship *Great Eastern*.

Elected Member of Parliament for Whitby in 1847, he was President of the Institution of Civil Engineers and also a Fellow of the Royal Society.

He was buried in Westminster Abbey, his funeral being a great public occasion. There is a bronze statue of him in Euston Square, erected 1871.

Biography
Rolt, L.T.C. *George and Robert Stephenson* (Longmans, 1960)

STEPHENSON, Rev. Thomas Bowman 1839-1912
Founder of the National Children's Homes

Thomas Stephenson was born near Newcastle-upon-Tyne. He entered the Methodist ministry. After a short time in the north of England he was sent to Waterloo Road Chapel, South London, where many of his congregation were children who slept rough around that district. He described them as 'ragged, shoeless, filthy, their faces pinched with hunger and premature wretchedness'.

Having read a book about a home for dockside boys in Hamburg, he resolved to do what he could to help the homeless children of Waterloo. With some financial help he was able to rent a house in what is now Exton Street, SE1 in 1869 and the first children moved in.

above Rev. Thomas Stephenson *below* National Children's Home, in Bonner Road, Bethnal Green *National Children's Home*

143

Within two years the need to expand was evident and in 1871 the home moved to a disused paving stone factory in Bonner Road, Bethnal Green, where it remained for over 40 years, housing 350 children at any one time.

The Home moved to Harpenden in 1912. All the time the work was expanding and there are now 50 branches throughout the country and the work has spread overseas.

When the National Children's Homes celebrated their centenary in 1969 it estimated that over 50,000 children had been provided with a home and an education. Dr. Stephenson was a member of the School Board for London, representing Hackney from 1873-76.

Pamphlet
National Children's Homes; One Hundred Years (NCH,1969)

STOTHARD, Thomas 1755-1834
Painter and Book Illustrator

Thomas Stothard was born at Long Acre, Westminster. At the age of 13 he was sent to a boarding school in Ilford, but when his father died in 1770 he returned to live with his mother in Stepney Green.

Thomas Stothard was apprenticed to a designer of flowered silk patterns in Spital Square, Spitalfields. On finishing his apprenticeship he returned home to his mother's apartments in Bethnal Green. He began painting portraits of his friends and acquaintances.

In 1777 he became a student at the Royal Academy Schools and he exhibited his painting of the Holy Family at the Royal Academy in 1779. He began book illustrations in the same year. There are examples in Boydell's *Shakespeare*, Bunyan's *The Pilgrims Progress*, Defoe's *The Life and Adventures of Robinson Crusoe* and Carey's *Critical Description of the Procession of Chaucer's Pilgrims to Canterbury*. He was elected Royal Academician in 1794 and in 1814 was appointed Librarian of the Royal Academy, holding the post until his death.

In 1814 Thomas Stothard won the competition for designing the armorial shield for the Duke of Wellington.

He is commemorated by Stothard House, Amiel Street, E1, and Stothard Street, E1.

Biography
Bray, Mrs E.A. *Life of Thomas Stothard, R.A.* (London, 1851)

DNB

STRYPE, Rev. John 1643-1737
Historian and Biographer

John Strype was born in Strypes Yard, Spitalfields which had been named after his father, who was a silk merchant. He was educated at St. Paul's School and Cambridge.

He became Vicar of Leyton in 1669, remaining there until his death.

He wrote the biographies of prominent clergymen of his time but his main achievement was the enlarging and editing of Stow's *Survey of the Cities of London and Westminster* which was published in 1720.

in 1929, a London County Council Blue Plaque was erected at 10 Leyden Street, E1, the nearest site to Strype's Yard.

DNB

SYMINGTON, William 1763-1831
Engineer - Pioneer of Steam Navigation

William Symington was born in Leadhills, Scotland and on leaving school he became a mechanic in a coal mine.

In 1787 he patented an engine for road locomotion and then constructed a similar engine for a boat which had trials on Dalwinston Loch. This engine, now in the Science Museum, London, is still in working order.

He designed the *Charlotte Dundas* at Grangemouth in 1802; this was the first workable steam boat.

On retirement William Symington received a small pension and moved to London to live with his son. He died in Burr Street, Aldgate.

He was buried in St. Botolph, Aldgate, Churchyard.

DNB

TATE, Beatrice Lilian 1896-1969
Borough Councillor

Beatrice was born at Shepherdess Walk, Hoxton. She met Henry TATE in 1915 and married him on 1st July 1918 at St. Mary's, Hoxton.

In 1924 she founded the women's section of the Bethnal Green Labour Party and remained its Secretary for 40 years.

A member of Bethnal Green Borough Council for 31 years, from 1934, and of the London County Council from 1949-1961, she took a great interest in housing and welfare services.

She was the first woman Councillor to be Mayoress, serving during the three periods when her husband was Mayor. Elected Mayor herself in 1952-1953, she chose her daughter, Mrs Dorothy Saunders, to be the Mayoress. She is commemorated by Beatrice Tate Nursery School, St. Jude's Road, E2.

Mayor Henry Edward Tate in 1949

TATE, Henry Edward 1883-1978
Borough Councillor

Henry Tate was born in Vyner Street, Bethnal Green and educated at Mowlem School, Bishops Way, Bethnal Green. When he was five, his father died, leaving his mother to raise six children. The then Liberal Board of Guardians refused to give help to his mother unless she parted with her children and, witnessing her condition of poverty, Henry Tate vowed to work with the socialist movement. Leaving school, he worked as a brushmaker. Having joined the Bethnal Green Labour Party he became its full time Secretary in 1922. At the time, the membership was 24; under him the number rose to 1,200. Elected to the Borough Council in 1934, he became Leader and was Mayor three times (1934-1936 and 1949-1950). He was the only Freeman of the Borough (1953). Altogether he served the Borough as a Councillor for 31 years. He was married to another Borough Councillor, Beatrice TATE. They are commemorated by Tate House, Roman Road, E2.

TAWNEY, Richard Henry
1880-1962
Historian

Richard Tawney was born in Calcutta, where his father was Principal of Presidency College. He was educated at Rugby School and Balliol College, Oxford. Richard Tawney came to Toynbee Hall, a university settlement as a resident in 1903 and was a leading pioneer of adult education. In 1908 as a resident he lectured in the Hall on 'Trade Unions', 'Co-operative Trading', 'Some Nineteenth Century Writers' and 'Social Aspects of Industry'. He was contemporary with Albert MANSBRIDGE and William BEVERIDGE, whose sister he married in 1909. It was Mansbridge who persuaded him to become a tutor for the recently formed Workers' Education Association. He later became a member of the Executive Committee and eventually President.

He was Professor of Economic History at London School of Economics 1931-1949. His works include *Religion and the Rise of Capitalism* (1926).

A portrait by Claude Rogers (1950) hangs in the London School of Economics and a drawing by John Mansbridge hangs in the National Portrait Gallery.

DNB

TELFORD, Thomas 1757-1834
Engineer

Thomas Telford was born at Westerkirk in Scotland; his father was a shepherd who died soon after he was born. Thomas Telford was educated at the parish school and at 15 was apprenticed to a mason, soon becoming a journeyman.

In 1780 he moved to Edinburgh and two years later came to London where he worked on the building of Somerset House in the Strand, Westminster.

In 1784 he received a commission to build a house for the superintendent of Portsmouth Dockyard. He then became Surveyor of Public Works for Shropshire. In 1793 he built the Ellesmere canal in Cheshire.

He was one of the country's leading engineers and altogether built more than 1,200 bridges and over 1,000 miles of roads. In East London he made the plans for St. Katharine's Dock, which opened in 1828.

145

Thomas Telford was the first President of the Institution of Civil Engineers and he was buried in Westminster Abbey, where there is a statue of him by Edward Baily.
Biography
Rolt, L.T.C. *Thomas Telford* (Longmans, Green, 1958)

DNB

Benjamin Tillett

TILLETT, Benjamin 1860-1943
Labour Leader

Benjamin Tillett was born in Bristol and his childhood was spent in extreme poverty. His mother died when he was one year old. When he was old enough he joined the Navy and later the Merchant service, afterwards working as a casual labourer in the docks.

He could hardly read or write until he was 17, but then he became a voracious reader and attended classes at the Bow and Bromley Evening Institute, Bow Road. He attended Bethnal Green Congregational Church, Pott Street and became a lay preacher. He married in 1882 and lived with his wife in a room in Bethnal Green.

Although physically a small man, he was a vigorous personality. He soon revealed himself as one of the great orators of the Labour movement. Working in a tea warehouse as a cooper, he was appointed Secretary of the Tea Operatives and General Workers' Union at a salary of £2 a week. With Tom MANN and John Burns he provided the leadership for dock workers.

The Dock strike of 1889 raised Tillett to a position of national importance, and after the strike his union was re-organised into the Dock, Riverside and General Labourers' Union, of which he became general secretary. In 1922 the union became part of the Transport and General Workers' Union. He was not a good administrator; his strength lay in his oratory.

Appointed Alderman of the London County Council 1892-98 and elected Member of Parliament for North Salford in 1917, 1924, and 1929, he was also a director of the *Daily Herald*.

He was so well known that he could go into the smallest town in Britain and be recognised immediately, while in Europe he would get an instant welcome in the streets.

In 1936 there was a presentation to him at Poplar Baths to which every man and his wife who had taken part in the Dock Strike were invited.

He is commemorated by Tillett Way, E2.
Autobiography
Memories and Reflections (J.Long, 1931)
Pamphlet
Dock, Wharf, Riverside and General Workers' Union (Twentieth Century Press, 1910)

DNB, DLB

TOMLINSON, Henry Major
1873-1958
Writer

Henry Tomlinson was born in Paynton Street (now Hind Grove) Poplar, his father was a cooper employed by the East and West India Dock Company.

Henry Tomlinson went to Byron Street School (now Langdon Park), Bromley-by-Bow until 1886, where his father died and the family moved to Spey Street, Bromley-by-Bow.

In 1904 he joined the editorial staff of the *Morning Leader* and his first book *The Sea and the Jungle* was published after a journey up the Amazon River.

During the first World War he was a war correspondent for the *Daily News*, afterwards becoming literary editor of *The Nation* and *The Atheneum*.

His first novel *Gallions Reach* was published in 1927 and he wrote a history of Trinity Congregational Church in 1952.
He died in London but was buried at Abbotsbury, Dorset.

Autobiography
A Mingled Yarn (Duckworth, 1953)

Book
Swinnerton, F. *The Georgian Literary Scene* (Heinemann, 1935)

DNB

TOYNBEE, Arnold 1852-1883
Economic Historian

Arnold Toynbee was born in London and was educated in Blackheath and at Oxford. He became lecturer in Economic History at the University and was also involved in arranging classes for workers.

A great friend of Samuel BARNETT he came frequently to Whitechapel to assist him in social work.

Arnold Toynbee died in March 1883. In December of the same year an informal meeting was held at Balliol College at which it was resolved to found a University settlement in East London. Samuel Barnett decided to call it Toynbee Hall and it was opened in 1884, and officially opened in January 1885.

Arnold Toynbee coined the phrase 'The Industrial Revolution', used in the title of his book *Lectures on the Industrial Revolution in England* (1884).

He is commemorated by Toynbee Street, E1, and Toynbee Hall, 28 Commercial Street, E1.

Biography
Milner, A. *Arnold Toynbee* (Edward Arnold, 1895)

TRAPNEL, ANNA circa 1642-1660
Prophet

Anna Trapnel was born in Poplar, the daughter of William Trapnel, shipwright, and of a 'godly' mother.

After visiting different Puritan congregations in her teens, she had a 'revelation' at the church of John Simpson in Aldgate, She joined that congregation in 1650 and became a 'Fifth Monarchist', an extremist sect of the Cromwellian period, who expected the imminent coming of Christ to take political power. There was an attempted rising in London in 1661, following which the movement subsided.

Anna Trapnel's first pamphlet *Strange and Wonderful Newes from Whitehall* chronicles the twelve day trance into which she fell on 7th January 1654. Large audiences gathered to hear her verse prophesies which she uttered from her bed. *The Cry of a Stone* also records these events. Her words were written down by recorders who she sometimes exhorted to write faster, to keep pace with her.

Anna declared God's displeasure at Oliver Cromwell being made Lord Protector on 16th December 1653. In the role of God's vessel, Anna Trapnel made public political criticisms alongside her spiritual predictions.

She went to Cornwall to preach and was arrested in March 1654 and imprisoned in Plymouth, then Portsmouth and finally, Bridewell, London, accused of witchcraft and madness. During her imprisonment, *A Legacy for Saints* was published by her congregation at All Hallows-the-Great, London, describing her conversion.

Her high public profile and her talent for talking her way out of tight corners seemed to have led to her release on 26th July.

In 1656 she re-visited Cornwall and from August 1657 to mid 1658 fell into another trance, so avoiding further arrest. Anna Trapnel condemned the Quakers as well as the politicians, her utterings were recorded in *A Voice for the King of Saints*. Anna Trapnel demonstrated that some women could make their voices heard on political as well as spiritual matters during the Interregnum.

DNB Missing Persons (1993)

TRAVERS, Nat 1875-1958
Music Hall Singer

Nat Travers started his career at the music halls in Hoxton and Shoreditch. In 1903 he appeared at the London Pavilion with Dan Leno and George Robey.

Travers was 'on the boards' for 74 years. He specialised in songs like *My Old Dutch* and *She was a sweet little Dickybird* and wrote many others himself, some of which he published from 307 Mile End Road.

Despite his dislike of using a microphone, Nat Travers also appeared on radio and television.

He was still topping the bill at the Metropolitan in Edgware Road, West London in 1958, in his 83rd year.

He lived at 265 Bancroft Road, E1 for sixty years.

TREVES, Sir Frederick 1853-1923
Surgeon

Frederick Treves was born at Dorchester, where his father was an upholsterer. He was educated at the Merchant Taylors' School in London.

He was at the London Hospital as a student, assistant surgeon, principal surgeon, and lecturer in anatomy. He did a great deal to improve the techniques of surgery.

During the Boer War he served with Buller's army and was present at the relief of Ladysmith.

In 1902, two days before the coronation of Edward VII, Frederick Treves was to operate on the King for acute appendicitis. The coronation had to be postponed until the following year.

Frederick Treves wrote *The Elephant Man and Other Reminiscences* about his time at the London Hospital. He became famous for his befriending of Joseph (John) MERRICK, 'The Elephant Man'. Treves wrote in the *British Medical Journal* about Merrick's condition and the nature of his disease. He also wrote a series of textbooks on surgery and anatomy and was one of the founders of the British Red Cross Society.

His portrait by Sir Luke Fields is in the London Hospital Medical College, and he is commemorated locally by Treves House, Vallance Road, E1.

Books
The Elephant Man and Other Reminiscences (Cassell, 1962)
Clark-Kennedy, A.E. *The London* (Pitman-Medical, 1962)
DNB

TREVITHICK, Richard 1771-1833
Engineer

Richard Trevithick was born at Redruth, Cornwall. He became a mining engineer at Penzance. In 1801 he constructed a road locomotive powered by steam to carry passengers, and in 1803 it ran from Leather Lane, Holborn, to Paddington via Oxford Street. He was also involved in the development of the high pressure engine.

In 1805 he was invited to succeed Robert Vazie as engineer in building a tunnel for the Thames Archway Company from St. Mary's, Rotherhithe to Limehouse. After driving 1,000 feet under the Thames, the project was abandoned as impracticable.

Tunnelling under the Thames had to wait another ten years until I.K. BRUNEL had invented the tunnelling shield, and a further decade until it had been perfected.

Richard Trevithick has a memorial window in Westminster Abbey.

Biography
Dickinson, H.W. and Titley, A. *Richard Trevithick* (Cambridge University Press, 1934)

Book
Pudney, J. *Crossing London's River* (Dent, 1972)
DNB

Sir Benjamin Truman

TRUMAN, Sir Benjamin
1690-1780
Brewer

Benjamin Truman was born in Brick Lane, Spitalfields. His father, Joseph Truman, had joined the brewing business soon after it was founded by Thomas Bucknall in 1666.

In 1737 when the Duchess of Brunswick (grand-daughter of George II) was born there was a celebration outside Carlton House, London. The beer provided by the royal brewer was judged by the crowd not to be good enough for the occasion and it was thrown over many present. A second celebration was ordered by the Prince of Wales for the next night and Ben Truman was asked to provide four barrels of better beer. His beer was judged excellent and became a very popular drink.

On the accession of George III, Ben Truman was knighted and to celebrate the occasion he had his portrait painted by Thomas Gainsborough in 1760. The portrait is now in the Tate Gallery.

During the 18th century fame came to the Brewery again through the brewing of 'porter', a black stout. It was the first beer which could be brewed in large quantities without deterioration.

When Grand Metropolitan took over the Brewery in 1971 they re-built part of it to establish their administrative headquarters (1975). The closure of the Brick Lane premises took place in 1989 and administration and brewing was transferred to the Mortlake site.

Books

Truman, Hanbury and Buxton *Truman's, the Brewers* (Newman Neame, 1966)

Barnard, A. *The Noted Breweries of Great Britain and Ireland* (Sir J. Causton & Sons, 1889-91)

TRUMAN, Charles Samuel
1892-1978
Local Historian

Charles Truman was born in Whitechapel. He qualified as a schoolmaster in 1914 and later took a correspondence course with Ruskin College, Oxford. A member of the Independent Labour Party and a Trades Council representative, he was also a member of Stepney Borough Council.

From 1932-1935 he was Head of the Evening Institute at Bow Creek and then at the Isle of Dogs 1936-1942. After a period in South London he returned to teach local history at Cephas Street School, Mile End (now John Scurr School).

In 1952 he was co-founder of the East London History Society and became its Chairman for a time. He was an authority on the area of Mile End and Stepney Green and wrote a pamphlet *The Hamlet of Mile End Old Town* (1963)

Charles Trueman showing school children an early map of Stepney in 1965

TURNER, Merfyn 1915-1991
Youth Worker and Penal Reformer

Merfyn Turner came to Oxford House, Bethnal Green shortly after the end of the war. One of his experiments was to run a club for adolescent boys on a barge, moored at Wapping. The club was designed to meet the needs of boys who would not join a conventional club. He wrote an account of the work in a book called *The Barge Experiment*.

It was while he was at Oxford House that he began visiting Pentonville Prison, north London, developing an interest which was to shape the remainder of his life.

He became an authority on penal affairs and was listened to with respect by Government officials and prison staff, as he outlined his vision for the care of prisoners.

His dedication and humanity ensured that every prison door was open to him because people recognised his warm personality and practical sensitivity.

In the 1950s he opened the first Norman House – a halfway house between prison and freedom, and became the first Warder. Many more Norman Houses followed, it was a new concept in the re-settlement of offenders He continued the work for forty years.

His father was a Methodist minister and Merfyn Turner inherited his style of Welsh oratory, making him a popular speaker, but with an uncomfortable message about the state of British prisons.

VALE, George Frederick 1890-1960
Librarian and Local Historian

George Vale was born in East London and began work at St. George's Library in Cable Street as a junior assistant in 1903. Following the success of his professional studies he was appointed deputy to the Borough Librarian for Bethnal Green in 1919 and in 1934 he became Borough Librarian.

He founded the local records collection for Bethnal Green and was also responsible for the creation of the 'Air Raid Shelter Library', at the tube station much used during the second World War. Under him the Bethnal Green Public Library became one of the best known in the country.

His little book on Bethnal Green contains a mine of information about its history and some of the Borough's characters.

He is commemorated by George Vale House, Mansford Street, E2.

Book
Old Bethnal Green (Blythenhale Press, 1934)

VALLANCE, William 1834-1909
Poor Law Reformer

William Vallance was born in Woolwich and became one of the shrewdest Poor Law Officers in London, pursuing reforming policies (to increase the independence and self help of those in poor circumstances) which later were to be adopted throughout the country.

He began his career as a youth in the office of the Clerk of the Board of Guardians of the Dunmow Union in Essex and in 1857 transferred to the Clerks Office of the Braintree Union in Essex.

When he was appointed to the post of Clerk of the Whitechapel Union in 1868 he also took on the duties of Super-

George Vale receives a testimonial from Mayor Clark after 31 years service, 25th January 1951

intendant Registrar and Clerk of the Union Assessment Committee. In 1902 he retired with 34 years of service.

Costly outdoor relief to the poor was reduced and a separate infirmary was built allowing the able bodied paupers to move to the workhouse. Widows and children were found help through arrangements made with the Tower Hamlets Pension Society and the Charity Organisation Society. Pauper children were sent to cottages in Grays in Essex and were educated.

William Vallance took an interest in the work of Clerk to the Forest Gate School District for 5 years, alongside his other duties and from 1884-1909 he was also a member of the East London Industrial School's Board at Lewisham having joined it when the institution moved there from Leman Street, Whitechapel.

He gave expert evidence to Poor Law and other inquiries relating to Poor Law administration.

In 1893 he read a paper at a Congress in Chicago, USA., during which time he also studied the best American Poor Law system at Buffalo, USA.

In 1885 he founded and was the first President of the National Poor Law Officers' Association which became an influential institution of 10,000 members by 1909. William Vallance made a significant contribution to the superannuation movement through the strength of the Association and after an 11 year campaign, achieved the Poor Law Officers' Superannuation Act of 1896.

In the same year, a tribute was paid to his work by the London County Council which made an exception to its rule never to name streets after living individuals, and Bakers Row, Nottingham Street and White Street, Whitechapel were re-named Vallance Road.

When William Vallance was a member of the Metropolitan Asylums Board he conceived the idea of a training ship for boys and became Chairman of the *Exmouth* training ship committee. At his funeral at Brockley Cemetery, South London, a party from the *Exmouth* fired 3 volleys in the air and a bugle sounded *The Last Post*.

Articles

East London Observer 31st. May 1902; 14th August 1909; 23rd October 1909

East London Advertiser 10th September 1892

VASSALL, John   died 1625
Sailor

John Vassall was a Protestant refugee from Normandy who lived on Ratcliff Wall. He was an authority on navigation.

He commanded a ship in the English fleet against the Spanish Armada, 1588, and was one of the founders of Virginia, USA, 1609. He married Judith, niece of Sir William BOROUGH and died of the plague in Stepney.

He was buried in St. Dunstan's Church.

He is commemorated by Vassall House, Grove Road, E3.

DNB

VATCHER, Marion   1850-1933
Philanthropist

Marion Vatcher lived in Newark Street, Stepney where her husband was vicar of St. Philip's Church from 1883-1920.

She was one of the founders of the East End Maternity Hospital formerly in Commercial Road, London E1, serving on its committee for over 50 years. She also founded a nurses' home in Rutland Street, Mile End Old Town and a hostel for nurses in Felixstowe.

VOISEY, William (Bill)   1891-1964
Footballer

William Voisey was born on the Isle of Dogs and attended Glengall Road School where he gained a reputation as a schoolboy footballer. He signed for Millwall in 1908 and played his first senior game for the club in 1910. His career was interrupted by the first World War, where he received decorations for bravery.

After the war he was selected for one of the Victory Internationals. He was made Captain of Millwall and retained his position as right half up to 1922.

He later had a successful career as a coach and scout.

WAINRIGHT, Rev. Lincoln Stanhope   1847-1929
Priest

Lincoln Wainwright was born near Guildford. His father, Major Henry Wainwright was retired from the army for taking part in a duel. It was the last ever duel to take place in the British Army.

Lincoln Wainwright was ordained in 1872 and came to St. Peter's Church, London Docks in 1884. He worked unsparingly for the poor of his parish for 45 years without a break. He provided them with schools, clubs, medicine, nursing facilities, clothing and holidays. He would sometimes take off his boots and shirt to give them to a needy person.

He was a member of Stepney Borough Council and St. George's Guardians for many years. He founded the Church of England Working Men's Society.

His funeral was followed by hundreds of working men and women.

A London County Council Blue Plaque was erected on the Vicarage, Wapping Lane, E1, in 1961 and he is further commemorated by Wainwright House, Garnet Street, E1.

WALEYS, Henry Le died 1302
Politician

Henry Le Waleys was an immigrant from Gascony in France who entered the wine trade. He became prosperous and influential, and was the Mayor of London three times, 1273, 1281-84, and 1298-1299, and Member of Parliament for London in 1283.

The rights, freedoms and liberties won from the Crown by the citizens and feudal barons, written into the Magna Carta (1216) were contested by the Crown afterwards. From time to time the London citizens were not permitted to elect a mayor, but by the time of Edward I, the Crown's political and financial weakness was apparent, and in 1298 the King agreed under pressure to allow the citizens to chose a mayor, and Henry Le Waleys was elected.

Edward I's war campaigns could only continue with political and financial support. Henry Le Waleys, amongst others gave Edward I the support he needed and was granted land by the King and served him in many projects.

In May 1299, because there had been a fire at Westminster, Edward I held a Parliament at Henry Le Waleys' house in Stepney. The 'Statute of Stepney' was issued by Parliament to prevent the import of imitation pennies (known as pollards and crockards) and stop the export of English coins. Magna Carta was probably discussed at the Stepney Parliament, and the following year Edward I confirmed his 1297 version, which included the principle of taxation by consent.

Henry Le Waleys was buried at St. Botolph's Church, Aldgate.

Books
Beavan, A.B. *The Alderman of the City of London* (Guildhall Library, 1908-13)

Stow, J. *A Survey of London; reprinted from the text of 1603* (Clarendon, 1908)
Stubbs, W. *Constitutional History of England* Vol. 2. (Clarendon, 1880)
Safford, E.W. (compiler) *Itinery of Edward I* Vols 1-3 (P & D Swift, 1974-77)
Prestwich, M. *Edward I* (Methuen, 1988)

Article
Sayles, G. and Richardson, H.G. 'The Early Records of the English Parliaments. Pt. 1. The English Parliaments of Edward I' in *Bulletin of the Institute of Historical Research* Vol. 5. 1927-28 pp. 129-154

DNB

WARDELL, William Wilkinson
1823-1899
Architect and Engineer

William Wardell was born at 60 Cotton Street, Poplar, the eldest of three sons of Thomas Wardell, baker, and his wife Mary. His parents subsequently became Master and Matron of Poplar Union Workhouse.

Following a spell at sea, William served in the offices of Mr Morris, surveyor to the Commissioners of London Sewers, and W.F. East, an architect. While surveying land for new railways he began measuring and drawing medieval buildings. The influence of the architect A.W.N. Pugin drew him to the Roman Catholic Church into which he was received in 1846.

William Wardell designed about thirty Catholic churches principally in London and South East England. He designed St. Mary and St. Michael's Church, 340a Commercial Road, in the parish of St George's-in-the-East, which opened in 1856.

He was elected FRIBA in 1850, a Freeman of the City of London in 1851 and an Associate of the Society of Civil Engineers, 1858

Owing to ill health William Wardell sold his practice to Hadfield and Goldie of Sheffield and emigrated to Australia with his family in 1858. He became Inspector General of Public Works in Victoria from 1861, responsible for docks and harbours as well as public buildings. He also designed churches and schools in and around Melbourne, his principal building being St. Patrick's Cathedral.

His career in Melbourne ended abruptly when all principal officers were dismissed on 'Black Wednesday' 1878; in a government upheaval. He then moved to Sydney where he confined himself to private practice, designing houses

DNB Missing Persons (1993)

WATERS, Elsie OBE 1896-1990 and WATERS, Doris OBE circa 1900-1978
Stars of Stage, Film and Radio

Elsie and Doris Waters were part of a family of six children born to Maud and Edward Waters who lived at 1 Rounton Road, Bow. One of their brothers was Jack Warner of *Dixon of Dock Green* television fame. He changed his name from Horace John WATERS to further the career of his two sisters. The two girls attended Coborn School for Girls.

Edward Waters was a funeral furnisher providing accessories for undertakers and was a keen musician. He insisted that each of his children should be able to play an instrument, and there was much music making in the home.

Elsie and Doris Waters went to the Guildhall School of Music, where they studied elocution, violin and the piano. Their career began as a musical act, playing at seaside concert parties singing comic songs to their own accompaniment. Needing to fill the second side of a record, they wrote a comic dialogue between two Cockney women watching a society wedding. They adopted the names 'Gert and Daisy' and were soon taken up by radio, putting across the feelings and frustrations of ordinary people. They wrote all their own scripts and boasted that they never used the same sketch twice.

Elsie and Doris Waters performed together for more than fifty years, beginning their professional career in 1923 and giving their first radio programme in 1927.

During the second World War they were much in demand. They entertained people sheltering in the London tube stations. They visited and entertained wounded soldiers in hospital, and went abroad to entertain troops in the Middle East and in Burma. They raised a great deal of money for charitable causes, never refusing a charity concert appearance if their engagements permitted. Continuing their interest in the Borough of Poplar, in 1941 with the help of their many audiences they presented the Borough with a mobile canteen for the benefit of local people. They also assisted the Ministry of Food during severe rationing in suggesting recipes and how to make the best use of available ingredients.

In 1942, Elsie and Doris Waters made a film *Gert and Daisy's Weekend* and in 1949 a radio programme entitled *Petticoat Lane* an imaginary tour of the market, meeting stallholders and customers. Doris also wrote the music for the show.

They were delighted when a pair of elephants at Maidstone Zoo were named 'Gert and Daisy'!

They were both awarded the OBE in 1946 and later the Burma Star, but for Doris it was posthumously.

The sisters were inseparable and claimed never to have had a cross word. Following their last stage appearance in 1973 during a tour of South Africa, they retired to their cottage in Steyning, Sussex where they enjoyed a daily round of golf.

'Gert' and 'Daisy' serve tea from mobile canteens they presented to Poplar during the second World War (October 1941) *Whiffin Collection*

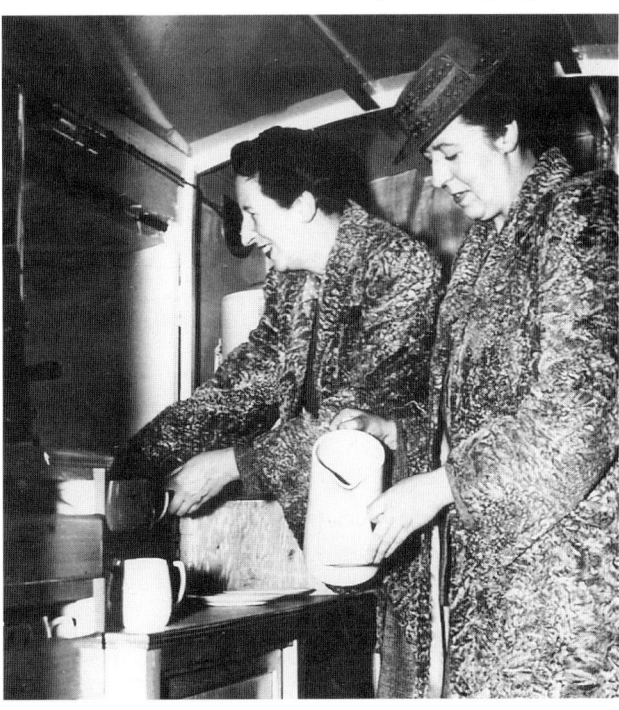

WATERS, Horace John OBE
1895-1981
Actor

Horace Waters was born at 1 Rounton Road, Bow. After being educated at Coopers' Company's School and London University, he began work in a garage.

His sisters Elsie and Doris WATERS, known as 'Gert' and 'Daisy' were variety comediennes and he followed them onto the stage. Assuming the name of 'Jack Warner' he began his career as a Cockney comedian, going on to become an actor.

During the second World War he took part in 'Garrison Theatre', a radio show for the troops in which he became well known for his phrase "mind my bike".

He was in a number of films – *Hue and Cry*, *It Always Rains on Sunday* and *The Captive Heart*. The film *The Blue Lamp* led the way to the popular television series *Dixon of Dock Green* written by Lord (Ted) Willis. Jack Warner's "Evenin all" catchphrase made him familiar to everyone as the friendly bobby.

After his retirement as 'Dixon' in 1976 he continued to work in cabaret. He raised large sums of money for charity and was awarded the OBE in 1965 and honorary D.Litt. by the City University in 1975.
Autobiography
Jack of All Trades (W.H.Allen, 1975)

WATTS, Dr. Isaac 1674-1748
Hymn Writer

Isaac Watts was born in Southampton, the eldest of nine children. He was the son of Isaac Watts, a clothier. His father was Deacon of an Independent Meeting House.

After a classical education he decided in 1660 to further his career with the dissenters by entering an academy at Stoke Newington. The young Isaac became Pastor, later Co-Pastor of a Dissenting Congregation in Mark Lane, London from 1702 to 1748. He preached the opening sermon of the re-built Old Gravel Lane Independent Meeting House in 1736.

He was one of the most popular writers of the day, with educational manuals such as *Catechisms* (1730) and philosophical books such as *Logic* (1725). Samuel Johnson eulogised over his *The Improvement of the Mind* (1741). Isaac Watts wrote over 600 hymns, the most well known of which are still in use, *Oh God, our help in ages past*, *Jesus shall reign where'er the sun* and *When I survey the wondrous cross*.

He lived at 3 Wood Street (later re-named 4 Wilkes Street), Spitalfields, and was associated with the Protestant Dissenting Charity School in Fashion Street, Spitalfields (later situated in Keate Street, Spitalfields). The School was founded in 1717, initially for 30 boys and continued until the 1840s. Sometime after his death, his house became the school building. The purchase of the property was made in 1796.

For much of his time from 1712 until his death he resided with the family of Sir Thomas Abney, firstly at Theobalds, in London and then at Stoke Newington. A statue was erected to Watts in 1845 in Abney Park Cemetery where the Abney mansion stood.

Isaac Watts was buried in Bunhill Fields, City Road, London. A monument was also erected to him in Westminster Abbey.

There is a portrait by Keller in the National Portrait Gallery, and an anonymously printed portrait and a bust in Dr. Williams' Library.
Articles
East London Observer 25th September 1915 and 2nd December 1911
Books
Scott, J.H. *A Short History of Spitalfields 1197-1894* (Privately Published, c.1895-6)
Mellor, H. *London Cemeteries* (Avebury, 1981)
Survey of London Vol.27. *Spitalfields and Mile End New Town* (Athlone, 1957)
The Church Hymnal (Oxford University Press, 3rd edn, 1973)

WEBB, George William 1888-1915
Footballer

George Webb was born at Devonshire Terrace, West Ferry Road, Millwall. He attended Shaftesbury Road School, East Ham, where he played football and afterwards turned out with local teams in junior club matches.

He made his first appearance for West Ham United towards the end of the 1908-9 season and remained the first choice for centre forward for the next three seasons, forming a good partnership with Danny SHEA, his inside right. He was capped for England several times as an amateur, and twice for the full England side. Despite his skills at the game he refused to turn professional.

He died of consumption at the early age of 27.

WEBB, Martha Beatrice
1858-1943
Social Reformer

Beatrice Webb was born near Gloucester, one of nine daughters of a wealthy industrialist, Richard Potter. As a young woman she became interested in social issues and from 1885 to 1887 she acted as manager and rent collector of Katharine Buildings, Cartwright Street, Whitechapel, tenement buildings just completed by the East End Dwellings Company. Between 1885 and 1892 she assisted Charles BOOTH in the research that led to his great work *An Inquiry into the Life and Labour of the People of London*. Charles Booth encouraged her as a social researcher and writer, and in 1887 she published *Dock Life in the East End of London* and conducted an enquiry into sweated labour in the tailoring trade in Stepney. Her book *The Co-operative Movement in Great Britain* was published in 1891.

In 1892 Beatrice married Sydney Webb (1857-1947) and began a famous partnership. Together, they wrote *The History of Trade Unionism* (1894), helped to found the London School of Economics (1895) and the journal *The New Statesman* (1913).

A portrait of Beatrice Webb by Edward Swinson is in the National Portrait Gallery. The ashes of Beatrice and Sidney Webb are buried in Westminster Abbey. She is commemorated locally by Beatrice Webb House, Chisenhale Street, E3.

Autobiographies
My Apprenticeship (Longmans Green, 1926)
Our Partnership (Longmans Green, 1948)
Biographies
Cole, M. *Beatrice Webb* (Longmans Green, 1945)
Muggeridge, K. and Adam, R. *Beatrice Webb* (Secker and Warburg, 1967)

WENTWORTH FAMILY
Lords of the Manor

Thomas Wentworth, 1501-1551 was created 1st Baron Wentworth in 1529. Edward VI made him Lord of the Manor of Stepney in 1550. He lived at Bishop's Hall, the site of which is near the present London Chest Hospital, Victoria Park. The Manorial rights remained the property of the Wentworth family until 1720.

Thomas Wentworth was Lord Chamberlain to the King and served in the Parliament of 1548.

The descendants of Thomas Wentworth include Thomas 4th Baron Wentworth who was created Earl of Cleveland by Charles I in 1626. There was also Sir William Wentworth, who was beheaded on Tower Hill 1641.

By 1720 the family was forced to sell the remnants of the Manor to pay off debts.

The family is commemorated in the Borough by Wentworth Street, E1, and Cleveland Way, E1.
Book
Fea, A. *The Loyal Wentworths* (John Lane, 1928)
DNB

WESLEY, Rev. John   1703-1791
Founder of Methodism

John Wesley was the son of the Rev. Samuel and Susannah WESLEY. He was born at Epworth in Lincolnshire and educated at Charterhouse School and Oxford. He was ordained into the Church of England in 1725, remained as a tutor at Oxford for ten years, and then went as a missionary to America from 1735-38.

In 1738, whilst at a meeting in Aldersgate Street, City of London, John Wesley underwent a religious experience when his 'heart was strangely warmed'.

John Wesley, and his brother, Samuel were the founders of Methodism.

Rather than taking work in a parish, John Wesley travelled throughout England, preaching in churches and in the open air. He attracted the opposition of the authorities, and was eventually expelled from the Church of England.

In building up the Methodist societies he frequently visited the Borough and preached at Spitalfields, St. John at Wapping, St. Paul's, Shadwell, and St. Matthew's, Bethnal Green.

In April 1772 he consecrated the new preaching house in Poplar.

He described what he saw in Bethnal Green – 'There is such poverty as few can conceive without seeing it. I have not found any such distress, no, not within the prison of Newgate'.

There is a statue of him by John Adams Acton in the forecourt of Wesley's Chapel, City Road, EC1. His tomb is in the burial ground behind the Chapel. He and his brother, Charles have a memorial in Westminster Abbey.
Biography
Ayling, S.E. *John Wesley* (Collins, 1979)

WESLEY, Susannah 1669-1742
Mother of John and Charles Wesley

Born in Spital Yard, Norton Folgate, the youngest daughter of Dr. Samuel Annesley, Dissenting Minister, who had been ejected from the living at St. Giles, Cripplegate, by the Act of Uniformity 1662.

Susannah married the Rev. Samuel Wesley and they had a family of nineteen children including John WESLEY and Charles Wesley.

After her husband's death she came to live with John Wesley at the Foundry in Moorfields. She was buried in Bunhill Fields, City Road, EC1.

WHIFFIN, William Thomas 1878-1957
Photographer

William Thomas Whiffin, the eldest son of William H. Whiffin, was born in Poplar. By 1908 he had left the East End and opened a studio in West Green Road, Kensal Rise, Middlesex. He moved back to Poplar in about 1911, and with his brother Ernest, and his father, opened a studio at 237 East India Dock Road, Poplar. William Whiffin worked there until he was called up for war service in 1914.

After intensive training with men much younger than himself, his health failed and instead of going overseas he was sent to Yarmouth for home service duties. After demobilisation he returned to the Studio in Poplar and resided at 231 East India Dock Road, Poplar.

Between both wars he took a keen interest in documentary photography in and around London. During this period he was recognised as a freelance press photographer; he was also engaged by the Poplar Borough Council to photograph buildings. In his commercial work, he dealt with the Port of London Authority, The Imperial Tobacco Co., Lusty's 'Lloyd Loom' furniture, and London Transport. He presented the London Museum, then situated in Kensington Palace, with a collection of London pictures. Portraiture and weddings also played a large part in his business.

From his studio he photographed some of the historical events of Poplar passing his door; such as the Poplar Councillors marching to prison in 1921 for non-payment of rates and the troops used to guard the convoys of food from the docks during the General Strike ef 1926.

His photographs appeared in two Poplar Borough *Official Guides* and *Wonderful London*, published in 1926-27. He completely illustrated *A Loiterer in London*, a book written by an American author, Helen Henderson.

In the great fires that devastated London during the second World War, William Whiffin lost hundreds of negatives, and towards the end of the war both home and studio were damaged by the rocket which fell on the 'Eagle' Public House opposite. He carried on with outdoor photography from his new home at 11 Woodstock Terrace, where the underground kitchen was converted into a darkroom. Subsequently his main occupation was the photography of post-war housing developments in the area.

He was made a Life Governor of Poplar Hospital in recognition of the photographic work he did for them.

William Whiffin died in Poplar Hospital and was buried at Manor Park Cemetery.

After his death, photographs and negatives were given to Libraries, Museums and Record Offices and they are known as 'The Whiffin Collection'. His photographs have been known through historical publications.

Sources
Richman, Geoff *Fly a Flag for Poplar* (Liberation Films, 1975)
Mrs Gladys Manister (nee Whiffin), and Sidney Whiffin

WHISTLER, James Abbott McNeill 1834-1903
Painter

James Whistler was born in America, educated in France and finally settled in London.

In 1859-1860 he stayed in Wapping and painted several pictures – *Thames on Ice, Black Lion Wharf, Thames Warehouses* and *Thames Police*, all of which are in the Tate Gallery. Other pictures are in The Louvre, Paris.

In 1877 John Ruskin, artist and social reformer, denounced his painting *Nocturne in Black and Gold* as 'flinging a pot of paint in the public's face'. Although Whistler won the lengthy libel case he only won one farthing damages and had to pay his own legal costs of £1,000. By 1879 he was bankrupt. Financial problems had arisen at about the same time through the loss of much credibility in the art world after an acrimonious dispute with his

patron and then the expenditure on his new house in Tite Street, Chelsea.
Now held in high regard, there have been many exhibitions of his work.
Biography
Pennell, E.R. and J.P. *Life of James McNeill Whistler* (Heinemann, 1908)
DNB

WIDGERY, David MB,BS
1947-1992
Doctor and Campaigner

David Widgery served as a doctor in Gill Street Health Centre for more than twenty years, pained always by the knowledge that much of the avoidable illness he was treating, was caused by bad housing, dangerous working conditions and too little money.

Fired by the struggle for civil rights in America and in the travels around the world, he had joined the Vietnam Solidarity Campaign while a medical student in London in the 1960s. He was a member of the Socialist Workers Party for twenty five years.

David Widgery wrote a succession of books on politics, rock music and the National Health Service, he edited the magazine *OZ* and contributed many articles to *The Guardian, The New Statesman, Time Out* and *City Limits*. He was also an active participant in 'Rock against Racism', a campaign to combat Neo-Nazism. He had been a supporter of the Miners' marches and of the campaign against closures of London hospitals. He is commemorated with a plaque in St. Anne's Churchyard, Three Colt Street, Limehouse.
Books
Some Lives (Sinclair Stevenson, 1991)
Beating Time (Chatto and Windus, 1986)

WIGRAM, Sir Robert 1743-1830
Ship Owner

Robert Wigram was born in Wexford. His father was drowned at sea before he was born. His mother and uncle apprenticed him to a doctor in London. On completion of his training he became a surgeon on East Indiamen – ships which differed from frigates, being shorter and wider in the beam. After some years he was forced by eye trouble into retirement.

He then began as a wholesale druggist selling medical supplies to ships' doctors from which he made a fortune. He invested his money in East Indiamen and at one time owned 23 ships. He bought part of Blackwall Shipyard and became the first Chairman of the East India Dock Company in 1810. His connection with the sea covered a period of sixty-six years.

Robert Wigram lived in Walthamstow and could often be seen riding to work in Blackwall, escorted by some of his 23 children.

He was Member of Parliament for Fowey 1802-1806 and for Wexford 1806-1807, and created a baronet 1805. He is commemorated by Wigram House, Wade's Place, E14.
Book
Green, H. and Wigram, R. *Chronicles of Blackwall Yard*, part 1. (Whitehead, Morris & Lowe, 1881)

WILD, Robert 1840-1916
Headmaster

Robert Wild was born in Heywood, Lancashire. He became Headmaster of St. Michael's Schools in 1862. The school became Byron Street in 1878, under the School Board of London, and in 1908 the London County Council re-named it Hay Currie School. It has been Langdon Park School since 1966. Robert Wild remained Head until his retirement in 1906.

Highly thought of locally as Head of an excellent school, he was known nationally for his work with the National Union of Teachers, of which he was President in 1885 and again in 1889.

He was an opponent of the system of payment by results, which was abolished in the 1890s largely due to his energies.

WILLIAMS, John 1797-1875
Scholar

John Williams was born in London. He was sent to Charterhouse School where he was known as a quiet and studious boy. He became a master at Christ Church School, Spitalfields and joined the Spitalfields Mathematical Society, an institution dating from the time of Isaac NEWTON. The Society was principally supported by weavers and dyers who met on Saturday evening in Crispin Street, Spitalfields, to solve mathematical problems. John Williams was appointed secretary and often gave lectures on mental arithmetic, electricity, botany and geology.

He collected rare gems and coins and it was estimated that he had 50,000 casts. One set of Roman brass coins is now in the Museum of Classical Archaeology, Cambridge. He also studied Egyptian hieroglyphics by copying all

John Williams

the inscriptions on sarcophagi and statues in the British Museum and elsewhere. He published his first book, *An Essay on the Hieroglyphics of the Ancieut Egyptian* in 1836.

In 1846 the Mathematical Society membership dwindled, and its library and other items were presented to the Royal Astronomical Society. John Williams was appointed assistant secretary to the Society.

He then turned to the study of Chinese and became an acknowledged authority on Chinese historical literature. His principal work was on the Chinese astronomer's observations of comets from 1611BC to 1640AD. In 1871 he published the *Chinese Celestial Atlas*, a standard reference on the subject.

He was also an archaeologist, Fellow of the Society of Antiquaries and secretary of the London Photographical Society.

WILLIAMSON, Father Joseph (Father Joe) MBE 1895-1988
Priest

Joseph Williamson was born at 75 Arcadia Street, Poplar. He felt drawn to the priesthood at an early age, and one day presented himself at the local vicarage to announce the fact. The vicar thanked him for the information and then dismissed him. He persevered, though and eventually entered St. Augustine's College, Canterbury. He was ordained in St. Paul's Cathedral in 1925.

He worked in two churches as a curate in this country and then went to South Africa to serve on the staff of Grahamstown Cathedral from 1828 to 1932.

Returning to England he worked part-time as a carpenter and bricklayer to restore and repair several village churches.

He came to St. Paul's Church, Dock Street, Stepney in 1952 where he undertook a major restoration of the church which had been damaged in the war. Joseph Williamson was appalled at the poor housing in his parish, believing many of the social problems were the result of conditions they had lived in. He challenged the Minister of Housing, Henry Brooke to join in a walk around the streets of Stepney.

In the 1950s the Cable Street area was a well known haunt of prostitutes. He was instrumental in getting the London County Council to demolish the slum housing in Cable Street in the 1960s. Father Joe began a campaign to offer support for the women and turned Church House, Wellclose Square, Stepney into a hostel for them. He founded the Wellclose Square Fund to provide money and toured the country raising funds and later opened two more hostels in Essex and one in Birmingham.

Troubled with failing eyesight he retired from the parish in 1962 but continued as Warden of the hostel.

He was also Chaplain to the Sailors' Home and the Red Ensign Club in Dock Street, E1.

He was appointed MBE in 1975.

Autobiography
Father Joe (Hodder and Stoughton, 1963)

WINNINGTON-INGRAM, Arthur Foley 1858-1946
Bishop of London

Arthur Winnington-Ingram was born in Worcestershire, one of ten children. His father was a clergyman. He was educated at Marlborough School and Oxford and ordained in 1884.

He was appointed Head of Oxford House, a University settlement which had been established in 1884 in the disused St. Andrew's National School, Bethnal Green. In 1895 he coupled this post with that of Rector of St. Matthew's Church, Bethnal Green. In 1892 he built a new building for Oxford House in Mape Street (now Derbyshire Street) with rooms for thirty residents. A large programme of activities included concerts and entertainments, parish work, 5 clubs, a boys' institute, a night school, a boys' home and co-operation with other educational and charity organisations. Every Sunday afternoon he spoke in Victoria Park.

In 1897 he was appointed Bishop of Stepney, during this time raising large sums of money for the East London Church fund.

Appointed Bishop of London in 1901, he served until 1939.

Autobiography
Fifty Years' Work in London (Longmans, Green, 1940)

Biography
Carpenter, S.C. *Winnington-Ingram* (Hodder and Stoughton,1949)

William Samuel Woodin

WOODIN, William Samuel
1825-1888
Entertainer
William Woodin lived at Lower Manor House, Brunswick Road, Bromley, from 1872-1888.

With his one man show he performed character entertainment, taking the parts of over 50 characters. His favourite sketches were *Carpet Bag, A Cabinet of Curiosities* and *Elephant Extraordinary*. He appeared in London at the Polygraphic Hall, King William Street, Strand. *The Illustrated London News* gave very full accounts of his performances.

WOOLMORE, Sir John 1755-1837
Ship Owner
John Woolmore was baptised at St. Mary's Church, Whitechapel. He began his career as a midshipman in the East India Company's *Granby*, sailing mainly in the Far East. In 1789 he became a manager and part owner of East India ships.

He became an Elder Brother of Trinity House, the navigational and pilotage Corporation in 1803, the year the Brethren undertook the defence of the Thames against a threatened French invasion. Trinity House moved to its present site at Trinity Gardens, Tower Hill in 1797. Trinity House has a full length portrait of Sir John Woolmore, who became deputy Master, 1825-1834.

He is commemorated in the Borough by Woolmore School, Bullivant Street, E14, and Woolmore Street, E14.

WYLLIE, George Cameron GC
1908 -1987
Royal Engineer
George Wyllie lived in Bow for most of his life. During the second World War he served in a Royal Engineer's bomb disposal team. After a heavy air raid on the night of 12th September 1940, he noticed an unexploded 2,000 kg. bomb embedded in the soil of Dean's Yard, threatening to wreck St. Paul's Cathedral.

The weight of the bomb forced it down in the soft soil, making excavation a difficult and arduous task. This was made even more hazardous by the proximity of fractured and burning gas mains. For three days, with the continual fear that the bomb would explode, George Wyllie and his team worked to prise the bomb out of the earth. They succeeded, and the bomb was taken to Hackney Marshes, where its controlled explosion caused a 100 ft. crater.

For his courage and skill he was awarded the George Cross, one of the first three to be given, after its instigation by King George VI.

In 1984 he came to the conclusion that his medal no longer represented the standards he had valued in wartime society, and he sold it. The medal was bought privately by a merchant bank which then presented it to St. Paul's Cathedral, where it is on permanent display.

Obituaries
The Daily Telegraph 3rd February 1987
The Times 7th February 1987

YARROW, Sir Alfred Fernandez
1842-1932
Shipbuilder

Alfred Yarrow was born in London and was educated at University College School. He was apprenticed to Ravenhills of Ratcliff, constructors of marine engines. With others he founded the Civil and Mechanical Engineers' Society which first met in Albert Square, Stepney. In 1861 he built a steam road car which could travel at 25 miles an hour.

In partnership with J.Hedley he purchased a small works on Folly Wall, Isle of Dogs, where they undertook ship repairs. The Company also built small steam launches for work on the river and by 1875 had built over 350. At that time he dissolved his partnership with Hedley and began to build larger vessels. Alfred Yarrow built boats for H.M. Stanley's exploration of the River Congo, for General Gordon's River Nile expedition and the boat *Ilala* for David Livingstone.

Alfred Yarrow developed and patented in 1889 the water tube boiler which increased the speed of vessels. He then began torpedo boats and destroyers. The business was transfered to the River Clyde in 1907.

He took advantage of new inventions. He was one of the first people to use a typewriter in business and during the first World War he manufactured artificial limbs. In a radio talk in 1930 he claimed to have contributed to the emancipation of women by the development of the cold drawn steel frame tube, used in making bicycles. He said they enabled the girls of the 1890's and their boy friends to escape from their chaperônes.

Book
Barnes, E.C. *Alfred Yarrow, his life and work* (Edward Arnold, 1923)

YOUNG, Canon Edwyn 1913-1988
Rector of Stepney

Edwyn Young was born in Colombo, Sri Lanka. He became a Curate at St. Peter's, Wapping, E1. During the early part of the war, he ministered to people in air-raid shelters, to those who had lost their homes, and their relatives, occasionally going to visit families who were evacuated.

In 1941 he moved to St. Francis Church, Paddington, and then to a country parish, but he returned to London as Vicar of St. Silas', Pentonville. It was here that he was invited to become Chaplain to Collins Music Hall, starting his association with the show business world.

He became Rector of St. Dunstan's, Stepney in 1953. He brought the church into every aspect of Stepney's community life and became familiar to many local residents through selling his parish magazine *Stepahoy* in public houses. He was Chairman of the Borough Youth Committee for five years. Every summer he moved down to Kent for three weeks to minister to workers in the hop fields.

He became Chaplain to the London Palladium and his study walls were filled with pictures of him with well known actors and actresses.

In 1964 he became Rector of Liverpool and developed a new form of pastoral work in departmental stores.

In 1973 he returned to London as Chaplain of the Queen's Chapel of the Savoy and of the Royal Victorian Order. He resumed his ministry in Theatre land.

In 1970 he published his autobiography *No Fun Like Work*.

YOUNG, George Frederick
1792-1870
Shipbuilder

George Young was probably born in Limehouse, the son of Vice-Admiral William Young. He was apprenticed as a shipwright and later became a shipbuilder in Limehouse. Young's Yard was next to Cox and Curling's Yard, and the firms amalgamated in about 1820 to become Curling, Young and Co.

In 1839 they built the *British Queen*, 1,700 tons, to carry 800 passengers. It was intended to be the first British ship to cross the Atlantic under her own steam and the first steamship designed for the Atlantic service. In the event, building delays prevented this from happening and the *Sirius* had the honour instead.

George Young was elected Member of Parliament for Tynmouth 1834-1837, and in 1851, Member for Scarborough. He was also a magistrate for Middlesex and Deputy Lieutenant of the Tower of London.

George Young was the prime mover in the creation of Victoria Park. He convened a meeting at his home in Limehouse in June 1840 and, having resolved the need for a park, the meeting declared itself a provisional committee to work for its formation.

A further meeting was held at the London Tavern, Bishopsgate, when George Young was entrusted with composing a petition to Queen Victoria. Over 30,000 signed the petition. There seems to have been no official opening of the park, and it was maintained by Her Majesty's Office of Works from the opening in 1845 until 1887.

Book
Poulsen, C. *Victoria Park* (Stepney Books, 1976)

ZANGWILL, Israel 1864-1926
Writer

Israel Zangwill was born at 10 Ebenezer Square, Stoney Lane, in the City. His father was a peddler from Latvia. Israel Zangwill lived in Fashion Street and later Princes Street, Spitalfields.

He was a pupil and later a teacher at the Jews' Free School, Bell Lane, Spitalfields; whilst working there he took a degree at London University and graduated with triple honours. During his time at the school he wrote *Motza Kleis* (Matzoh Balls) an account of market days in the Spitalfields Jewish community. As a novelist and playwright he is best known for his studies of Jewish life. The most famous of his books, *Children of the Ghetto* set in Whitechapel, was published in 1892.

Israel Zangwill was a radical and humanitarian, and much of his later writing was devoted to political causes. He was a supporter of women's suffrage, and of the Zionist movement, and in 1905 became founder and president of the Jewish Territorial Organisation, set up to encourage the settlement of Jews within the then British Empire. One of his plays, *The Melting Pot* (1908) on the theme of Jewish immigration to America, gave its symbolic title to the concept of the USA as a land where all nationalities might be absorbed into a new harmonious national character.

A GLC blue plaque marks his house at 288 Old Ford Road, E2. He is also commemorated by Zangwill House, Carr Street, E14.

Biographies
Leftwich, J. *Israel Zangwill* (James Clarke, 1957)
Wohlgelernter, M. *Israel Zangwill* (Columbia University Press, 1964)
DNB

Israel Zangwill

APPENDICES

General References

Banbury, P. *Shipbuilders of the Thames and Medway* (David & Charles,1971)
Bermant, C. *Point of Arrival* (Macmillan,1975)
Besant, Sir M. *East London* (Chatto & Windus,1903)
Bethnal Green Official Guide (Metroplitan Borough of Bethnal Green, 1921-62)
Bolt, D. (compiler) *List of Streets and Places in Poplar* (Metropolitan Borough of Poplar, 1938)
Branson, N. *Poplarism 1919-1925* (Lawrence & Wishart, 1979)
Briggs, A. & Macartney, A. *Toynbee Hall; the First Hundred Years* (Routledge & Kegan Paul,1984)
Carr, R.J.M.(ed.) *Dockland* (North East London Polytechnic, 1986)
Chambers' Biographical Dictionary (W. & R. Chambers, 1974)
Churchett, C. *Coopers' Company and Coborn School Anniversary History* (Coopers' Company & Coborn Educational Foundation, 1986)
Clark-Kennedy, A.E. *The London* (Pitman-Medical, 1962-63)
Cobb, G. *London City Churches* (Batsford, 1977)
Cox, J. *London's East End; Life and Traditions* (Weidenfeld & Nicolson, 1994)
Darby, M. *Waeppa's People* (History of Wapping Trust, 1988)
Daunton, C. (ed.) *The London Hospital Illustrated; 250 Years* (Batsford, 1990)
Davies, A. *The East End Nobody Knows* (Macmillan, 1990)
Dictionary of Labour Biography (Macmillan, 1972–)
Dictionary of National Biography (Smith, Elder & Co; Oxford University Pr.,1885–)
Fishman, W.J. *East End 1888* (Duckworth, 1988)
– *East End Jewish Radicals* (Duckworth, 1975)
– *The Streets of East London* (Duckworth, 1979)
Gautrey, T. *Lux Mihi Laus; School Board Memories* (Link House Publications, 1938)
Groves Dictionary of Music ed. by Eric Blom (5th edn.,Macmillan, 1954)
Hall, M. *Blue Plaque Guide to London Homes* (Queen Anne Press, 1976)
Hill, G.W. & Frere, W.H. *Memorials of Stepney Parish* (Privately Published, 1890-91)
Jackson, W.E. *Achievement; a Short History of the London County Council* (Longmans,1968)
Keay, J. *The Honourable Company; a History of the English East India Company* (Harper-Collins, 1991)
Kent, W. (revised by Thompson, G.) *Encyclopaedia of London* (Dent, 1970)
Kerrigan, C. *A History of Tower Hamlets* (London Borough of Tower Hamlets, 1982)
Lazarus, M. *A Club called Brady* (New Cavendish Books, 1995)
Leff, V. and Blunden, G.H. *The Story of Tower Hamlets* (Research Writers Publications, 1967)
Llewellyn Smith, Sir H. *History of East London* (Macmillan, 1939)
Lysons, D. *The Environs of London* (Routledge, Warne & Routledge, 1792)

Moss, G.P. and Saville, M.V. *From Palace To College; an Illustrated Account of Queen Mary College* (Queen Mary College, 1985)

Murray, V. *Echoes of the East End* (Viking, 1989)

Palmer, A. *The East End; Four Centuries of London Life* (J. Murray, 1989)

Pepys, W.C. & Godman, E. *The Church of St. Dunstan, Stepney* (London Survey Committee, 1905)

Poplar Official Guide (Metropolitan Borough of Poplar, 1927-63)

Poulsen, C. *Victoria Park* (Stepney Books, 1976)

Pudney, J. *London's Docks* (Thames & Hudson, 1975)

Richman, G. *Fly a Flag for Poplar* (Liberation Films, 1975)

Ritchie, L.A. *The Shipbuilding Industry* (Manchester University Press, 1992)

Robinson, A.J. & Chesshyre, D.H.B. *The Green* (London Borough of Tower Hamlets, 1986)

Rose, M. *The East End of London* (Cresset Press, 1951)

Rubinstein, S. *Historians of London* (Peter Owen, 1968)

Rumbelow, D. *The Houndsditch Murders* (Macmillan, 1973)

Service, A. *Architects of London and Their Building From 1066 to Present Day* (Architectural Press, 1979)

Simmons, A. (Compiler) *History of the Parish of All Saints Poplar* (Thomas Boutell, 1870)

Sinclair, R. *East London* (Robert Hale, 1950)

Stepney Official Guide (Metropolitan Bororough of Stepney, 1922-64)

Survey of London Vol. 27; Spitalfields and Mile End New Town (Athlone, 1957)

Survey of London Vols. 43-44; Poplar, Blackwall and the Isle of Dogs (Athlone, 1994)

Taylor, R. and Lloyd, C. *Stepney, Bethnal Green and Poplar in Old Photographs* (Alan Sutton Publishing, 1995)

Thompson, G. *London's Statues* (J.M.Dent, 1971)

Timbs, J. *Curiosities of London* (Longmans, 1868)

Tower Hamlets Official Guide (London Borough of Tower Hamlets, 1966-86)

Vale, G.F. *Old Bethnal Green* (Blythenhale Press,1934)

Walker, H. *East London* (Religious Tract Society, 1896)

Weinrab, B. & Hibbert, C. *The London Encyclopaedia* (Macmillan, 1983)

Wilks, H. C. *George Green's School 1828-1978; a History* (Edward Arnold, 1979)

Wilson, A.E. *East End Entertainment* (Arthur Barker, 1954)

Bishops of Stepney

George Forrest Browne	1895-1897	Francis Evered Lunt	1957-1968
Arthur Winnington-Ingram	1897-1901	Trevor Huddleston	1968-1978
Cosmo Gordon Lang	1901-1909	James Thompson	1978-1992
Henry Luke Paget	1909-1919	Richard J.C. Chartres	1992-1996
Henry Moseley	1919-1928	John Sematu	1996-
Charles Edward Curzon	1928-1936		
Robert Hamilton Moberley	1936-1952		
Joost de Blank	1952-1957		

Book

Rowles, G. *Diamond Jubilee* (London Diocesan Fund, 1955)

Mayors of Bethnal Green
1900-1965

Felix Loughlin	1900 - 1901	Lydia Benoly	1933 - 1934
Charles Fox	1901 - 1902	Henry Tate	1934 - 1935
James Walker	1902 - 1903	Henry Tate	1935 - 1936
Charles Wood	1903 - 1904	Henry Wilson	1936 - 1937
Charles Wood	1904 - 1905	Percival Bridger	1937 - 1938
Charles Wood	1905 - 1906	Percival Bridger	1938 - 1939
Charles Fox	1906 - 1907	James Edwards	1939 - 1940
Garnham Edmonds	1907 - 1908	James Edwards	1940 - 1941
Alfred Barnard	1908 - 1909	James Edwards	1941 - 1942
Charles Fox	1909 - 1910	Margaret Bridger	1942 - 1943
Charles Fox	1910 - 1911	Allen McAuliffe	1943 - 1944
William Clark	1911 - 1912	Henry Stubbs	1944 - 1945
William Rawles	1912 - 1913	Albert Turpin	1945 - 1946
William Lewis	1913 - 1914	Henry Hooke	1946 - 1947
William Lewis	1914 - 1915	George Hemsley	1947 - 1948
William Lewis	1915 - 1916	George Hemsley	1948 - 1949
William Lewis	1916 - 1917	Henry Tate	1949 - 1950
William Lewis	1917 - 1918	Alfred Clark	1950 - 1951
William Lewis	1918 - 1919	Alfred Gilbert	1951 - 1952
Joseph Vaughan	1919 - 1920	Beatrice Tate	1952 - 1953
Joseph Vaughan	1920 - 1921	Frederick Sanders	1953 - 1954
Joseph Vaughan	1921 - 1922	Henry Wilson	1954 - 1955
Rev. George Whitworth	1922 - 1923	George Hadley	1955 - 1956
Thomas Boyce	1923 - 1924	William Johnson	1956 - 1957
Charles Hovell	1924 - 1925	Alice Sivill	1957 - 1958
Charles Hovell	1925 - 1926	Alfred Hastings	1958 - 1959
Charles Hovell	1926 - 1927	William Hart	1959 - 1960
Michael Seymour	1927 - 1928	George Browne	1960 - 1961
Wesley Chandler	1928 - 1929	Robert Hare	1961 - 1962
George Bayley	1929 - 1930	Alfred Stocks	1962 - 1963
Richard Pearson	1930 - 1931	Robert Rosamond	1963 - 1964
Thomas Brooks	1931 - 1932	Leonard Coan	1964 - 1965
Charles Bennett	1932 - 1933		

Mayors of Poplar
1900-1965

Richard Green	1900 - 1901	Alfred Yeo	1903 - 1904
William Crooks	1901 - 1902	Mark Dalton	1904 - 1905
John Bussey	1902 - 1903	Joseph Cahill	1905 - 1906

Frederick Thorne	1906 - 1907		George Lansbury	1936 - 1937
Henry Barge	1907 - 1908		Ethel Lambert	1937 - 1938
John Le Manquais	1908 - 1909		John Gilbertson	1938 - 1939
Robert Brown	1909 - 1910		James Jones	1939 - 1940
Frederick Sedgwick	1910 - 1911		Albert Overland	1940 - 1941
Frederick Sedgwick	1911 - 1912		Frederick Baldock	1941 - 1942
Edwin Aldrick	1912 - 1913		Elizabeth Stavers	1942 - 1943
Alfred Warren	1913 - 1914		Nellie Cressall	1943 - 1944
Alfred Warren	1914 - 1915		Lilian Sadler	1944 - 1945
Alfred Warren	1915 - 1916		Alice Shepherd	1945 - 1946
Alfred Warren	1916 - 1917		Joseph Ashley	1946 - 1947
Alfred Warren	1917 - 1918		William Thomas Guy	1947 - 1948
Rev. William Lax	1918 - 1919		William Thomas Guy	1948 - 1949
George Lansbury	1919 - 1920		Charles Blaber	1949 - 1950
Samuel March	1920 - 1921		George Mills	1950 - 1951
Charles Sumner	1921 - 1922		John Bond	1951 - 1952
John Scurr	1922 - 1923		William Brinson	1952 - 1953
Charles Key	1923 - 1924		William Henry Guy	1953 - 1954
Edgar Lansbury	1924 - 1925		Ebenezer Caudwell	1954 - 1955
Joseph Hammond	1925 - 1926		William Tuson	1955 - 1956
Thomas Goodway	1926 - 1927		Alfred Atkins	1956 - 1957
John Wooster	1927 - 1928		Maud Saunders	1957 - 1958
Charles Key	1928 - 1929		Edward Smith	1958 - 1959
Peter Hubbart	1929 - 1930		Patrick Connolly	1959 - 1960
Thomas Blacketer	1930 - 1931		Thomas Phillips	1960 - 1961
George Cressall	1931 - 1932		Frederick Philp	1961 - 1962
Charles Key	1932 - 1933		Thomas Beningfield	1962 - 1963
Albert Baker	1933 - 1934		Joseph Gillender	1963 - 1964
David Adams	1934 - 1935		John Tucker	1964 - 1965
Albert Easteal	1935 - 1936			

Mayors of Stepney
1900-1965

Edward Mann	1900 - 1901		Oscar Tobin	1921 - 1922
Edward Mann	1901 - 1902		Harry Kosky	1922 - 1923
Henry Potter	1902 - 1903		Alfred Prevost	1923 - 1924
William Barker	1903 - 1904		Jack Somper	1924 - 1925
Rowland Hirst	1904 - 1905		Joseph Hurley	1925 - 1926
Rowland Hirst	1905 - 1906		John Sullivan	1926 - 1927
Rowland Hirst	1906 - 1907		George Groves	1927 - 1928
Harry Lawson	1907 - 1908		Daniel Franklin	1928 - 1929
Harry Lawson	1908 - 1909		Henry Lazarus	1929 - 1930
George Dutfield	1909 - 1910		Morris Davis	1930 - 1931
Henry Potter	1910 - 1911		Miriam Moses	1931 - 1932
Henry Potter	1911 - 1912		Robert Mullan	1932 - 1933
Walter Jones	1912 - 1913		Richard Woodham	1933 - 1934
Hugh Chidgey	1913 - 1914		Isidore Vogler	1934 - 1935
Hugh Chidgey	1914 - 1915		Helena Roberts	1935 - 1936
James Kiley	1915 - 1916		John Lawder	1936 - 1937
Hugh Chidgey	1916 - 1917		Jeremiah Long	1937 - 1938
Jerome Reidy	1917 - 1918		Joseph Johnson	1938 - 1939
Francis Miles	1918 - 1919		Frank Lewey	1939 - 1940
Clement Attlee	1919 - 1920		George Chamberlain	1940 - 1941
Joseph Cahill	1920 - 1921		John Pritchard	1941 - 1942

Henry Roeder	1942 - 1943	Joseph McCarthy	1954 - 1955
Edward O'Brien	1943 - 1944	James Sambrook	1955 - 1956
Walter Edwards	1944 - 1945	Albert Sealey	1956 - 1957
Joseph O'Connor	1945 - 1946	John Reardon	1957 - 1958
Maurice Zeital	1946 - 1947	William Sullivan	1958 - 1959
Thomas Aylward	1947 - 19¢8	James Calnan	1959 - 1960
Thomas Aylward	1948 - 1949	Annie Elboz	1960 - 1961
Frederick Tyrrell	1949 - 1950	Kathleen O'Connor	1961 - 1962
Frederick Spearing	1950 - 1951	Ellen Aylward	1962 - 1963
William Humphries	1951 - 1952	Ernest Hill	1963 - 1964
Alfred Bermel	1952 - 1953	James Olley	1964 - 1965
John Long	1953 - 1954		

Mayors of Tower Hamlets
1965-1997

Thomas Mitchell	1965 - 1966	John O'Neill	1982 - 1983
John Orwell (BG)	1966 - 1967	Emmanuel Penner	1983 - 1984
Matthew Durell	1967 - 1968	Robert Ashkettle	1984 - 1985
Frederick Briden	1968 - 1969	Paul Beasley	1985 - 1986
Edwin Walker	1969 - 1970	Brian Williams	1986 - 1987
John Orwell (S)	1970 - 1971	Brian Williams	1987 - 1988
William Harris	1971 - 1972	Barrie Duffey	1988 - 1989
Herbert Rackley	1972 - 1973	Jeremy Shaw	1989 - 1990
George Desmond	1973 - 1974	Janet Ludlow	1990 - 1991
George Chaney	1974 - 1975	Barry Blandford	1991 - 1992
Benjamin Holmes	1975 - 1976	Kofi Appiah	1992 - 1993
Daniel Kelly	1976 - 1977	John Snooks	1993 - 1994
John Riley	1977 - 1978	Arthur Downes	1994 - 1995
Arthur Dorrell	1978 - 1979	Ghulam Mortuza	1995 - 1996
Eva Armsby	1979 - 1980	Albert Jacob	1996 - 1997
Lilian Crooks	1980 - 1981		
Patricia Thompson	1981 - 1982	BG = Bethnal Green	S = Stepney

The Metropolitan Board of Works 1855-1889
Tower Hamlets Representatives

Bethnal Green

T. Bevan	1855 - 1879
A. Ewin	1879 - 1889

Limehouse

B. Dixon	1855 - 1872
W. Nathan	1872 - 1880
J. Abbot	1880 - 1889

Mile End Old Town

W.E. Snow	1855 - 1862
W. Newton	1862 - 1876
R. Jones	1876 - 1879
T. Moore	1879 - 1880
R. Jones	1880 - 1886
F. J. Wood	1886 - 1887
H. Cushen	1887 - 1889

Poplar

S. Knight	1855 - 1861
J. D'A Samuda	1861 - 1889
E.R. Cook	1865 - 1889
J. Lenanton	1885 - 1889

St. George-in-the-East

P. Crellin	1855 - 1865
W. Clark	1865 - 1875
T.M. Fairclough	1876 - 1888
R.S. Sly	1888 - 1889

Whitechapel

G.S. Wallis	1855 - 1864
T. Brushfield	1864 - 1875
Col. D. Munro	1875 - 1888
G. Ilsley	1888 - 1889

The London County Council 1889-1965
Tower Hamlets Representatives

1889-1892

J. Ambrose	P	Limehouse
W.S. Beaumont	Mod	Stepney
J. Branch	P	SW Bethnal Green
W.P. Bullivant	Mod	Poplar
F.N. Charrington	P	Mile End
B.F.C. Costelloe	P	Stepney
C. Harrison	P	S W Bethnal Green
A.J. Hollington	P	Mile End
W. Hunter	Mod	Bow & Bromley
A. L.Leon	P	Limehouse
J. McDougall	P	Poplar
P.M. Martineau	P	St. George's
S.M. Samuel	P	Whitechapel
R.S. Sly	P	St. George's
C. Tarling	P	Whitechapel
J.F. Torr	P	NE Bethnal Green
W. Wren	P	NE Bethnal Green
Mrs. J.F. Unwin	P	Bow & Bromley

1892-1895

J. Branch	P	SW Bethnal Green
W.W. Bruce	P	Bow & Bromley
T. Catmur	P	Whitechapel
F.N. Charrington	P	Mile End
B. Cooper	P	Bow & Bromley
W. Crooks	P	Poplar
C. Freak	P	NE Bethnal Green.
C. Harrison	P	SW Bethnal Green
A.J. Hollington	P	Mile End
A.L. Leon	P	Limehouse
J. McDougall	P	Poplar
P.M. Martineau	P	St. George's
A. Mercer	P	St. George's
W. Pearce	P	Limehouse
W.C. Steadman	P	Stepney
C. Tarling	P	Whitechapel
B. Tillett	P	Alderman
J.F. Torr	P	NE Bethnal Green
W.B. Yates	P	Stepney

1895-1898

M. Abrahams	Mod	Whitechapel
G. Bicker-Caarten	Mod	Mile End
J. Branch	P	SW Bethnal Green
W.W. Bruce	P	Bow & Bromley
Viscount Burnham CH	Mod	Whitechapel
T. Catmur	P	Whitechapel
B. Cooper	P	Bow & Bromley
W. Crooks	P	Poplar
C. Freak	P	NE Bethnal Green
C. Harrison	P	SW Bethnal Green
A. L. Leon	P	Limehouse
J. McDougall	P	Poplar
H.H. Marks	Mod	St. George's
Rev. Viscount Mountmorres	Mod	Mile End
W. Pearce	P	Limehouse
C. Rose-Innes	Mod	NE Bethnal Green
W.C. Steadman	P	Stepney
B. Tillett	P	Alderman
D. Williams	Mod	St. George's
W. Yates	P	Stepney

1898-1901

C. Balian	P	St. George's
C. Barratt	P	St. George's
J. Branch	P	SW Bethnal Green
W.W. Bruce	P	Bow & Bromley
Viscount Burnham CH	Mod	Whitechapel
B. Cooper	P	Bow & Bromley
E. Cornwall	P	NE Bethnal Green
B.F.C. Costelloe	P	SW Bethnal Green
W. Crooks	P	Poplar
C. Freak	P	N.E. Bethnal Green
H. Gosling CH	Lab	St. George's
W.C. Johnson	Lib	Whitechapel
A.L. Leon	P	Limehouse
J. McDougall	P	Poplar
J.E. Matthews	Mod	St. George's
W. Pearce	P	Limehouse
J. R. Seager	P	Mile End
W. C. Steadman	P	Stepney
B. S. Straus	P	Mile End
T. Wiles	P	SW Bethnal Green
W.B. Yates	P	Stepney

1901-1904

W.B. Bawn	P	Limehouse
J. Branch	P	SW Bethnal Green
W.W. Bruce	P	Bow & Bromley
Viscount Burnham CH	Mod	Whitechapel
B. Cooper	P	Bow & Bromley
E. Cornwall	P	NE Bethnal Green
W. Crooks	P	Poplar
G. Foster	Mod	St. George's
Capt. A.O. Goodrich	MR	Mile End
H. Gosling CH	Lab	Alderman
W.C. Johnson	Lib	Whitechapel
A.L. Leon	P	Limehouse
Sir J. McDougall	P	Poplar

J.R. Seager	P	Mile End
E. Smith	P	NE Bethnal Green
J. Smith	P	St. George's
W.C. Steadman	P	Stepney
B.S. Straus	P	Mile End
T.Wiles	P	SW Bethnal Green
A.T. Williams	Mod	Stepney
W.B. Yates	P	Alderman

1904-1907

W.B. Bawn	P	Limehouse
J. Branch	P	SW Bethnal Green
W.W. Bruce	P	Bow & Bromley
B. Cooper	P	Bow & Bromley
Sir E. Cornwall	P	NE Bethnal Green
W. Crooks	P	Poplar
Capt. A.E.Goodrich	MR	Stepney
H.H. Gordon	P	Whitechapel
H. Gosling CH	Lab	St. George's
W.C. Johnson	Lib	Whitechapel
A.L. Leon	P	Limehouse
Sir J. McDougall	P	Poplar
Earl of Malmesbury	Mod	Stepney
E. Smith	P	NE Bethnal Green
J. Smith	P	St. George's
W.C. Steadman	P	Stepney
B.S. Straus	P	Mile Rnd
G.J. Warren	P	Mile End
T.Wiles	P	SW Bethnal Green
W.B. Yates	P	Alderman

1907-1910

B. Cooper	P	Alderman
Sir E. Cornwall	P	NE Bethnal Green
Major E.H. Coumbe	MR	Mile End
W. Crooks	P	Poplar
Capt. A.O. Goodrich	MR	Stepney
H.H. Gordon	P	Whitechapel
H. Gosling CH	Lab	St. George's
F.L. Harris	MR	Stepney
P.A. Harris	Lib	SW Bethnal Green
Rev. S. Headlam	P	SW Bethnal Green
C. Jackson	MR	Limehouse
W.C. Johnson	Lib	Whitechapel
W.S.M. Knight	MR	Bow & Bromley
J.R. Lort-Williams	MR	Limehouse
Sir J. McDougall	P	Poplar
R.H. Montgomery	MR	Mile End
H.V. Rowe	MR	Bow & Bromley
P.C. Simmons	MR	St. George's
E. Smith	P	NE Bethnal Green.

1910-1913

G.L. Bruce	P	Bow & Bromley
G. Edmonds	P	NE Bethnal Green
R.C.K. Ensor	Lab	Poplar
Capt. A.O.Goodrich	MR	Stepney
H.H. Gordon	P	Whitechapel
H. Gosling CH	Lab	St. George's
P.A. Harris	Lib	SW Bethnal Green
Rev. S. Headlam	P	SW Bethnal Green
C. Jackson	MR	Limehouse
W.C. Johnson	Lib	Whitechapel
G. Lansbury	Lab	Bow & Bromley
Sir J. McDougall	P	Poplar
C.J. Mathew KC	P	St. George's
J. May	P	Mile End
H.V. Rowe	MR	Alderman
J. Sankey KC	MR	Stepney
P.C. Simmons	MR	Alderman
E. Smith	P	NE Bethnal Green
C. Stettauer	P	Mile End
A.W. Yeo	P	Limehouse

1913-1919

F.H.J. Baber	MR	Bow & Bromley
W.C. Bersey	MR	Bow & Bromley
G.A. Dutfield	MR	Mile End
G. Edmonds	P	NE Bethnal Green
B.B. Evans	P	Limehouse
Capt. A.O.Goodrich	MR	Stepney
H.H. Gordon	P	Whitechapel
H. Gosling CH	Lab	St. George's
P.A. Harris	Lib	SW Bethnal Green
D. Hazel	MR	Stepney
Rev. S. Headlam	P	SW Bethnal Green
M. Hilbery	MR	Bow & Bromley
St.J. Hutchinson	P	Poplar
Sir C. Jackson KBE	MR	Alderman
W.C. Johnson	Lib	Whitechapel
Miss A.S. Lawrence	Lab	Poplar
H. Marks	P	Limehouse
C.J. Mathew CBE KC	P	St. George's
Sir G. Piggott KBE	MR	Mile End
H.V. Rowe	MR	Alderman
P.C. Simmons	MR	Alderman
Sir E. Smith	P	NE Bethnal Green
Lord Templemore KCVO	MR	Stepney
T.W. Wickham	P	Mile End
Sir A.W. Yeo	P	Limehouse

1919-1922

R. Bryan	Lab	Limehouse
E. Cruse	Lab	Bow & Bromley
G. Edmonds	P	NE Bethnal Green
Capt. A.O. Goodrich	MR	Mile End

H.H. Gordon	P	W'chapel & St. George's
P.A. Harris	Lib	SW Bethnal Green
D. Hazel	MR	Mile End
Rev S. Headlam	P	SW Bethnal Green
Sir C. Jackson KBE	MR	Alderman
W.C. Johnson	Lib	W'chapel & St. George's
Miss A.S. Lawrence	Lab	S Poplar
S. March	Lab	S Poplar
H. Marks	P	Limehouse
C.J. Mathew CBE KC	Lab	Alderman
Sir E. Smith	P	NE Bethnal Green
C.E. Sumner	Lab	Bow & Bromley

1922-1925

Sir E. Bonham-Carter	P	NE Bethnal Green
E. Cruse	Lab	Bow & Bromley
Capt. A.O. Goodrich	MR	Alderman
P.A. Harris	Lib	SW Bethnal Green
Rev. S. Headlam	P	SW Bethnal Green
Sir C. Jackson KBE	MR	Alderman
W.C. Johnson	Lib	W'chapel & St. George's
C.J. Kelly	Lab	W'chapel & St. George's
Mrs. C.B. Lankester	MR	Limehouse
Miss A.S. Lawrence	Lab	S Poplar
J.C.G. Leigh	MR	Mile End
S. March	Lab	S Poplar
H. Marks	P	Limehouse
Mrs. C.V. Mathew	Lab	Alderman
C.J. Mathew CBE KC	Lab	Alderman
W. Shadforth	P	NE Bethnal Green
C.E. Sumner	Lab	Bow & Bromley
Sir O. Wakeman	MR	Mile End

1925-1928

G. Belt	Lab	NE Bethnal Green
T.J. Blacketer	Lab	Bow & Bromley
R. Coppock	Lab	Alderman
E. Cruse	Lab	Bow & Bromley
M.H. Davis	Lab	W'chapel & St. George's
Lieut.Col.J.B.Dodge DSO	MR	Mile End
Capt.A.O. Goodrich	MR	Alderman
P.A. Harris	Lib	SW Bethnal Green
W.C. Johnson	Lib	Alderman
R.P. Jones	Lib	SW Bethnal Green
C.J. Kelly	Lab	W'chapel & St. George's
Mrs.C.B. Lankester	MR	Alderman
Miss A.S. Lawrence	Lab	S Poplar
I.Lyons	Lab	Limehouse
H.T. Macdonald	Lab	NE Bethnal Green
Mrs. C.J. Mathew	Lab	Limehouse
G.W. Mills	Lab	S Poplar
H. Roberts	Lab	Mile End
J. Scurr	Lab	Alderman
Mrs. J. Scurr	Lab	Mile End

1928-1931

D.M. Adams	Lab	S Poplar
T.J. Blacketer	Lab	Bow & Bromley
R. Coppock	Lab	Alderman
E. Cruse	Lab	Bow & Bromley
M.H. Davis	Lab	W'chapel & St. George's
Lieut.Col.J.B.Dodge DSO	MR	Mile End
Hon. L. Guest OBE	MR	Mile End
P.A. Harris	Lib	SW Bethnal Green
W.C. Johnson	Lib	Alderman
R.P. Jones	Lib	SW Bethnal Green
Mrs. C.B. Lankester	MR	Alderman
M. MacDonald	Lab	Limehouse
Mrs. C.J. Mathew	Lab	Limehouse
G.W. Mills	Lab	S Poplar
Lady E. Nathan	Lib	NE Bethnal Green
R.E. Pearson	Lib	NE Bethnal Green
Mrs. J. C. Peterkin	Lab	S Poplar
J. Scurr	Lab	Alderman
J. Sullivan	Lab	W'chapel & St. George's

1931-1934

D.M. Adams	Lab	S Poplar
T.J. Blacketer	Lab	Bow & Bromley
E. Cruse	Lab	Bow & Bromley
M.H. Davis	Lab	W'chapel & St. George's
D. Frankel	Lab	Mile End
P.A. Harris	Lib	SW Bethnal Green
S. Hastings FRCS	Lab	Mile End
R.P. Jones	Lib	SW Bethnal Green
H. Lazarus	Lab	Limehouse
Mrs. C.J. Mathew	Lab	Limehouse
Lady E. Nathan	Lib	NE Bethnal Green
J.R.A. Oldfield	Lab	W'chapel & St. George's
R.E. Pearson	Lib	NE Bethnal Green
Mrs. J.C. Peterkin	Ind Soc	S Poplar
J. Scurr	Lab	Mile End

1934-1937

D.M. Adams	Lab	S Poplar
R. Coppock	Lab	Limehouse
E. Cruse	Lab	Bow & Bromley
M.H. Davis	Lab	W'chapel & St. George's
T. Dawson	Lab	NE Bethnal Green
D. Frankel	Lab	Mile End
W.H. Guy	Lab	S Poplar
S. Hastings FRCS	Lab	Mile End
Mrs. R. Keeling	Lab	NE Bethnal Green
J.E.A. King	Lab	SW Bethnal Green
Mrs. E.M. Lambert	Lab	Bow & Bromley
Mrs. C.J. Mathew	Lab	Limehouse
J.R.A.Oldfield	Lab	W'chapel & St. George's
A.R. Stamp	Lab	SW Bethnal Green

1937-1940

F.T. Baldock	Lab	S Poplar
R. Coppock	Lab	Limehouse
E. Cruse	Lab	Bow & Bromley
M.H. Davis	Lab	W'chapel & St. George's
T. Dawson	Lab	NE Bethnal Green
D. Frankel	Lab	Mile End
T.J. Goodway	Lab	Bow & Bromley
W. H. Guy	Lab	S Poplar
S. Hastings FRCS	Lab	Mile End
Mrs. R. Keeling	Lab	NE Bethnal Green
J.E.A. King	Lab	SW Bethnal Green
Mrs. E.M. Lambert	Lab	Bow & Bromley
J.R.A. Oldfield	Lab	W'chapel & St. George's
A.R. Stamp	Lab	SW Bethnal Green
Miss M. Whately	Lab	Limehouse

1940-1943

F.T. Baldock	Lab	S Poplar
R. Coppock CBE	Lab	Limehouse
M.H. Davis	Lab	W'chapel & St. George's
T. Dawson	Lab	NE Bethnal Green
Sir W. Deedes CMG	Lab	NE Bethnal Green
D. Frankel	Lab	Mile End
T.J. Goodway	Lab	Bow & Bromley
W.H. Guy	Lab	S Poplar
S. Hastings FRCS	Lab	Mile End
Mrs. R. Keeling	Lab	NE Bethnal Green
J.E.A. King	Lab	SW Bethnal Green
Mrs. E.M. Lambert	Lab	Bow & Bromley
J.R.A. Oldfield	Lab	W'chapel & St. George's
A.R. Stamp	Lab	SW Bethnal Green
Miss M. Whately	Lab	Limehouse

1943-1946

F.T. Baldock	Lab	S Poplar
R. Clements OBE	Lab	W'chapel & St. George's
R. Coppock CBE	Lab	Limehouse
M.H. Davis	Lab	W'chapel & St. George's
T. Dawson	Lab	NE Bethnal Green
Sir W. Deedes CMG	Lab	NE Bethnal Green
D. Frankel	Lab	Mile End
T.J. Goodway	Lab	Bow & Bromley
W.H. Guy	Lab	S Poplar
S. Hastings FRCS	Lab	Mile End
J.E.A. King	Lab	SW Bethnal Green
Mrs. E.M. Lambert	Lab	Bow & Bromley
J.R.A. Oldfield	Lab	W'chapel & St. George's
E.H. Smith GM	Lab	Bow & Bromley
A.R. Stamp	Lab	SW Bethnal Green
Miss M. Whately	Lab	Limehouse

1946 - 1949

F.T. Baldock	Lab	S Poplar
Mrs. H.C. Bentwich	Lab	NE Bethnal Green
E.F. Bramley	Comm	Mile End
R. Clements OBE	Lab	W'chapel & St. George's
R. Coppock CBE	Lab	Limehouse
J. Gaster	Comm	Mile End
W.H. Guy	Lab	S Poplar
Sir P.A. Harris	Lib	SW Bethnal Green
S. Hastings FRCS	Lab	Alderman
E. Martell	Lib	SW Bethnal Green
J.R.A. Oldfield	Lab	W'chapel & St. George's
Mrs. A.L. Reeve	Lab	Limehouse
Mrs. L.M. Sadler	Lab	Bow & Bromley
E.H. Smith GM	Lab	Bow & Bromley
A.R. Stamp	Lab	Alderman
R.M. Wood OBE	Lab	NE Bethnal Green

1949 - 1952

F.T. Baldock MBE	Lab	Poplar
Mrs. H.C. Bentwich	Lab	Alderman
J. Branagan	Lab	Poplar
Sir R. Coppock CBE	Lab	Alderman
W.H. Guy	Lab	Poplar
Sir P.A. Harris	Lib	Bethnal Green
S. Hastings FRCS	Lab	Alderman
J.J.A. Long	Lab	Stepney
J.R.A. Oldfield	Lab	Stepney
Mrs. A.L. Reeve	Lab	Stepney
A.R. Stamp	Lab	Alderman
Mrs. B.L. Tate	Lab	Bethnal Green
R. M. Wood OBE	Lab	Bethnal Green

1952 - 1955

Mrs. H.C. Bentwich	Lab	Alderman
J. Branagan	Lab	Poplar
W.H. Guy	Lab	Poplar
S. Hastings FRCS	Lab	Alderman
Mrs. D. Holman	Lab	Bethnal Green
J.J.A. Long	Lab	Stepney
A.C. Niederman	Lab	Poplar
J.R.A. Oldfield	Lab	Stepney
Mrs. A.L. Reeve	Lab	Stepney
A.R. Stamp	Lab	Alderman
Mrs. B.L. Tate	Lab	Bethnal Green
R.M. Wood OBE	Lab	Bethnal Green

1955 - 1958

J. Branagan	Lab	Poplar
W.H. Guy	Lab	Poplar
S. Hastings	Lab	Alderman
Mrs. D. Holman	Lab	Bethnal Green
J.J.A. Long	Lab	Stepney

A.C. Niederman	Lab	Poplar
J.R.A. Oldfield	Lab	Stepney
Mrs. A.L. Reeve	Lab	Stepney
Mrs. B.L. Tate	Lab	Bethnal Green
R.M. Wood OBE	Lab	Bethnal Green

1958 - 1961

Mrs. H.C. Bentwich	Lab	Alderman
J. Branagan KSG	Lab	Poplar
W.H. Guy	Lab	Poplar
S. Hastings	Lab	Alderman
Mrs. D. Holman	Lab	Bethnal Green
Mrs. A.P. King	Lab	Stepney
A.D. Kirby	Lab	Stepney
A.C. Niederman	Lab	Poplar
A.E. Sealey	Lab	Stepney
Mrs. B.L. Tate	Lab	Bethnal Green
R.M. Wood OBE	Lab	Bethnal Green

1961 - 1965

Mrs. H.C. Bentwich	Lab	Alderman
C.W.J. Bird	Lab	Stepney

Sir A. Bramall	Lab	Bethnal Green
J. Branagan KSG	Lab	Poplar
W.H. Guy	Lab	Poplar
S. Hastings	Lab	Alderman
Mrs. D. Holman	Lab	Bethnal Green
A.D. Kirby	Lab	Stepney
A. McLaughlin	Lab	Bethnal Green
A.C. Niederman	Lab	Poplar
W. Sullivan	Lab	Stepney

Political parties are indicated as follows:

Comm	Communist
Ind Soc	Independent Socialist
Lab	Labour
Lib	Liberal
Mod	Moderate
MR	Municipal Reform
P	Progressive

The Greater London Council 1964-1986
Elected Representatives

1964-1967	E.A. Bramall	Lab	Tower Hamlets
	J.P. Branagan	Lab	Tower Hamlets
1967-1970	E.A. Bramall	Lab	Tower Hamlets
	J.P. Branagan	Lab	Tower Hamlets
1970-1973	E.A. Bramall	Lab	Tower Hamlets
	J.P. Branagan	Lab	Tower Hamlets
1973-1977	E.A. Bramall	Lab	Bethnal Green & Bow
	J.P. Branagan	Lab	Poplar & Stepney
1977-1981	Sir E.A. Bramall	Lab	Bethnal Green & Bow
	J.P. Branagan	Lab	Poplar & Stepney
1981-1986	Sir E.A. Bramall	Lab	Poplar & Stepney
	J.P. Branagan	Lab	Bethnal Green & Bow

The London Residuary Body succeeded the GLC, 1986-1995 with no elected constituency representatives, and was Chaired by Sir Godfrey Taylor. Responsibilities undertaken by The GLC are now devolved to the individual London Boroughs.

School Board for London 1870–1904
Tower Hamlets Representatives

First Board 1870–1873
Edward North Buxton
Sir Edmund Hay Currie
Arthur Langdale
William Pearce
Thomas Scrutton

Second Board 1873–1876
Rev. Joseph Bardsley
Edward North Buxton
Sir Edmund Hay Currie
Arthur Langdale
Thomas Scrutton

Third Board 1876–1879
Rev. Joseph Bardsley
Edward North Buxton
Rev. Angelo Lucas
William Pearce
Thomas Scrutton

Fourth Board 1879–1882
Edward Bond
Edward North Buxton
Spencer C. Charrington
William Pearce
Col. Lenox Prendergast
Thomas Scrutton (Resigned)

Fifth Board 1882–1885
Edward North Buxton (Chairman)
Sir Edmund Hay Currie
Miss Frances Hastings
William Pearce
Col. Lenox Prendergast

Sixth Board 1885–1888
Edward North Buxton (Chairman)
Frederick J.W. Dellow
Rev. W.P. Jay
Claude S. Montefiore
Rev. John F. Porter
Col. Lenox Prendergast

Seventh Board 1888–1891
Mrs. Annie Besant
Sir Edmund Hay Currie (Resigned)
Frederick J.W. Dellow
Rev. W.P. Jay (Resigned)
Sir Philip Magnus
Rev. John F. Porter
Col. Lenox Prendergast

Eighth Board 1891–1894
George L. Bruce
Mrs. Frances Homan
Cyril Jackson
Rev. Rowland T. Plummer
Rev. Edward Schnadhorst

Ninth Board 1894–1897
George L. Bruce
Sir Charles Elliott
Mrs. Frances Homan
Cyril Jackson (Resigned)
Rev. Rowland T. Plummer
Rev. Edward Schnadhorst

Tenth Board 1897–1900
Rev. Francis C. Beckley
Benjamin Costelloe (Died)
Sir Charles Elliott
Ernest F.S. Flower MP
Mrs. Frances Homan
Rev. Edward Schnadhorst

Eleventh Board 1900–1904
Rev. Francis Beckley
George L. Bruce
Sir Charles Elliott
Mrs. Frances Homan
Rev. Edward Schnadhorst

Members of Parliament for the Borough 1832-1997

1832	W. Clay	Lib	Tower Hamlets
	S. Lushington	Lib	Tower Hamlets
1835	W. Clay	Lib	Tower Hamlets
	S. Lushington	Lib	Tower Hamlets
1837	W. Clay	Lib	Tower Hamlets
	S. Lushington	Lib	Tower Hamlets
1839*	S. Lushington	Lib	Tower Hamlets
1841	C. R. Fox	Lib	Tower Hamlets
	W. Clay	Lib	Tower Hamlets
1846*	C. R. Fox	Lib	Tower Hamlets
1847	G. Thompson	Lib	Tower Hamlets
	Sir W. Clay	Lib	Tower Hamlets
1852	Sir W. Clay	Lib	Tower Hamlets
	C.S. Butler	Lib	Tower Hamlets
1857	A.S. Ayrton	Lib	Tower Hamlets
	C.S. Butler	Lib	Tower Hamlets
1859	A.S. Ayrton	Lib	Tower Hamlets
1865	C.S. Butler	Lib	Tower Hamlets
	A.S. Ayrton	Lib	Tower Hamlets
	C.S. Butler	Lib	Tower Hamlets
1868	A.S. Ayrton	Lib	Tower Hamlets
	J.D'A. Samuda	Lib	Tower Hamlets
1869*	A. S. Ayrton	Lib	Tower Hamlets
1874	C.T. Ritchie	Con	Tower Hamlets
	J.D'A Samuda	Lib	Tower Hamlets
1880	J. Bryce	Lib	Tower Hamlets
	C.T. Ritchie	Con	Tower Hamlets
1885	S. Charrington	Con	Mile End
	J.C. Durant	Lib	Stepney
	H. Green	Lib	Poplar
	G. Howell	Lib/Lab	Bethnal Green NE
	E. S. Norris	Con	Limehouse
	S. Montagu	Lib	Whitechapel
	E.H. Pickersgill	Lib	Bethnal Green SW
	C.T. Ritchie	Con	St. George's
	W.S. Robson	Lib	Bow & Bromley
1886	S.C. Buxton	Lib	Poplar
	S. Charrington	Con	Mile End
	J.C.R. Columb	Con	Bow & Bromley
	J.C. Durant	Lib	Stepney
	G. Howell	Lib/Lab	Bethnal Green NE
	F.W. Isaacson	Con	Stepney
	S. Montagu	Lib	Whitechapel
	E. S. Norris	Con	Limehouse
	E.H. Pickersgill	Lib	Bethnal Green SW
1886*	C.T. Ritchie	Con	St. George's
	C.T. Ritchie	Con	St. George's
1892	J.W. Benn	Lib	St. George's
	S.C. Buxton	Lib	Poplar
	S. Charrington	Con	Mile End
	G. Howell	Lib/Lab	Bethnal Green NE
	F.W. Isaacson	Con	Stepney
	J.A.M. MacDonald	Lib	Bow & Bromley
	S. Montagu	Lib	Whitechapel

	E.H. Pickersgill	Lib	Bethnal Green SW
	J.S. Wallace	Lib	Limehouse
1895	Sir M.M. Bhownaggree	Con	Bethnal Green NE
	S.C. Buxton	Lib	Poplar
	S. Charrington	Con	Mile End
	L.R. Holland	Con	Bow & Bromley
	F.W. Isaacson	Con	Stepney
	H.H. Marks	Con	St. George's
	Sir S. Montagu	Lib	Whitechapel
	E.H. Pickersgill	Lib	Bethnal Green SW
	H.S. Samuel	Con	Limehouse
1898	W.C. Steadman	Lib/Lab	Stepney (By)
1899	W.M. Guthrie	Con	Bow & Bromley (By)
1900	Sir M.M. Bhownaggree	Con	Bethnal Green NE
	S.C. Buxton	Lib	Poplar
	S. Charrington	Con	Mile End
	T.R. Dewar	Con	St. George's
	W.E. Evans-Gordon	Con	Stepney
	W.M. Guthrie	Con	Bow & Bromley
	S.F. Ridley	Con	Bethnal Green SW
	H.S. Samuel	Con	Limehouse
	S.M. Samuel	Lib	Whitechapel
1905	H.L.W. Lawson	Lib/Union	Mile End (By)
1906	W.W. Benn	Lib	St. George's
	S.W.W. Brooke	Lib	Bow & Bromley
	S.C. Buxton	Lib	Poplar
	Sir E.A. Cornwall	Lib	Bethnal Green NE
	Sir W.E. Evans-Gordon	Con	Stepney
	W. Pearce	Lib	Limehouse
	E.H. Pickersgill	Lib	Bethnal Green SW
	S.M. Samuel	Lib	Whitechapel
	B. S. Straus	Lib	Mile End
1907	F.L. Harris	Con	Stepney (By)
1910	W.W. Benn	Lib	St. George's
	S.C. Buxton	Lib	Poplar
	Sir E.A. Cornwall	Lib	Bethnal Green NE
	A. Du Cros	Con	Bow & Bromley
	F.L. Harris	Con	Stepney
	H.L.W. Lawson	Lib/Union	Mile End
	W. Pearce	Lib	Limehouse
	E.H. Pickersgill	Lib	Bethnal Green SW
	S.M. Samuel	Lib	Whitechapel
1910	W.W. Benn	Lib	St. George's
	S.C. Buxton	Lib	Poplar
	Sir E.A. Cornwall	Lib	Bethnal Green NE
	W.S. Glyn-Jones	Lib	Stepney
	G. Lansbury	Lab	Bow & Bromley
	H.R.W. Lawson	Lib/Union	Mile End
	E.H. Pickersgill	Lib	Bethnal Green SW
	S.M. Samuel	Lib	Whitechapel
	W. Pearce	Lib	Limehouse
1911*	C.F.G. Masterman	Lib	Bethnal Green SW (By)
1912	R. Blair	Con	Bow & Bromley (By)
1913	Sir S.M. Samuel	Lib	Whitechapel (By)
1914*	Sir M.R.H. Wilson	Con	Bethnal Green SW
*	A.W. Yeo	Lib	Poplar

Year	Name	Party	Constituency
1916	J.D. Kiley	Lib	Whitechapel (By)
	W. Brookes	Con	Mile End (By)
1918	R. Blair	Co Con	Bow & Bromley
	Sir E.A. Cornwall	Lib	Bethnal Green NE
	J.D. Kiley	Lib	Whitechapel & St. George's
	Sir W. Pearce	Co Lib	Limehouse
	W.R. Preston	Co Con	Mile End
	Sir M.R.H. Wilson	Con	Bethnal Green SW
	Sir A.W. Yeo	Co Lib	S Poplar
1922	C.R. Attlee	Lab	Limehouse
	G. Edmonds	Lib	Bethnal Green NE
	P.A. Harris	Lib	Bethnal Green SW
	G. Lansbury	Lab	Bow & Bromley
	S. March	Lab	S Poplar
	C.J. Mathew	Lab	Whitechapel & St. George's
	Sir W.R. Preston	Con	Mile End
1923	C.R. Attlee	Lab	Limehouse
	H. Gosling	Lab	Whitechapel & St. George's (By)
	P.A. Harris	Lib	Bethnal Green SW
	G. Lansbury	Lab	Bow & Bromley
	S. March	Lab	S Poplar
	J. Scurr	Lab	Mile End
	W. Windsor	Lab	Bethnal Green NE
1924	C.R. Attlee	Lab	Limehouse
	H. Gosling	Lab	Whitechapel & St. George's
	P.A. Harris	Lib	Bethnal Green SW
	G. Lansbury	Lab	Bow & Bromley
	S. March	Lab	S Poplar
	J. Scurr	Lab	Mile End
	W. Windsor	Lab	Bethnal Green NE
1929	C.R. Attlee	Lab	Limehouse
	H. Gosling	Lab	Whitechapel & St. George's
	P.A. Harris	Lib	Bethnal Green SW
	G. Lansbury	Lab	Bow & Bromley
	S. March	Lab	S Poplar
	H.L. Nathan	Lib	Bethnal Green NE
	J. Scurr	Lab	Mile End
1930	J.H. Hall	Lab	Whitechapel & St. George's
1931	D.M. Adams	Lab	S Poplar
	C.R. Attlee	Lab	Limehouse
	P.A. Harris	Lib	Bethnal Green SW
	B.R. Janner	Lib	Whitechapel & St. George's
	G. Lansbury	Lab	Bow & Bromley
	H.L. Nathan	Ind/Lib	Bethnal Green NE
	Dr. W.J. O'Donovan	Con	Mile End
1935	D.M. Adams	Lab	S Poplar
	C.R. Attlee	Lab	Limehouse
	D. Chater	Lab/Co-op	Bethnal Green NE
	D. Frankel	Lab	Mile End
	J.H. Hall	Lab	Whitechapel & St. George's
	Sir P.A. Harris	Lib	Bethnal Green SW
	G. Lansbury	Lab	Bow & Bromley
1940	C. W. Key	Lab	Bow & Bromley (By)
1942	W.J. Edwards	Lab	Whitechapel & St. George's (By)
	W.H. Guy	Lab	S Poplar (By)
1945	C.R. Attlee	Lab	Limehouse

	D. Chater	Lab/Co-op	Bethnal Green NE
	W.J. Edwards	Lab	Whitechapel & St. George's
	W.H. Guy	Lab	S Poplar
	P. Holman	Lab/Co-op	Bethnal Green SW
	C.W. Key	Lab	Bow & Bromley
	P. Piratin	Comm	Mile End
1950	W.J. Edwards	Lab	Stepney
	P. Holman	Lab/Co-op	Bethnal Green
	C.W. Key	Lab	Poplar
1951	W.J. Edwards	Lab	Stepney
	P. Holman	Lab/Co-op	Bethnal Green
	C.W. Key	Lab	Poplar
1955	W.J. Edwards	Lab	Stepney
	P. Holman	Lab/Co-op	Bethnal Green
	C.W. Key	Lab	Poplar
1959	W.J. Edwards	Lab	Stepney
	P. Holman	Lab/Co-op	Bethnal Green
	C.W. Key	Lab	Poplar
1964	I. Mikardo	Lab	Poplar
	P. Holman	Lab/Co-op	Bethnal Green
	P.D. Shore	Lab	Stepney
1966	W. S. Hilton	Lab/Co-op	Bethnal Green
	I. Mikardo	Lab	Poplar
	P.D. Shore	Lab	Stepney
1970	W. S. Hilton	Lab/Co-op	Bethnal Green
	I. Mikardo	Lab	Poplar
	P.D. Shore	Lab	Stepney
1974	I. Mikardo	Lab	Bethnal Green & Bow
	P.D. Shore	Lab	Stepney & Poplar
1979	I. Mikardo	Lab	Bethnal Green & Bow
	P.D. Shore	Lab	Stepney & Poplar
1983	C. Mikardo	Lab	Bow & Poplar
	P.D. Shore	Lab	Bethnal Green & Stepney
1987	M. Gordon	Lab	Bow & Poplar
	P.D. Shore	Lab	Bethnal Green & Stepney
1992	M. Gordon	Lab	Bow & Poplar
	P.D. Shore	Lab	Bethnal Green & Stepney

* Under the provisions of the Succession to the Crown Act, 1707 and a number of subsequent acts, MPs appointed to certain ministerial and legal offices were required to seek re-election.

Political parties are indicated as follows:

Co Con	Coalition Conservative
Co Lib	Coalition Liberal
Comm	Communist
Con	Conservative
Ind	Independent (indicates an unofficial candidate when placed before a party abbreviation)
Lab	Labour
Lab/Coop	Labour/Co-operative joint candidate
Lib	Liberal or Radical or Whig
Lib/Union	Liberal/Unionist joint candidate